INDIA
A Nation of
Fear and Prejudice

INDIA
A Nation of
Fear and Prejudice

RACE OF THE THIRD KIND

Kumar, Fisher and Subba

To order additional copies of this book, contact:
Xlibris
1-800-455-039
www.Xlibris.com.au
Orders@Xlibris.com.au
794790

DEDICATED TO...

We dedicate this book as a wake-up call for those whose lives have been paralyzed in the name of lower caste fate and untouchable status for thousands of years. Wake up! All in India and beyond now can arise to a new fate with a new dawning of the 21st century.

CONTENTS

Part 2 R. Michael Fisher

Part 3 Desh Subba

Part 4 B. Maria Kumar, R. Michael Fisher
Desh Subba

ACKNOWLEDGEMENTS

I (Maria) am extremely grateful to my wife Vijayalakshmi for her unfailing inspiration to all of my endeavors. I thank my son William Salim Aditya and my daughter Susan Sushmita for their constant encouragement and secretarial support during the course of doing Part 1 for this book. I would also like to place on record my deep sense of appreciation to P. Surendra Nath and Suhasini Ramchander for their valuable suggestions on the manuscript.

I (Desh), with many fond memories of my mother, I thank her for surrounding me with a healthy environment of family and community, which are the bricks, concrete and iron to build a house, which is my pyramid. I (Michael), acknowledge the great working relationship with my colleagues Maria and Desh and for their faith in my work.

INTRODUCTION

B. Maria Kumar, R. Michael Fisher, Desh Subba

India is not, as people keep calling it, an underdeveloped country, but rather, in the context of its history and cultural heritage, a highly developed one in an advanced state of decay.

—Shashi Tharoor [1]

To make an accurate assessment and prescription for a better future, India needs renewed and *exceptional* leadership with vision. We see that as coming both from the top down *and* from the bottom up—a two way integrative flow of intention, energy and action, of thinking and feeling. Rekindling the spirit of a nation is ultimately latent in everyone's heart and responsibility. The vision of renewal has to holistically integrate the past, present and future—sorting out what ought to be left behind, what ought to be explored further, and what ought to be taken action upon. Of course, the hardest part is to get everyone to agree on this. That's where exceptional leadership, on many levels of a society, is required to guide the learning required to work through finding the best solutions.

And, such vision and working through as a learning process, has to be not only free from fear-based prisons of the mind, it must be critical of what referent comparisons are made from outside of India. Should India always compare itself to the West? Who is to ultimately hold the truth about whether India is a "developed" nation or not? Maybe that is not even the right question? To us as authors, it certainly is *not* the only question. In this light of cautionary assessment, as thinkers/writers, we take on this responsibility ourselves in this book to free our minds yet also to share experiences and strong impressions of what are the strengths and weaknesses of this great nation. It is with excitement, in the face of a daunting task, we step-up into the dimension of vision and realities before us, and we do so from different locations (Kumar in India, Fisher in Canada, Subba in Hong Kong) and at times different perspectives.

We do not write as experts on India but rather as serious and curious inquirers, each offering a platter of ideas for the soup pot. And we invite others to add their ideas as well. We hope this eclectic pot of ideas will assist those working on the multidimensional ways to solve India's great challenges and create abundant opportunities for all. Again, from the bottom up *and* the top down, in tandem. We suggest it may be a good starting place for leaders to acknowledge the nations' places of decay and to use that as fertilizer for awareness, learning and transformation to a new level of development that has no doubt surprises no one can truly predict. Anyone could be wrong, as much as right, about the future of India in a rapidly changing world. A good task of leaders is to find some universal general agreements to move forward, and then start to prioritize desires and needs. It is best, we suggest, not to over-assume that 'all things have already been tried' and to fall back on only tradition. Vibrancy of a nation's healthy growth in a dynamic world will mean, to some degree, challenging traditions, taboos and prisons of the mind that hold back people as 'slaves' of one kind or another.

We think H. G. Wells, said it prophetically well in 1920, that general history and the future (e.g., India's future) is a "race between education and catastrophe" [2]. Though useful as literary hyperbole, perhaps Wells was creating a binary option and pitting "education" on one-side against "catastrophe" (or chaos) on the other-side. We search in our thoughts, philosophies, and ideas in this book to not fall *only* prey to either/or oppositions and dualism like Wells. We look for third options in between and other than within only the frame of the exaggerative and polarizing solutions—because, typically Wells, like so many others, will potentially end up creating a fear-based motivation that can breed its own fear-based solutions. Finding a balanced fear as motivation to face reality, to spark attention to issues of concern, of course, is a better way to go. Ultimately, all three of us can agree that "education" and learning is the better way to go.

Nothing in reality is ever simple only. Even education and learning can be fraught with controversy and even deception or unreasonable competition that aids some and harms others. We think of a traditional story. What made the ancient author Zeno of Elea, 5th century BC, to pit the small, slow and lethargic tortoise in the grand race against the muscular, athletic and mighty Achilles? Didn't Zeno know that it would be a grotesque instance of a seemingly unreasonable competition?

What (mythic) ancient wisdom is within this story to draw from today? In our view, Zeno's intention in his race (of the first kind) was otherwise to a seemingly unreasonable competition—it was something deeper, intriguing and well-conceived. He played to tortoise's demand for a special package, stuck to his idea and proved what the people generally hold to be, wrong. Achilles lost the race to the tortoise because tortoise intervened in the 'game' rather than played victim to fate. Tortoise argued logically that his obvious slow walk was demanding of a fair need for a head-start. Such a handicap would ensure that he kept just far enough ahead of the athletic Achilles at every gap of distance between the two. Because whenever Achilles finally caught up to tortoise and was passing, tortoise reminded him of the fair need for a head-start. Achilles repeatedly submitted to the logic. Tortoise won the race.

There was again an imaginary second race as a possible alternative to tortoise's argument. Because, in Zeno's (first) race, the logic-ridden argument of the tortoise overshadowed the reality of Achilles' speed. The logic that dominated was fallacious. The head start conception was a fallacy. Being privileged was a fallacy. Being ever-ahead at each gap for infinity was a fallacy. Hence, observed reality failed to show up as in synch with the logical reality. Tricked by the witty tortoise, Zeno too (perhaps) fell to his charms. Zeno in this context, metaphorically represents authoritarianism in the society. In the second race, Zeno was conspicuous by his absence. And the race was held on rational parameters with a view to convincing the world as to how the results of the race would have been righteous had it been on transparent and honest lines and flawless logic. Also in the Second Race, there was target distance that was fixed, finite and the logical consequence gave in to reality. Achilles overtook the tortoise and won the race as observed reality triumphed over fallacious logic.

Then, in the third race, the real and practical one, which has been under way in India since long ago, Achilles metaphorically represents the numerically abounding backward and lower castes with the largest vote bank (majority), whereas tortoise denotes the minority forward castes with born status and other ascribed special privileges. In this third kind of race, whenever Indian elections happen, the vote bank becomes subservient to the power of the few elite socially privileged—and, every time, the privileged forward caste tortoise seized power and authority while subduing the powerless backward, lower caste Achilles, as has been the case since time immemorial.

Of the four castes of ancient India, the first three namely the priests, rulers and the business clans, commonly known as forward or upper castes, not only usurped common natural resources and other means of production but also anointed themselves with self-proclaimed social privileges. The fourth caste, known also as backward castes, was relegated to that of serving the upper castes. Living below the upper and backward castes were the later addition as fifth category at the lowest rung of the society, termed as the lower castes.

So what unfair 'race' is still lurking upon the nation? The lower castes typically have been condemned to perform the most gruesome and menial jobs and thus have suffered routine oppression and discrimination for millennia. The tortoise has assumed the same fallacious logic in Zeno's paradox. It is a grand narrative of fate, of a history that privileges one-side and hurts the other-side. What then happens to the "whole" of a society—which is both sides? Wilber, the integral philosopher, suggests such a fallacious, divisive and oppressive logic has deep roots in the very dualism of thought and imagination itself. The very way reality is perceived, processed and conceptualized is decayed and in need of an educative reclamation and transformation. He wrote,

> [T]hrough the [everyday, often unconscious] process of
> *maya*, of dualistic thought, we introduce illusory dualities
> of divisions [as in the 'race' of Zeno's imagination],
> 'creating two worlds from one.' These divisions are not

real, but only seemingly, yet man behaves in every way *as if* they were real; and being thus duped, man clings to... primordial dualism." [3]

Any holisitic-integral education will, while racing against catastrophe, on one level, have to look at the mind and the problems it creates, and will have to critically look at the leaders and the problems they have created and disproportionately used power to cast their story ('race') upon the land, the people, the nation.

However, the 'race' looks to be flawed from the start—that is, the use of and privileging of a biased way of knowing—that is, dualism. Of course, there is not only this philosophical task at hand in revealing this problem in cognition at its base, there is also the practical tasks at reforming the systems and politics of culture and society that perpetuate the cognitive dominating dualism of 'making one into two' and pretending they are really two. No future, and no society will flourish sustainably, in fairness, harmony or with justice under that (false) regime of 'truth.' It is an illusion to think such dualism will lead one (or some group) to "win" ultimately over the others. There has to be a radically different conscious conception of the rules of the 'race' whereby all may find meaning and a way to peace. This book will offer some guidance in that preferred and authentic direction towards wholeness and a better and democratic 'game.'

The problem with the castes is that the said ancient system is still continuing to impact the contemporary Indian social-economic scene though not always formally; rather, mostly informally. The 'game' is played overtly at times and covertly often. In the just position of Dr. B. R. Ambedkar's terms, perpetuating inequality on the ground that whatever is once settled, is settled for all times, is opposed to all morality. Hence, the annals of Indian history, replete with fear-driven social inequalities (*via* dualism), have been masked by a clever 'game' gilding of the so-called rich ancient heritage and legacy of the nation.

In this book, the three of us have not fallen into any illusions or overly-romanticizing tendencies in our view of India's golden great past and potential. We are optimistic-realists, as is the very dialectic *philosophy of fearism* that Desh Subba has brought, *via* a fearist lens, into this critical discourse regarding the nation of India—it's legacy and its future. As the

Part 1, 2, 3 and 4 in this book unfold, we aimed high in our ideals for India and we aimed low at pointing to the deepest roots of the problems in this nation. We introduce some new territory of exploration or at least some new combinations that will stimulate thinking critically, and stir the stale imaginations that need shaking up. Our new language within the philosophy of fearism is later explained and references are added for readers to pursue more in depth.

We do not pretend to bring a fully united front on our understanding and theorizing on the nature and use of fear (and its management) because our goal was to keep our voices related but independent in each Part of the book; although in Part 4 Quo Vadis readers will be presented an opportunity to hear us in a lively dialogue with tensions over some of the points raised earlier in the book.

In the below section of the Introduction (Fear Management) we proceed. We let the ideas and words, especially from Kumar as lead author, who has lived and worked in India all his life, take us part way down a road of this co-inquiry as the topic *fear* comes more and more central in our investigation.

Fear Management, Reforms and Transformations

Any focus on the ubiquitous nature and role of *fear* [4] is underpinned by an interest to better manage fear [5]. The topic of fear management ought to be high on any nation's priority list. Such management needs reform in most nations today because of many serious factors threatening stability of systems. India, is no exception. Generally, fear is two-pronged as its mechanism uses both *insecurity* and *uncertainty*. Regarding insecurity as its primary vehicle, fear alerts and/or drives an individual to feel threatened and act to survive when there is real risk to its being. Regarding uncertainty, it is a secondary vehicle, whereby fear takes on the feeling of anxiousness when there are unknowns and uncontrollable aspects surrounding what is perceived to be going to potentially happen in future. In simpler terms, it can be said that insecurity, to a large extent, deals with one's current survival state and uncertainty is concerned with ambiguity and precarity regarding the future about survival and its associated components.

The insecurity aspect of fearmongering operates at three spatial dimensions in the real physical world, namely height, width and depth of the human body. The body survives when it is secured in terms of being able to access its life processes in three dimensions. Otherwise, danger is sensed or felt from sensing real unsafety for the physical body or other relevant things existing in space. But the existing dispensations provided for the people in general, say by governments or society, do not seem to make citizens secure about survival. Facts are, the rate of poverty or starvation doesn't show declining trends, as far as Indian statistical data is concerned.

From the insecurity wing of fear, the growing disparity between the minute numbers of haves and the astronomical have-nots only proliferates the symptoms, for example the rising number of nefarious elements such as insurgents, militants, terrorists, extremists and the like to continue posing threats to society as a whole. The insecurity wing of fear exacerbates the uncertainty wing—thus, fear grows in a *fear cycle*. The explosions and shootings that occur off and on are an ongoing testimony to the increasing trends. On the other hand, the uncertainty facet of the fear mechanism manoeuvres in the temporal co-ordinate of the future, through time, beyond mere physical bodies. It is now in the mind, which is the fourth dimension of reality.

In India, for a long time, lack of constructive policies at the behest of the government drove the people to despair in uncertainty as they have been rendered to fend for themselves not only without equal opportunities but also without being equipped with requisite skills and knowledge to seize growth opportunities. Survival based on fear trumps the growth-related potentials of any human being. And when such is chronic, it leaves one barely able to advance. It is this uncertainty that acts as a catalyst for anxiety which in turn tends to trigger motives and actions resulting in corrupt practices in governmental as well as socio-economic-political circles. It is also this uncertainty that kindles the spark of the fear of unknown, which typically takes away the self-confidence of the people. Under such pressures of fear's wings, at top and bottom, the entire nation does not fly well—there is little unity in the social fabric, in social trust, and social innovation that supports technological and other types of innovations. India must look at its foundation in the social sphere, the psychological sphere, and how fearmongering is causing havoc that can be largely prevented by good fear management policies and resources.

Whereas many nations have handled the two prongs of fear at the governmental level quite satisfactorily, and some are on top of the lists of happiness, and good country indices; all the while, India is struggling still to make any recognizable real headway. The main reason for this fiasco regarding Indian policy-making is that the efforts, which were and are being made, aimed at dealing with economic equality are done without touching social equality reforms in a thoroughgoing manner. The highly developed (albeit, perhaps out-dated) social-cultural-religious spheres of India contain and reproduce a regime of tradition and conformity that over-takes contemporary economic efforts. The progress is very slow and likely Indian leadership overall is lacking a vision or map of a "leadership journey" of development for leaders and for followers, and the nation altogether. The Economic dimension requires at least four others: Intellectual dimension, Moral dimension, Aesthetic dimension and Spiritual dimension for a holistic approach towards "exceptional leadership," according to Chaudhry [6].

With less than exceptional leadership as the seeming goal, or even projected 'norm,' the trend still continues. This subverted growth is like an anchor on a ship trying to sail. It has to move but does so without much progress, even despite the advent of scientific temper, industrialisation, urbanisation, modernisation and the current digital and attention economy, which India is partaking in.

Unfortunately, too often, the privileged minority turns means into ends to win the electoral battle. For example, elections and government formation are only means to achieve public good. But as means become ends, priorities get misunderstood and lopsided. Eventually, the fundamentals such as life, liberty, freedom, justice, equality, dignity, fearlessness and well-being have been sidelined to the extent that secondary issues like belief systems, rituals, customs, traditions etc. took precedence over life matters. The resultant culture that developed accordingly over the centuries has become not only the subject of false glorification for the upper castes but at the same time the element of fear for the lower castes remains inhibitive—to toe the line.

Rabindranath Tagore, the first Asian Nobel Laureate (1913, for Literature) wrote the poem, *Where the Mind is Without Fear* in 1910, when India was under British rule. It reads prophetically:

Where the mind is without fear
And the head is held high;
Where knowledge is free;
Where the world has not been
Broken up into fragments
By narrow domestic walls;
Where words came out from
The depth of truth;
Where tireless striving
Stretches its arms towards perfection;
Where the clear stream of reason
Has not lost its way
Into the dreary desert sand of dead habit;
Where the mind is led forward by thee
Into ever-widening thought and action;
Into that heaven of freedom, my Father!
Let my country awake!

Tagore longed for freedom not only on the political front but most importantly in the socio-ethical-intellectual domain. Even after seventy two years of independence, India could not, and has not, lived up to the vision of the great poet-sage, especially as far as freedom from fear is concerned.

Juxtaposed with Tagore's idea of free knowledge, India still abounds with ignorance and illiteracy. Narrow domestic walls of casteism, fundamentalism and regionalism have fragmented the fabric of the nation into mutually fearing groups (see Part 1). The stream of reason, a precious gift of the mind, has not yet impacted on so many minds in order to eschew long-held superstitions; as a result of which the self-imposed fear haunts at every step. Perhaps, a philosophical revolution of wide-awakeness and seeing dualism's fallacious logic will help reorient humanity towards a better path, a better 'race.' For now, most of the Indians seem trapped in the traditional past and habits even today, all of which continues to block their own thoughts and actions from widening their horizon to possible and actual outstanding achievements beyond the norm.

Has India realised Tagore's heaven of freedom?

A race for freedom from fear, is that too far, too much, to ask?

****

NOTES

1. Quote from https://en.wikiquote.org/wiki/Shashi_Tharoor
2. Ritter, D. (2010). The race between education and catastrophe. Retrieved from https://www.globalpolicyjournal.com/blog/03/06/2010/race-between-education-and-catastrophe
3. Excerpt from Wilber, K. (1977/2012). *The spectrum of consciousness.* Wheaton, IL: Quest Books, p. 94.
4. See Subba, D. (2014). *Philosophy of fearism: Life is conducted, directed and controlled by the fear.* Australia: Xlibris.
5. Fisher (2010) has made a case for this, while emphasizing "fear and fearlessness are dialectical conceptions and phenomena, neither of which can be understood well without knowing the other" (p. xii)—thus, any good fear management has to go beyond fear as its focus of interest, towards "freedom from fear" (e.g., *a la* Erich Fromm). Fisher, R. M. (2010). *The world's fearlessness teachings: A critical integral approach to fear management/education in the 21ˢᵗ century.* Lanham, MD: University Press of America.
6. See Chaudhry, R. (2011). *Quest for exceptional leadership: Mirage to reality.* Los Angeles, CA: Sage, pp. 166-67.

****

PART 1
B. MARIA KUMAR

CHAPTER 1

THE OLD THAT WAS NOT GOLD

Ancient Indians

When India was constructing the Tajmahal, America's colonisation was just under way, at least more than a century prior to its Independence. The scenario has changed to an unimaginable extent after less than 400 years.

North America has risen from a relatively primitive culture to an ultra-modern civilization, whereas the Indian situation has not altered much except for a minor degree of modernization in the minds of a very few people and in some pockets here and there across the country. The present general condition of Indian society seems to hold no better prospects as far as public outlook is concerned. Many historians have documented America's quick progress, whereas vert few have touched upon the crucial aspects of the underlying reasons for the overall backwardness of India.

Most of the writers over the ages went on glorifying a handful of the best facets of ancient Indian culture, but they left out the causative factors that led to the continuous retrogressive metamorphosis of Indian destiny. It is because of this critical issue that the age old psyche encompassing typical mindsets remains intact as far as caste system, poverty, superstitions, and ignorance are concerned.

If we go deep into the history of ancient India; some millennia ago, we observe that the struggle for survival led to the division of people based primarily upon muscle strength. Those who were strong physically, socially or intellectually, unfortunately exploited the situation in their favor. Here, the word *intellectual* connotes the negative-side of intelligence, in terms of conning or destroying behavior. Like in the jungle rule, might was used to exploit for selfish grandeur. The strong men controlled the society, occupied the lands and kept natural resources for themselves.

The remaining weak people did not dare to question the strong for their excesses because they were afraid of their lives at the cruel intent and retaliation of the strong. Therefore, the weak surrendered themselves to the dictates of the strong or faced the consequences. The strong few realized the efficiency of the *power of fear* which they inflicted on the weak people, fearmongering for continuity of their control over human and natural resources for their easy survival without struggle.

The Strong and the Weak

The strong few institutionalized the resultant situation by making unwritten laws. They enjoyed immunity from their own laws, and they awarded punishments to the weak for violations.

As the very ancient people always wondered at the environmental phenomena in a natural state, they also maintained their lack of the scientific approach and mostly everyone remained relatively ignorant. All were, more or less, fearful of great forces of destruction or potential destruction *via* natural occurrences like thunder, lightning, cloudbursts, cyclones, eclipses, and earthquakes.

Some self-styled intellectuals among the strong few reasoned with explanations, in their own biased ways, about the reasons for such climatic events. In doing so they held the power of explanation. They created their model of supreme power in the form of human, animal, and/or plant dynamics and wove this into myths in a mesmerizing and convincing manner. They imagined different worlds like heaven or upper world or hell or netherworld or sometimes multiple worlds existing in the upper skies or lower underground. When there was a rainbow, they popularized it as a road from the heaven to earth across the skies. When there was thunder, they meant it as the roaring sound of divine chariots and when there were floods or earthquakes, they conceptualised that the supreme powerful beings called gods were angry with the mortals. These self-fabricated notions became handy for the strong to control the weak through *fear mechanisms*. Superstitions and irrational fears reinforced each other to become the basis of a worldview.

Emergence of a Body Politic

As a social species, humans wanted to be gregarious beings for their feelings of mutual security and assurance, in large part because they mostly feared environmental disasters like forest fires, tremors, volcanic eruptions and also the natural threats from wild animals. Their migration pattern and activities living in groups ensured them not only safety and support but hope and confidence too. The strong manipulated their own position systematically in such a way as to provide extra security to others against the attacks of the wild animals.

This basic security-driven manipulation by the strong groups led to a kind of arrangement which slowly led to the institutionalization of a body politic. In successive periods, there emerged leaders among the groups for taking decisions as to where to hunt for food or how to settle the disputes within the groups or to take any further course of action in the future. In the process, body politic evolved into an autocratic form of rulership over a mass of more and more disempowered people. The system in due course transformed itself into dynastic kingdoms.

CHAPTER 2

RULERS & PRIESTS OF ANCIENT INDIA

Gods, Goddesses and Demigods

As the first body politic was formalized in the form of a monarchy or autocracy, the ruling strongman, who was a leader earlier, strove to stabilize his authority over the community. To achieve this purpose, he enlisted the support of his loyalists, who interpreted the natural phenomena as largely fearful, which served their own whims and fancies. These people subsequently assumed the garb of priests, inventing their professed chants and hymns to invoke the supreme power, the supreme security. Depending upon the type of natural phenomena like rains, winter, lightning etc, they conceived and coined different supernatural powers that came to be known as gods, goddesses, demigods etc.

Eventually, whatever the priests advised, the rulers abided by them, making it an order, decree, rule or regulation of necessary observance by the people. The ruler even believed in the prophecies of priests, as at least half of what the priest said came to be true as *per* the general probability theory would predict. Whenever there was no luck of occurrence due to lack of coincidence, the priest attributed the cause to the wrath of gods or else to the faulty procedures, negligently or inadvertently committed by the concerned. For the sake of royal convenience, the priests formulated the scriptures comprising not only holy procedures but also legal provisions for maintaining law and order by suppressing the common masses.

Formation of Castes

The main bureaucracy of the kingdom comprised more or less of those belonging to royal and priestly clans. Yet the people of middle and lower strata of the society accounted for the largest chunk of total populace in the kingdom. As conceived and documented by the ruler and priests in the scriptures, all were divided on the basis of labour as *per* which nature and type of work was determined. The people who were assigned to a particular type of work were categorised as a *caste* and consequently umpteen castes came into currency.

The ruler and priests felt it necessary and convenient for grouping the people by the methodology of castes and in order to make it incontrovertible, they incorporated a provision to that effect in the religious scriptures. Certain works which were of managerial nature were usurped by the royal and priestly clans.

The rulers felt it necessary and convenient for grouping the people by the methodology of division of labour. Certain works which were of managerial nature were usurped by the ruler, his family and relatives, whereas other supervisory positions were taken over by the priestly community. Certain vocations involving financial dealings were held by some other community members designated as business clans. In order to maintain the factors of production, the fourth type of community called common masses were assigned the functions of tilling the land, raising the crops, making household implements and serving the rulers, priests and business clans called as upper castes or forward castes and the fourth type of community came to be known as backward castes.

Those commoners who had no land were given the menial jobs of serving the other communities by working in the fields, forging the agricultural implements, taking care of pottery work, washing the clothes or utensils, sweeping the streets, making footwear and so on – all designated as lower castes. Since most of them were deliberately and forcefully kept away from owning the lands, they relied exclusively on their labor and body for their survival. Some times their own labor was also not helpful to earn them food because other communities did not provide work. Depending upon the nature of work, a large number of castes came into existence among the common masses, of whom majority were landless. They were the worst sufferers as their survival was always at stake.

The rulers and priestly community were usually under suspicion regarding the possibility of dissent and disaffection among the lower castes. In order to preempt such disruptive contingencies, stringent penal provisions were created to instill constant fear in the members of the lower castes. The people of higher castes like the ruling class, the priestly community, and the business families who were involved in financial dealings, were bestowed with special privileges of immunity to the penal provisions. The priests legitimized this concept by scripting in the texts that the three upper castes were born out of upper parts of the body of supreme power, whereas the backward and lower castes emerged from the lowly feet. The scriptures did not make any provision for dissemination of knowledge to lower castes, as a result of which they remained illiterate and ignorant and this drawback largely incapacitated development of their rational mind and reasoning abilities.

In order to give authenticity to this differential treatment and ghastly arrangement, many legends and fables were fabricated. When the stories were narrated to the younger generations during their childhood, they readily believed them. When grown up, the same generation among the lower castes taught in turn their own children the myths and legends and the tradition continued.

The mindset of the upper castes was finely attuned to control backward lower castes, whose mindset was already shaped to carry out whatever was instructed to them. To facilitate the perpetuity of the system, religion was institutionalized with the unseen supreme power as the central power entity and other gods and goddesses as auxiliary figures. The notions of religiosity spewed sentiments and hushed-up the emotional ingredients of people's personalities whenever there was resentment due to survival struggles. The common masses tolerated their exasperation or suppressed their angst, attributing the cause of their misfortune to the karmic action which was again a creation of the man-made scriptures of upper castes; hence the ancient Indian society did not witness any significant form of revolt such as a Marxian model of class struggles.

CHAPTER 3

FEAR FACTOR

The Fearful vs. the Fearsome

In general, the upper castes comprising the royal clans, priestly community and business families accounted for less than one-third of the total populace and even then they embarked on domineering the backward and lower castes consisting of the lowly artisans, menial workers, etc. Fear was resorted to by the upper castes to subjugate the lower castes. The lower castes, being enslaved psychologically as well as socially, were chronically fearful. Fear of punishments like excommunication, banishment, confinement, physical violence or even death made them categorically subservient to all passing moods and whims of the ruling castes. With fear institutionalized routinely, the specific fears of lower castes became collectively self-debilitating because of their demotivating nature.

Less obvious perhaps, on the other hand, is that the upper castes also had their own fears. The rulers were apprehensive about their continuity on the throne of power. The members of the priestly community were sceptical about their own influence over others whether the commoners would continue to believe in them. Unfortunately, such fears drove them to further fortify their powers. Juxtaposed to the fears of the lower castes, the fears of the upper castes were self-strengthening for their unceasing dominance.

The everyday survival concerns of the lower castes made them to feel fearful for life, whereas the power-mongering anxieties of the upper castes emboldened them to be fearsome. Therefore, *negative fear* dominated the existence of the lower castes because their worries and their feelings of uncertainty and insecurity permeated throughout their lives in a disempowering manner. Such thoughts also propelled them to become pessimistic about their future. Resultantly, almost every member of the lower castes felt demoralized as far as their hopes and dreams were concerned.

Emptiness percolated down to their line of thinking rendering the lower caste people dejected not only within themselves but also with their fraternity of the same kinship or fellowship. Fear of penalties for dissension shoved them into a stressful living that in turn led to self-pity and ill health. Life itself seemed disconsolate and inadequacy of fulfillment reigned throughout their caste professions. The lower castes because of their menial jobs were kept at a distance from the upper caste members on the basis of the so-called 'purity' notions. Over the years, the lower castes also came to be designated as the untouchables, all the way back to times BC.

Wages of Fear

Benevolent or *positive fear* motivated the members of the royal clan to learn a variety of effective skills like sports, military exercises, and activities of physical robustness. They believed that such skills would ensure their strength and supremacy to continue. Military skills involved raising the army's capacity and its preparation for facing dissent or any invasions. Their planning abilities sharpened their expertise in strategizing and tactical approaches. Fear of failure in war made them alert and cautious while making decisions. Positive fear helped the members of the royal, priestly and business castes seek more knowledge and information *via* systematic education. Such motivational factors turned them not only worldly-wise but also skilled manipulative tacticians.

As time passed, there were changes in the outlook of the kings. Some kings were altruistic whereas other successors were cruel in their approaches to rule over their territories. Mostly, there was no people-oriented governance. The rulers fortified the institutions of caste, religion, family, marriage, education etc., by promoting their policies and methods on the basis of exploiting superstitions and irrationality of the people. Whatever the king uttered was a law.

The advice of the priestly caste was largely based on prejudices and illogical practices, based on fear. There was no invited cooperative consent of the subjects taken as part of policy-making. Governance was carried out through dogmatism and a less than human fear management paradigm. The people were extra intimidated from time to time lest they start questioning the system. Whatever natural resentment existed on the part of the common people, it was nipped in the bud through increasing threats.

When taken together, all these brutal measures forced the lower castes to surrender their freedoms to the wishes of the ruler and upper castes. The upper caste members tried to project themselves as paternalistic protectors of the land; and yet, the commoners' fears grew unmindful of logic and failed in reason. There was, and still is, widespread ignorance that resulted in the maintenance of baseless traditions, blind customs, and unscientific practices. *Fear* became the multi-edged weapon through which the upper castes exploited every aspect of the socio-economic and political situation to benefit their vested interests and power.

CHAPTER 4

FEAR OF FAILURE

Inconvenient Statistics: Poverty & Youth Unemployment

Either in ancient India or modern India, the people belonging to the lower castes have not realized their full potential. Of the various reasons, one of utmost importance is *fear* and its role. How fear has been whimsical in the development of their lower caste psyches and how that fear had negatively shaped their destiny can be understood from different perspectives.

In this regard, here is one aspect of concern that has ample examples to cite. They were unable to *visualize* their future regarding certain goals or ambitions above daily survival needs and suffering—like for example, unable to envision achievement, satisfaction, success or meaning of life etc. A good deal of this lack was because most of the time they were engaged in body based labour but that led to pessimistic attitudes in the sense that they could not dream positively. They were fearful to such an extent that they could not think of imagining a *good life*.

This kind of negative fear-ridden attitude has been all pervasive in the minds of the people of lower castes since ancient times. Though there has been a trend to show that a little improvement took place because of Dr. B. R. Ambedkar's efforts of modernization and education on the part of these deprived castes, these people, on an overall scale, could only achieve to some negligible extent, that too limited to a few people of the lower castes.

Still, much of the downtrodden population, due to their backwardness in terms of survival aspects and intellectual levels, could not think of a better life and its actualization. They are still unable to visualize a good experience in the current day digital India.

If we go by government statistics to date, there are about 330 million people in India who have been starving, and likely this is increasing day-by-day. This figure might be on the rise at *par* with the escalating population. The people below poverty line (BPL) category always face unfortunate prospects. The total population that is roughly 135 crores now, shows an increasing trend in producing unproductive youth as a consequence of which economic backwardness, coupled with socio-political maladies, have been playing havoc in the lives of majority of the masses.

The population of India consists mainly of youth. Young persons are numbering about 90 crores, i.e., nearly 70%. Of them, the youth below that of average age, that is 26 years as *per* recent statistics is 50%, and if the maximum limit for youth is taken up as the age of 35 years, the population of the youth goes up to 90 crores, and most of these young persons could be classified as *precariats*, of which is discussed in greater detail in *The Youth Don't Cry* [1] book by Kumar and Sushmita (2018). Youth then are unable to pursue productive employment because of lack of opportunities. These opportunities are not being made available from outside, again because of continuous shortcomings in the policies that have been made by the authorities and on account of certain criteria like self-made negativistic attitudes thrust upon them by themselves. If the analysis is made clear, the realization is very startling. The unproductive youth roughly comes to around 70 crores of the population. So, out of 90 crores of the youth population, only 20 crores seem to be productively employed.

Youth can contribute their might to the socioeconomic development of the nation, if they are supported to do so. The maximum number of youth who are unproductive and still unemployed are at the almost receiving end of the society because of lack of vision and hope due to fear. "[T]he issue of handling fear [well] assumes critical significance on the part of the youth's agenda to advance progressively" [2].

The first blockade to the opportunity is *unmindful attitude*. Because it renders a mind lost in irrelevance. Productivity is nothing but achieving success in fulfilment of one's ambitions. How does success happen? Success happens when there are efforts and when these efforts are in place in the right manner such that these very efforts meet the opportunities. Then only will there be realization of the ambition. That means the success has happened. In this equation, if we look at the current situation, the concept of effort plays a pivotal role. One should go on attempting and putting his or her honest attempts in whatever ethical manner he or she wishes to achieve. When efforts are absent, there is no possibility of meeting the opportunity. There should be perfect sync and a sort of rendezvous between effort and the opportunity. How does that rendezvous happen? It is a kind of probable concept. More probability exists if the efforts are more and continuous. Whenever efforts cease to exist, the probability of winning also decreases in descending order. Again coming to efforts, how does one put in efforts, and how will we determine whether effort results in a conscientious attempt *vis-a-vis* the precariat youth?

Fear is the Bad Luck

If we go by an experiment conducted by Richard Wiseman, we can conclude that the attitude of mindfulness takes a greater prominence in shaping the conscientious efforts. Richard Wiseman is a psychologist who conducted a unique type of perception experiment on his subjects, mixed male and female adults. He distributed copies of the local newspaper to them. He simply asked them to enumerate the number of pictures or images in the newspaper and he declared that the person who could give the correct number of pictures within the shortest possible time would get a prize. So, what had happened during the course of experiment was that a few persons were able to answer correctly within a short time but most of the persons were not able to give the answers timely. Then Wiseman analyzed the whole status and went through each subject's profile and interviewed them. Then he came to know that the people who were able to give the right answer at the earliest were those who were going through each page of the newspaper with mindfulness because on the second page of the newspaper there was one message in big letters, about the size of few inches, visible boldly to the reader mentioning that there were 43 pictures in that newspaper. At the end of the message was the experimenter's name, as though he quoted. That meant it was a clear proof that the total number of pictures could be 43 and there was no need to count the pictures going through each page of the newspaper.

Here Wiseman concluded that the people whom he called as *lucky* people, winning the prize, were lucky in the sense that they were *mindful* while going through the newspaper and as they turned to the second page, immediately they could catch the message. Because they were watching not only the pictures, they were also scanning other news reports. Everything was being done very consciously. However, the other group of subjects could not do that even though they were trying very hard to figure out the number of the pictures in the whole newspaper. For this latter group, their efforts largely went in vain because they were not cautious while going through each page of the newspaper, and they lost sight of the very crucial message. This experiment reveals that mindfulness plays a vital role during the course of any effort. When the effort is in place with mindfulness that is a real effort. When there is no mindfulness in the effort, it is devoid of direction as it could not lead the subject towards the opportunity. Anxiety and fear blur mindfulness.

Extrinsic Blockades of Opportunities

Opportunity is like time. Time is flowing everywhere. And it is equally available to each and every being in the same manner. Though the opportunities are available, the people who have been searching for them are unable to grab them because they are out of mindfulness. Again, regarding opportunities, there are certain factors which block the person from approaching the opportunities. They become a type of mental barrier to a person's efforts when they are in pursuit of opportunities. These blockades can be broadly categorized into two, one is *intrinsic blockades* and the second one is *extrinsic blockades.*

Extrinsic blockades are those which are externally coerced. Here one example from the great epic of Mahabharata could be cited. There was Ekalavya, a hunter, a youth, who wanted to achieve excellence in archery and learn more. One day he happened to go to the great teacher, Drona. Drona was the guru of the royal siblings, the Kauravas, and the Pandavas.

Ekalavya being a youth from the jungles and he being not of royal blood, was refused to join the class. He prayed to Drona to make him his disciple, but he faced disappointment. Drona did not entertain his request simply because he was not eligible as he was not of royal blood. Drona's decision was as *per* the customs and traditions prescribed during those days in ancient India. Depending upon this contextual reason, the youth of jungles, Ekalavya was not able to achieve excellence. Otherwise, he would have reached his full potential having as much mastery as Arjuna might have got. Even though the legends eulogised Ekalavya for his highly skilful archery, history denied him opportunity. Despite his well-meaning efforts, Ekalavya could not seize the opportunity because of certain extrinsic blockades put forth during his way to the path of success, and these blockades were created by none other than the socially enforced customs, rules, and traditions. This is known as externally imposed restriction. They act as obstruction to the chances as a result of which the efforts could not be in a position to have rendezvous with.

Intrinsic Blockades of Opportunities

The second type of obstruction is the intrinsic blockade. Here we can cite an example of a great runner, Eric Liddell. He was a British racer. At that point of time, very few could match his prowess in the athletics as running champion. For the 1924 Paris Olympics he was selected as a participant from Britain to represent the country. One thing about Eric Liddell was that he was a devout Christian. He followed the teachings of the Bible to the letter and spirit.

He resumed his practice and already he was a medal hopeful in 100 meters race. Everybody was sure of his winning a gold medal. When the time came, the heats of the 100 meters run were held on a Sunday. Having come to know about it in the schedule, he refused to run because for him Sunday was a rest day and he did not want to work on Sunday, because according to Bible, Sunday is for praying and resting. On hearing this, his officers who were in charge of the British team goaded him to participate, and despite many pleas and requests from his friends and other co-athletes of the team, he was stuck on his conviction. Hence, he could not get Olympic medal in 100 meters race.

If we analyze this instance, we see that Eric Riddell was a promising youth and had he participated, he would have surely won the championship in 100 meters, because opportunity was there. His efforts were there. He was practicing. He had prepared for the event as a mindful practitioner, but even then he could not succeed because he created a blockade for himself. Even though there was an opportunity, his efforts could not meet the opportunity, due to his self -imposed restriction. These situations normally happen in the lives of most of the people in India because of fear, superstitions and blind belief systems.

Fear, Efforts and Opportunities

Irrational fear can be observed in efforts and also in barriers to opportunities. As regards to efforts, how irrational fear becomes an impediment to mindfulness can be found in the experiment done by Richard Wiseman (as mentioned in the preceding pages). The people who could not enumerate the number of pictures in the newspaper and those who had taken longer time were actually anxious and psychologically perturbed because of mental strains or tensions with the task or life in general. This can be attributed to irrational fear as a result of which they were unable to observe or perceive the things, while going through or turning the pages of the newspaper. However, on the other hand, the people who succeeded in figuring out the right number of pictures timely were relatively without anxiety or fear. When there are no irrational fears, one could see things clearly. That is what has happened with the people who have succeeded in winning the prize.

If we come to opportunities, again fears are there in both extrinsic blockades and intrinsic blockades. When Drona refused Ekalavya, he could not react to that. Ekalavya merely obeyed his orders and went away. He was afraid of the consequences. Moreover, his personality imbibed the inculcation of fear regarding complying with orders of the royal court. Because even though the fear was irrational, he felt fearful of repercussions of violation and just walked away. Also, even in case of the intrinsic blockades, irrational fear exists. Eric Liddell was afraid of non-adherence to the teachings of the Bible and he had no intention to analyze his decision in the light of rationality. His mind was oriented towards blind following of the scriptures. As a result of his adherence to socially-sanctioned self-imposed religious rules, he could not win the medal for 100 meters. So, it is also a clear example of irrational fear that has led Eric Liddell to fail in his desire to achieve success.

Beset by such fears, the people of lower castes have been losing opportunities on various platforms despite constitutional provisions, because socio-psychologically indoctrinated and inculcated irrational mindsets based on fear often tend to supersede even legal empowerments. Change and development of human potential can be undermined by fear of the fearful and the fearsome (see Chapter 3).

NOTES

1. See Kumar, B. M., & Sushmita, B. S. (2018). *The youth don't cry: A critical commentary on the youth about their fears and hopes amidst adversities and opportunities.* Bhopal, India: Indra Publishing House.
2. Ibid., p. 166.

CHAPTER 5

INEQUALITY & FEAR

Literals and Laterals

Dr. B. R. Ambedkar said,

To idealize the real, which more often than not is full of inequities, is a very selfish thing to do. Only when a person finds a personal advantage in things as they are that he tries to idealize the real. To proceed to make such an ideal real is nothing short of criminal. It means perpetuating inequity on the ground that whatever once settled is settled for all times. Such a view is opposed to all morality. [1]

This quote describes the general situation even today in Indian society. Dr. B. R. Ambedkar was referring to the days of British Raj. If we take all the people, both the rich upper castes and the poor backward and lower castes as the survivors, we may broadly divide them into two groups. One group is the people who need not bother about their basic livelihoods. We may call them as lateral survivors or *laterals*. The other group, which is naturally a much larger group, who had to make both ends meet with much difficulty, may be called as literal survivors or *literals*.

In other words, the literals are have-nots, the biggest chunk of the Indian population, comprising mostly the members of backward and lower castes and including backward and the erstwhile untouchables. They are hungry and thirsty, struggling with chronic uncertainty to survive the insecure socio-economic-political conditions at all odds. On the other hand, the laterals continue to survive their privileged lives. They are the members of the upper castes, born with social privileges of ascribed status and economic privileges of ancestral properties and ease of doing any type of business or entrepreneurship. They want to survive their current elite status. That means not going down below the current standard of living. Also they are too ambitious to earn more to be more secure. These laterals do not need to survive literally. They have to survive the sophistication.

Poverty and Ignorance

No doubt, the status of *literals* has improved over the years. The condemned communities that once were forced to reside at the outskirts of settlements began making their habitats inside the villages and towns. Those who were not permitted to read and write once upon a time came over the obstacles to some extent thanks to social reformers and benevolent legislations. Though untouchability was eradicated on paper, far-flung corners of the country still experience its practice even now. Often reports emerge from the public that the educated literals either encountered problems in getting or could not get houses for rent for living in the central areas of towns and cities. From a health point of view of everyone, both literals and laterals gained much due to access to proper nutrition and medical facilities. Advanced facilities again were available only to the affordable laterals but *not* to the literals, who cannot cope with expenses due to lack of resources.

Once Swami Vivekananda lamented at the severity of starvation and reprimanded his fellow Indian citizens for their indifference towards poverty and ignorance on the part of masses. The current scenario is better than those earlier days, but the official statistics declare that there are about 330 million starving people in recent years. If ignorance level is stipulated, the status is again not encouraging. As much as 30% of the

Indian population is illiterate. However, one of the recent studies shows that those young persons who did schooling were found to be wanting in simple general knowledge. Unfamiliar with their surroundings, most of the pupils could not answer to most straightforward questions regarding the state's capital or national capital and the like, when asked. It shows that they are namesake literates.

In another research study, the young college students were found to be orthodox and traditional in their attitudes. Their thinking has been oriented towards *irrational* practices even though they are being taught modern science in colleges. Though their way of dressing and manner of eating are quite modern, their attitudes are still of acute fear-based superstitions. This tendency has roots in the unshakeable foundations of blind belief systems. Unfortunately, most people and leaders often ignore the insidious negative impact of such irrational notions on the young generation.

Unseen or Unreal

The *literals* believe that their inferior position in the society is due to their birth status as *per* scriptures or sutras. They hardly resent the discrimination shown upon them by the laterals because they have already come to terms of fateful acceptance with their place in society.

Their only hope is the unseen gods and goddesses, who in their faith can grant them with upper status and security in the next birth. This is one of the fundamental reasons that the spirit of religiosity thrives among the people of backward lower castes. The *laterals* also promote religiosity to the hilt and their advantage of power. They have already had the benefit of enjoying the status they desired, both social and economic. The remaining status that they crave for is political status. Power along with fear forms the core of their agenda, be it explicit or implicit. The democratic system in India is best suited for them to grab votes for winning in the elections. Because of their standing on the higher rungs of the society, they feel that the existing system of majority voting is convenient. They have already attributed the cause of their ascribed elevated status to the gods, and hence they firmly believe in divine blessings, so religious spirit is further reinforced in the minds of the laterals.

Tragically, religiosity forms the crux of cause for inequality as well as acquiescence to continue in India. Inequality is imposed from within and from outside. When born, humans are equal in their outlook, free from prejudice. The socialization process through myths, customs and rituals easily distorts the instinctual form of equality to become self-prejudiced forms of inequality.

External imposition occurs through the propagation of self-prejudiced inequality from individual to individual. *Social inequality* dominates over other inequalities, economic, legal and political. The act of hierarchical *domination* thrives on the existence and continuance of ascribed status. There is inequality between the oppressor and the oppressed. In the words of Steven Biko, one's acquiescence to inequality becomes the weapon of the oppressor. This is silent submissiveness without serious effort to critically analyze the causes and consequences on the part of the oppressed—namely, the literals and the oppressor being the laterals.

This type of apathy *via* an oppressive tendency was observed during Hitler's Nazi period. Whatever the dictates came from the Fuhrer, compliance was done not only by the German soldiers but also by the so-called right-thinking citizens. Edmund Burke reasoned that the fundamental cause for the triumph of evil is non-action on the part of passive good citizens in terms of submissive silence.

Historians opine that such a Holocaust during the Nazi tyranny resulted in genocide, just because of such diabolical tolerance. Einstein said, "The world is in greater peril from those who tolerate or encourage evil than from those who actually commit." Such instances in lower degree are a common sight in India where megalomania is quite visible in the upper strata of society. Such megalomaniacs in large number are obsessed with the delusions of self- superiority and enforce their will on the submissive literals. Whenever there occurs some small degree of resistance, riots ensue in which the weak submissive literals have to fend for themselves for their survival. The silent, powerless, acquiescent and submissive majority of literals obey the tyrannical rulings of the elite minority of laterals who manoeuvre through various fear mechanisms.

Steven Biko's phrase of the *oppressed mind* refers to *fear*, both rational and irrational. Rational, in a sense that the oppressed knows the eventualities in case of non-compliance of the oppressor's dictates. Irrational in a sense that the oppressed imagines the unwarranted anxious scenarios so as to inflict in mind more tensions and more worries. These fears, inequalities and submissive attitudes coupled with ignorance, illiteracy, and poverty are causing havoc to democratic processes. Democracy, as a principle and concept as such, is not suitable for those countries comprising poor and ignorant majority of the population. Because the leaders are elected on the basis of majority vote.

Dunning and Kruger's findings reveal that the leaders, elected on the majority vote of the unwise and less knowledgeable electorates would be unwise and incapable. The decisions made by such bad leaders hardly lead to any real progress. Since the first general elections in 1952, the fate of India has been still unchanged in regards to poverty and caste inequality without proper social security measures. Pensions are a strange word that has not yet occurred in the minds of the leaders in the correct sense. Despite huge revenues through imposition and collection of a multitude of taxes and cesses, the essential aspects of human life have been ignored. This ignorance on the part of the democratically elected leaders may not be deliberate or unmindful. However, it is due to sheer lack of knowledge, vision, and wisdom as to how to manage the affairs of the nation in equity perspective.

Penny Wise, Pound Foolish

Mistaken assumptions, misplaced priorities, and irrational rules and unnecessary socially-sanctioned procedures have been resulting in the criminal wastage of energy, time and budget. The unfortunate aspect of the top leadership is that there is no common sense involved in their decision making. There's no impetus among them for vision of exceptional leadership. Disappointingly, when there is not a wide and deep vision for society, one decision taken in one area of management may cause a little benefit leading to considerable losses in another area.

Holistic spectral thinking seems to be lacking. There are many instances which illustrate that the policy made on liquor trade, for example, led to a loss of millions of jobs. One rule implemented in the food dimension left lakhs of private vendors without work. A decision taken in the industrial sector made thousands of villages thirsty. Such blind approaches do not appear to be intentional. It is quite inferable to say that most of the leaders in power are as ignorant as the illiterate masses as far as policy making for the whole nation is concerned. The dictum, "penny wise, pound foolish," sounds apt in the Indian scenario of planning.

With official statistics of 30% illiteracy in the masses, an unprecedented emphasis in initiatives by government goes to digital literacy. All procedural formalities are being digitalized. The worrisome factor is how the illiterate masses can cope with the trend. School admission percentage is still discouraging. The same stress, as given to digital literacy has not yet been accorded to functional literacy. Due to the ongoing trend in the same manner, more and more people are unable to reap the benefits of a digital economy since an illiterate villager has to become literate functionally first and foremost, which is not happening. The worst affected are the illiterate literals, who are neither capable of participating in e-tenders nor able to make independent e-transactions.

Height of Ignorance

The overall position in India is that the culmination of negative factors, like non-adherence to the principle of economic determinism (of Karl Marx), making too many laws and rules to administer (as Thoreau feared), creating more inequalities due to incompatible balance between growing joblessness and increasing automation (as Stephen Hawking worried) etc., have led to much bigger problems.

Diagnostics has always been a significant drawback to policy makers and planners. When the real cause is economical in nature they diagnosed it to be of fundamentalism or fanaticism. If the youth are going astray due to joblessness, they reasoned that the youngsters are addicted to digital gadgets. If corruption is escalating because of growing insecurity and uncertainty, they thought that the existing laws are not sufficient. If the rapes and molestations are on the rise as a result of the non-availability of ventilating mechanisms in the world of growing isolation, they felt that they are the effects of Kaliyug (the era of doom).

When diagnostics are such a misconceived and least priority issue, what to assess re: prognostics is far away from the minds of the policymakers. Added to all these maladies are a proliferation of rules, regulations, and procedures, on a day-to-day basis, causing more restrictions, more confusions and more fears. These rules and procedures have not only curbed the freedom of citizens but also created additional avenues to the unscrupulous public servants for unethical practices. The more the laws and rules are, the more the stipulations and the less the opportunities are. The more the procedures are, the more the corruption is. Thoreau and Jefferson advocated for a minimal number of laws which are essential for safety, security, and liberty of the individuals. They visualized the dangers of the impact of too much of curtailment on individual freedoms.

There are new laws framed in every session of Indian assembly or parliament. With each law comes a multitude of rules and procedures. Such a continuous scenario has only resulted in a sort of Arachne's never-ending dragnet in which more and more victims tend to be hooked and included; among the victims are those who turn out to be innocents in due course.

Digging Their Own Graves

It is also perceptible that an increasing number of legislators and parliamentarians themselves are unwittingly falling prey to their own design when they happen to get hooked in the dragnet. Such instances are on the rise day-by-day as though they are digging their own graves.

Though it is legally and ethically proper to take every possible course of action while bringing such nefarious elements to justice, there is an inherent shortcoming regarding abuse and misuse of the dragnet on the part of enforcers, who mostly are not judicious as *per* general probability. Such dragnets at the local level through the laws of local bodies, at the state level through the state laws and at the national level through the laws of central government have proven to be causing excess fear and stress among the general public. This anxious climate is engulfing every tender mind. It has created a discouraging tendency among the youth in particular, while taking initiatives in realizing the existing opportunities.

Ultimately, the whole events, building up into a complex grid-like vicious circle called *chakravyuha*, emerged on the current Indian scene. With the advent of advanced technology, which is proliferating and making inroads into the depths of socioeconomic-political lives, the resultant situations have become more alarming. Privacy has been affected by the digital foot print, and the hitherto concealed casteist and fundamentalistic undercurrents have surfaced with the result that the maximum of Indian social environment has not only been polluted but poisoned, even to the extent of civil war like conditions at times, albeit, at regional levels. Such indicators point at internal animosity as far as oft-quoted "unity in diversity" and "national integration" are interpreted in practical sense. As security has been being warranted for more and more significant persons (VIPs), the notion of liberty is impaired. Because of security management operations, the general public began to face increasing constraints to move at their will. Therefore, public liberty has been adversely impacted.

Because of mounting restrictions in the guise of public order regulations, people are accordingly left with little choice to realize their potential or element of free well. More laws created more work, including that which is unnecessary; hence Stephen Hawking's vision of luxurious leisure seems to be doomed in India.

NOTES

1.   Excerpt from Ambedkar, B. R. (1990). *Writings and speeches.* Volume 7.

CHAPTER 6

THE RACE OF THE THIRD KIND

Achilles and Tortoise

The archetypal race started long ago. It was in the ancient times of Indian civilization. Achilles raced with the tortoise. One may wonder how Achilles figured on Indian scene. However, it was true, Achilles was alive then also and is alive even today in memory. How Achilles had existed since then is a long, long story.

Let us talk about the race. It was not Achilles who wanted to run the race. He was conditioned not to compete in any contest. However, it was tortoise who provoked him to race him. Tortoise might have had a different motive to instigate him into the race because of some vested interest.

Competition did not mean any other purpose than achieve its selfish reason. Achilles was crude mentally as he already physically was. Well-built, tough and robust bodied, Achilles was living a life of the animal within the niceties of his livelihood. The situation was quite the opposite to that of tortoise. Tortoise was gentlemanly. Small, smart, yet witty, the tortoise had a sophisticated life with all comforts, rights, and privileges. When instigated, goaded and motivated, Achilles also thought that he had to be like the tortoise. However, the intentions of tortoise were evil, selfish and megalomaniacal. By contrast, Achilles was illiterate, ignorant, unrefined in thought and straightforward.

For the race, tortoise wanted a head start. Achilles thought that tortoise had already been much ahead of him. Therefore, he nodded in usual temper. The tortoise was very sweet in talking. He said that his pad-like legs hardly allowed it to run faster, by comparison with human legs.

Achilles, despite his pitiable state, pitied for clever tortoise. And the race started. Within no time, Achilles realized that even in the real sport, he was no match to tortoise because tortoise began flying whereas he was still on foot race. The tortoise did not inform that its shell bore wings on either side. Achilles understood that the wings of tortoise, by metaphor, were made of social privileges. Earlier too, tortoise kept him in the dark on many occasions. Achilles felt for a while as though he was deceived but when he remembered the history of his life since childhood, he felt it normal in his senses as it was the same in every aspect, every time.

First and Second Races

Unlike Zeno's race of mythical Achilles and mythical tortoise, the competition between the real Achilles and real tortoise involved gaps between the two at every stage that began increasing and increasing. This current race is the third one, prior to which Zeno and mathematicians conducted both the first and second races, respectively. Zeno was impartial in the sense that he put Achilles and tortoise under equal conditions with no privileges to either of the two. Comforts and rights were the same to both of them. Since tortoise was small, he gave extra advantage of the head start in the race, with the voluntary consent of Achilles.

Zeno played a trick, of course, not deliberately, but amusingly. Achilles was an acknowledged athlete. He was ten times faster than tortoise. Fixing the target as already agreed upon with governable treatment, the tortoise was given a head start. Every one-furlong tortoise covered in the distance, Achilles had already done ten furlongs. In successive intervals, gaps between tortoise and Achilles began diminishing, yet tortoise was ahead of him towards the target. Zeno, the referee, logically adjudged the tortoise winner as Achilles could not reach the distance of equivalence because of the fact that the gap was smaller and smaller and as small as a hair's width at the end. The target looked comprising infinite number of gaps. This was the first race, where logic triumphed.

A second race ensued under the alert supervision of mathematicians who assisted Zeno in refereeing. Mathematicians extended their expert advice to Zeno in measuring the target distance. Since distance was a fixed, finite one, there was no chance for both the racers to run the race infinitely and indefinitely. The defined target would always be achievable, hence achieved when Achilles overtook the tortoise. Here, observed reality made Achilles triumphant.

Race of the Third Kind

The third race is still in progress. Zeno had disappeared from the scene. Mathematicians also did not understand as to how the adjudication of the third race could materialise with the existing logic and equations. Not only the mathematicians, economists, sociologists, scientists, political analysts, but even the bureaucrats and policymakers have not yet been able to understand how to supervise the timely execution of the race.

The racers, of course, are known by different names now. Achilles represents the literals, encompassing the largest proportion of the Indian population categorized as marginal classes, weaker sections, disadvantaged classes, downtrodden masses or have-nots. Tortoise, on the other hand, denotes the laterals, having all social privileges with ascribed higher status. In this third race, neither logic nor observed reality seems to be winning. In the first race, Zeno's logic of infinite number of gaps won; whereas, in the third race the logic of majority of literals winning majority of seats in the parliament failed. In the second race, observed reality was unanimously positive, whereas in the third race, the observed reality was negativistic, rendering the majority literals poor, unproductive and still cursed.

The race between them is precisely not against each other. It is for achieving the target. The target is not a post as in the initial case of Achilles and tortoise. The objective is something which goes on as a process of advancing. Whosoever is reaching it or within the vicinity, literals or laterals or all together would have already achieved much and would be advancing ahead. Those whose position on the track of the race is still much behind in time and civilization are struggling for existence. The target denotes the real, practical and attainable goals of life, liberty, freedom, dignity, equality, fraternity, justice, fearlessness, and happiness.

The laterals did not encounter hurdles over the centuries and millennia towards the target, for having enjoyed most of the fruits. As the target is advancing with technological revolution, and with corresponding social change, the benefits in the form of ultra-modern comforts with additional perks like luxurious leisure, self- actualization, the meaning of life and so forth have already reached most of the laterals or the remaining are almost at their doorstep.

Contrarily, the target is moving farther and farther away from the literals. Their position might have surely moved a bit from their original locale towards the direction of the goals but there was no perceptible improvement. One of the main reasons for this gulf of difference between the standings of laterals and literals is because of the said privileges associated with the former since birth. The ascribed status has been inbuilt in their social standing. Since Indian society became a closed system, social standings have continued to be indelible. Known as 'born with privileges,' they are akin to 'blue blood' or 'royal lineage' system of incontrovertible tradition.

Such privileges have bestowed upon the laterals almost every possible advantage over the literals in the third race. Opportunities included not only intangible perquisites like ascribed higher status in society, caste tag, respect, dignity, certain immunities but also tangible assets like land, capital, entrepreneurship opportunities, knowledge acquiring facilities etc. These privileges had automatically provided the laterals with a remarkable head start on the track towards the target, since birth.

The Short Arm of the Law

Because of hue and cry on the part of literals at times, the laterals who dominated the echelons of hierarchy in the government or power structure socially and economically, provided to literals with some *pro tem largesse* in law to silence them. Such generosity comprised certain relaxations in limited form for educational and employment purposes and a few positions in democratic process and set-up. Now the race has donned a modern avatar in the sense that it is not between the socially privileged laterals and the legally empowered literals. The crucial aspect of how the equity and equality to be achieved would depend upon the intriguing question of whether legal empowerment would enable the literals to reach the equivalence at *par* with the social privileges, not to speak of the ultimate goal of target fulfilment. The indisputable fact is that laws are made by the society *via* the elite, but not the other way round. The primacy of *culture* has been innate in the collective nature of human groups since the beginning of the human race. Laws are not permanent or absolute, they are relative to the times. The law that existed earlier may have been repealed today. The code which is not existent in the present may come into being in the future.

However, society and much of cultural tradition is quite permanent. The privileges bestowed by the community even in unwritten form by sheer force of fear and taboo are almost impossible to wither away unless structural metamorphosis of society occurs. This is relevant to change in India, because the social structure is the foundation on which human relations stand.

Legal empowerment, being limited in its operation and jurisdiction concerning subjects and objects of life, is also generally short-term oriented as it gets extended from time to time. This kind of thought has instilled the feeling of general uncertainty and insecurity in the minds of the literals. From the beginning, ambiguity grew in intensity as the literals had already been living otherwise also in the grip of uncertainty since long due to social ostracisation.

Fear-stricken due to this steady uncertainty the literals hardly made any further progress towards the target. They lagged in almost all spheres of a social life due to blockades to opportunities. They didn't have the privilege of owning lands nor did they possess the capital to invest in economic activities. Forced imposition of work allocations as a permanent feature of caste scuttled all the chances to aspire for the calling of their choice. The only factor of production that has been in their abilities is physical labor and labor became their everything, not only a means of survival but also a source of their exploitation at the hands of the strong privileged laterals.

The age-old custom of adhering to one's caste vocation is still in practice to a considerable extent. As a result, a shoe mending literal can hardly open a tea stall, or a low caste farm labourer cannot dream of becoming a priest at a temple. Since inter-caste marriages were prohibited as *per* the age-old scriptures, legal authorization of such has hardly taken precedence over the religious texts. Culture again, rules over law in practical ways. Ancient customs and traditions continued to prevail relegating legal provisions to namesake formalities in most of the interior regions of India.

Caste Casting Aspersions

Modern India does not see the visible change in many literals as their castes are still the basis for their social status. Caste names suffixed to individual names automatically lead to apparent inequality in prejudiced feelings and external impressions — that way, individual degradation is being practiced if not overtly at least at psychological level even in urban areas.

The literals tend to accept their so-called socially-sanctioned fate of being born in the lower castes because of karmic effect, as they believe so. This belief had resulted effectively in their voluntary self-degradation. In the same way, the laterals also reflect the same ideas assuming that their so-called karma in the previous birth was responsible for their current upper status. This is the perpetually in-built inequality. Strange, yet the truth is that both the oppressed as well as the oppressors do accept their status, with little critical questioning.

This riddle of caste observance made the social status of literals remain at the backward and lower strata, rendering them unacceptable in full sense in the mainstream of social life. Therefore, social exclusions impacted freedom on the part of literals as regards to the pursuance of their future. A negligible number of literals who gained acceptance in the mainstream were able to take part in economic activities of their choice but it is rare.

Likewise, the acquiescence of the literals set their minds in such a way as to view inter-caste marriages as a strange, if not taboo phenomena. Hence, their intermingling with other caste communities remained minimal. This leads to lesser interactions and subsequent poor exchange of ideas blocking their visions negatively. Most of the technical jobs like weaving, cobbling, blacksmithing, pottery etc. are the hallmark of literals' professions which needed innovations from time to time. Due to lack of open-mindedness and lack of worldly exposure, the traditional technology didn't make any encouraging headway in India—and, most of all technologies, to large extent, had to be imported from Western countries. This built a dependency on foreigners which is not always to the advantage of India's self-reliance and development.

Winged Tortoise Always Ahead

From an educational point of view, the literals have been the worst sufferers. They comprise by far most of the illiterates of the country. As were already deprived of land and capital, the only available source of production they had is their bodies and labor. Unfortunately, literals could not fully make use of it due to lack of education and access of to power in the society.

If educated, literals would have long ago turned into creative inventors and innovators. They could have managed their fears more rationally. Ignorance coupled with superstitions played havoc with their future as their earlier status continued to be the same in the present. Uneducated parents could not guide their children toward better health and improved livelihoods. They lost countless opportunities only because they didn't have 3 Rs.

Consequently, there was no mechanism to upgrade literals' knowledge. Their mindset was based on the continued systems of submissive, subdued and confined living. There was no change in their manner of working and living. In fact, there was not an iota of radical transformation. Changelessness continued century after century whereas the laterals experienced continuous advances, thereby progressing further nearer towards the target. The gap between the foot racing Achilles of literals and the winged tortoise of laterals went on widening.

With the explosion of information technology, came along the realities of the knowledge economy and digital society. The literals, who had the maximum chunk of functional illiterates, are entirely uninformed about digital operations. The laterals who have been born with land, capital, entrepreneurship and education had a significant advantage to fully exploit digital resources as there is no competition from the multitudinous literals.

The digital economy as such requires limited human resources but the dividends are unimaginably gigantic. Stephen Hawking has already warned about the emergence of widening disparities as a result of huge profits, pocketed by the digital technocrats, leaving the rest at a much lower level in the ladder of the economy. Digitally ignorant literals would naturally remain at the bottom.

The Demon of Democracy

On the overt political front, the state of the literals has never been encouraging neither in the past nor in the present. The democratic system opened its doors for all to become part of the process but the necessary evil kind of majority rule suited more favorably the educated rich laterals.

Though the electorate comprises more of literals, the winning candidates belong to the group of laterals. Despite largesse to the literals in the form of limited earmarked positions of legislators and parliamentarians, they formed a tiny minority in the assembly or parliament or on the cabinet. That too, the small number of legislator literals could not assert their share of political power in policy-making due to fear and domination from the side of the domineering laterals.

The so-called ideals of modern secularism and/or traditional religiosity could not deliver the desired outcome regarding equality, fraternity, liberty, and freedom. The rights and privileges of the literals were not always secure. The lack of respect for tolerance towards individual rights continued to drag the overall little progress down. The wrong prioritization of the budget allocation made the developmental process upside down.

The rich had become more productive and the poor had become more impoverished. The widening disparity could be attributed among other things primarily to a lopsided formulation of plans as regards to the individual freedoms of the literals.

India has always boasted of its secular credentials. Indian planners forgot that individual rights assume primacy over other factors like secularism, religiosity, democracy, nuclear energy, space technology or industrialization.

When personal freedom is secure, the people are naturally able to grasp the opportunities. Otherwise as is the case in India, the literals are dispossessed of such opportunities, as a result of which there is neither social equity, economic parity nor national unity in true spirit.

CHAPTER 7

FEAR & RELIGIOSITY

Unspiritual Rituals

The concept of *god* was conceived by humans as a means of self-assurance, especially in times of difficulties, worries and uneasy discomfort. Associated with the conception, were diverse rituals, traditions, procedures, and customs.

Over a period of time in history, sentiments of attachments grew in the minds of people in connection with customs, whether in verbal or non-verbal forms. Social evolution leapt on with an accompanying *theomania* to such an extent that god became secondary and rituals became primary in the valuation process. This situation leads to become habitual routine at least in India as far as a majority of the population is concerned. Rituals also multiplied in tune with the increasing number of gods. The earliest forms of *fear of god* or *theophobia* seemed to give way to *fear of rituals* or *fear of religiosity*. The fear-driven formalities assumed a significant role in the routine religious life of most Indians.

If any critical analysis is made as to what extent the concept of god or religious rituals became useful in uplifting human welfare, it glaringly suggests that benefits are not encouraging *vis-à-vis* costs overall. The investment made by Indians concerning time, costs, energy and intellect towards institutionalization of blind belief systems looks unwise and irrational because damages have occurred more in quantity and intensity in comparison to intentions held.

The number of superstitions increased the number of barriers to unlimited opportunities, which otherwise would have led to much economic progress. For example, restrictions put on crossing the seas during the medieval period created a type of confinement to people without free mobility. Designation of days and times as good and bad disabled the spirit of initiative and entrepreneurship. Monitoring and scanning on the observance of unfounded rigid practices escalated the degree of fear in the minds and actions of most of the people. The irrational rituals took away the physical time and energy whereas the *fear of non-observance* crippled the mental powers. Even a good thing, like a spiritual perspective, can be distorted by obsessive fear that goes with it. The sacred, spiritual realm and religiosity, as with culture itself, are apparently not immune to such an invasive degree of fear perpetuation.

Inflicting Conflicts

The shadow-side of religiosity in India continues. Dissimilarities in practices of different religious groups or sects gave rise to recurring ideological conflicts. Whenever the festivals of different religions happen to occur on the same day, one religious procession which is solemn and sombre and the other religion a rally of frolic and hilarity will likely trigger anxious moments while they cross each other. Apart from causing a tense atmosphere such differences also paved the way for physical conflicts as well as fear of conflicts.

Pew Research Center's report of 2017 says that India is ranked fourth worst in religious conflicts, trailing only after Syria, Nigeria and Iraq, from 198 countries surveyed and analyzed. India, being the second most populous in the world, has the highest number of people inflicted with the virus of religious intolerance. This has affected and comprised mostly the literals since they account for a substantial majority portion of the total population.

As literals were already divided into numerous groups by castes and sub-castes, religion exacerbated further divisions. The laterals were also categorized on the lines of castes and sub-castes. Faith and fate doctrine again became a cause for new division among the laterals. Modern India has inherited the divisive status of the population as a whole even after independence. As such, the Indian subcontinent is a home of the world's significant religious differences in practice and observance of rituals of every religion and this tendency has led to overall disunity orientation among Indians themselves.

Even though modern *secularism* was adopted by the Indian Constitution to uphold the ideals of "*Vasudhaivakutumbakam*," the practical and cultural atmosphere in Indian society seems to be vitiated on grounds of an intractable hatred and intolerance. The thinking that religion would keep India integrated proved otherwise, as suspicions and prejudices got ingrained in the public mind. The independence of the country took its birth in the midst of communal religion-based tensions, disturbances, and violent riots, of which Mahatma Gandhi was only barely able to soothe temporarily. The partition, as the British India divided into two independent nations of India and Pakistan, that coincided with the political freedom also witnessed hundreds of thousands dead. Such traumatic memories were retained not only in history but are still replayed in mental images of the public from time to time as *per* certain events or sudden sporadic occasions. India is far from fully healing its past.

Religiosity also obstructs entrepreneurship. The people adhering to different faiths and following their practices at a different time as *per* their ritualistic timings, hardly find themselves together for group meetings because if one is observing some ritual on a specific day, some other will stay confined to another activity without honoring the engagement or commitment as previously scheduled. That way, most of the people do not enjoy team spirit. They allow restrictions to rule their lives because they believe in what continues, howsoever irrational or illogical it might be. The more the intensity of religiosity is, the lesser the individual's freedom is. It does not make much difference even though the name-sake secularism involves religiosity in a different form. How one can enjoy rights is the crux of the issue, that people ought to know.

Secularism and Tolerance

As *per* some research studies, it is neither religiosity nor secularism that decides the course of human welfare in regard to safeguarding human rights and dignity. Though these two suppositions are characteristically mutually opposing, they don't offer actual overall benefit for harmony and progress. What matters, irrespective of religious practices or secular traditions, are tolerance and respect for individual freedom.

They each chart the path of human development. Some countries are not secular as they accord primacy to certain faith or creed. They have been found to be promising in uplifting the status of human dignity as we observe in western European nations. There are other countries (e.g., Scandinavia) which profess secularism, even to the extent of promoting an atheistic way of life. Both types of systems have shown tremendous progress in socioeconomic terms. The analysis infers that the common factor among these nations is the immense importance given to tolerance to uphold human rights, coupled with respect for individual freedom. Damien Ruck did elaborate research on such parameters and reasoned that tolerance for freedom and rights mattered most for human growth but not secularisation.

Another complexity of Indian religiosity is that it is not exactly a reflection of any of major religions. Sometimes, the practices of different faiths are mixed up in a way that one religious community also visits the worship place of another community and performs rituals. Most often traditions of folk religious sects are mingled up and it becomes difficult to distinguish between which ceremony belongs to which sect. Over the period, such mixtures of practices get embedded in the rituals of various faiths and they all together, to a large extent, conform to unfounded notions.

Then the real problem arises when the feelings associated with rituals show up and influence the general cultural and social life. Even though the idea of secularism delinks religion from politics, the social damages that are occurring continue unabated. This is because of the fact that the principles of secularism are not complete in vision. Indian secularism lacked holistic vision and ignored the fact that politics is nothing but a part of social life. Hence the problems crop up every time and everywhere, whether it is during elections or festival seasons.

Perils of Religiosity

Long back while defining bureaucracy, Max Weber stressed that office work ought to be impersonal. He envisioned the dangers of fusion between official duties and personal issues. Such a situation hampers the work on the official front and also affects personal life at home. Same way, the approach should be that religiosity needs to be detached not only from politics but also from all other aspects of social life. Humans are social animals. Group size varies with the number of members in a family or clan or community. Like individual dignity and individual life, individual conscience is personal. For example, wars were fought between the siblings when one sibling belonged to Protestant faith, and the other was a Catholic because conscience took a back seat—whereas an utterly new entity called politics linked with religiosity took over in its guise. The religious rituals are mostly mechanical, which hardly rely on reasoning and mental application. On the contrary, conscience is individualist reflecting inner sense. Moreover, it manifests ethical and moral aspects of righteous behaviour, whereas rituals are mostly social in nature and influence mob behaviour.

Religiosity also plays a disastrous role not only in spoiling interpersonal relations at a larger level but also in triggering unwanted emotions such as egoism, retaliation, enmity, revengefulness and so on. On a broader perspective, religiosity indoctrinates more damaging behavioural patterns than instilling good traits in tender minds. The same holds in the Indian context. Some studies were conducted in Western countries to find the impact of theism and atheism on the behaviour of children. The children born to and raised by devout theist parents showed to larger degree retaliatory, aggressive and unkind emotional tendencies. When questions like forgiving others, tolerating the opinions of other children and the like were asked, they exhibited unkind, unforgiving and punitive sort of attitudes. This was inferred to be due to the socialization process that primarily focussed on god penalizing the bad people and so on.

The continuous fight, so-called an eternal phenomenon between *good and evil* seemed to have dominated other mental traits of the religious theists. The idea of forgiving and the values of compassion were relegated to lesser value as god himself, as shown in various scriptures took the lead to enforce punishment on the immoral, guilty individual, or brought down wrath and calamity of horrific proportion on the cities of sin. Ingrained with such insensitive discourses and lessons, the children grew up with the same wrong ideals fixated in their minds.

On the other hand, the children of those parents who had no such religious background were found to be kind, adjusting, compromising and generous in their thinking towards certain persons of questionable character or of maladjusted behaviour. As a whole, these children exhibited sympathy and a more humanitarian approach reflecting correctional aspects in behaviour molding. Therefore, it surmises that any social mechanism, whether it is a political decision or religious convention or educational intervention or so, does not result in a benevolent outcome in the end unless *humanistic values* are embedded in it. If humanism reigns even over atheism, it matters most in achieving a general benevolent future for any nation.

To Be Loved, Be Lovely

As long as religiosity continues to dominate any society, humanism cannot thrive. That is what has been happening in India since ancient times. Religiously-oriented people tend to prioritize superstitious rituals over humanistic values. Sacrificing ritual is a significant example. In ancient India, it was almost routine to kill children or animals in the name of sacrifice that was believed to be an act of religious appeasement to deities. There was scant respect for human life due to the continuous practice of superstitions.

Why are most of the people or governments in India less humanistic in their approach in comparison to their counterparts in Western countries? In simple logic, Indians are *more fearful*, and Westerners are *less afraid*. Indians feel more *chronic uncertainty* about their lives. They are unsure about many aspects of their lives like means of livelihood, job opportunities, medical treatment, future of their children and the like. This feeling of uncertainty drives them to be negatively over-anxious and fearful.

Conversely, Westerners to a large extent do not need to bother much about such feelings because their governments have made, in many situations, systematic arrangements to alleviate such fears in the minds of their citizens. They are eligible to many benefits that let them feel sure about their survival. Experiments are underway in the West, this may include policies of unconditional basic income to every citizen, free health and medical care and free education. Such plans are humanistic.

When uncertainty shrinks, fear also diminishes. Consequently, irrationality declines because they are aware that their state of well-being depends upon the functioning of the government but not on imaginary beliefs. Hence respect towards government increases and patriotic feelings get cemented. As Edmund Burke said long back, "To make us love our country, our country ought to be lovely." Whereas in India, lack of such rational arrangements made citizens' lives uncertain and fearful. And as a way of defence mechanism, citizens turned to irrational belief systems involving superstitions, rituals, observance of religiosity and so on. As a corollary of religiosity, the spirit of humanism has been waning. This is not the best future direction to go.

CHAPTER 8

WHOSE FAULT IS IT ANYWAY?

How Government is at Fault?

As observed in ancient India, the conflicts between the laterals and the literals used to develop to the extent of frequent, open, and fearsome warlike circumstances. That means, one group was *afraid* of the other group and again in the same group one person was not able to feel secure with the other person as far as their livelihoods are concerned because everywhere there was a struggle that was overtly existent for the sake of survival.

In a way, it can be surmised that both the groups were *fearful* of each other. And, they were fearful in the past, like in medieval times and they continue fearful even in the present. With the growing concerns for secure life, the *quantum of fear* [1] kept on increasing with the availability of modern technology in the hands of precariats and egotist zealots.

What is the reason for such a pitiable condition that the nation is still passing through? A deep analysis infers that the bad things are set to continue. As Dr. B. R. Ambedkar had pointed out, that unless something to structurally reverse the situation is done, the people are condemned to continue living in the same state affairs of the present society.

So, ultimately who is to be blamed? In a democratic setup, as is the case, everything is, more or less, set up by rules and regulations, and everybody is beset by the climate of competition and confrontation to fend for oneself for survival. Each chaotic condition persists as long as the individual is left for himself or herself, being uncared for by the state. The meaning of *democratic process* seems unfortunately limited to election of particular ideologists or a party by majority vote. There is nothing substantive as regards to assurance of safe and secure living conditions for all.

How can the meaning of such a democratic setup be reset to usher in a new meaningful democracy is a big question. The only powerful organ in the society that can affect change structurally for an equitable society, as dreamt by all the great thinkers, is the government itself. Because it has every possible means of resources to affect change. It has got its revenue. It has got the army and paramilitary forces. It has got constitutional powers to legislate, to implement through its law enforcement wing and in times of emergencies, the government can also utilise the services of every wing of the government.

Then why is the government not able to affect positive and systemic change? Why is it letting the inequitable state of affairs continue in perpetuity? What are the basic reasons behind it? Is it mainly due to some vested interests on the part of the top political decision makers? Or, is it in the minds of the electorate who, unmindfully go to polls and whimsically elect their candidates, who form their governments for the sake of the government, not for the sake of the true people's needs and desires?

Ultimately what is the reason for this kind of confusion in the country? To bring the change that is required is not far from reality, provided the government takes it seriously. However, the people forget about it because of their ignorance or illiteracy or being conditioned to look the other way, rather than transforming the ethos of governance. This is due to the people's superstitious nature because of their age-old accustomed enculturated mindset, which makes them to blame themselves for whatever the evils and travails that they are facing within their lives. This situation can be explained by some illustrations.

The Curse That is Caste

The curse of caste had adversely impacted the Indian nation to an unimaginable extent. Otherwise, India which has a history of notable economic and cultural exuberance, as had been recorded by medieval foreign travellers like Marco Polo and Ibn Battuta, would have reached the pinnacles of glory by the 21st century.

Caste is a peculiar system which is unique to India, not known anywhere in the world. Other countries, having *class systems*, moved ahead through economic opportunities and experienced progressive strides because the class is not sacrosanct nor is it a closed system. However, in the Indian context, the caste is such an aberrant phenomenon that has closed its doors to every person in the other group of the society. This is the reason that there are thousands of castes and sub-castes that have surfaced in India since ancient times and the same pattern has continued from generation to generation.

Caste has survived over the millennia with much more pernicious, traditionalistic, religious and deplorable attitudes on the part of everybody because the very caste idea spews out inequality, hatred, prejudice, differentiation, separation and isolation amongst the people. The people's unity is rarely feasible when casteist feelings have been in prominence because it becomes an ingredient of the socialisation process since birth. Its status is an ascribed one, and it can never change. The people belonging to one caste who have been there in the pre-Christian era have been continuing to remain in the same group of people even today. Due to this peculiar feature, the traditions of respective castes have been indelibly associated with their members, professing their casteist allegiances that have been different to the members of the other castes. The divergence in loyalties resulted in estrangement in most instances. Hence there were examples when the foreign rulers in the medieval periods of Indian history fully exploited the situation, because the people belonging to one particular caste were not maintaining close or cordial relations with the members of the other caste and *vice-versa*.

There have been glaring contrasts concerning the vocations, livelihood patterns, education systems, ritualistic manners and so on, that had demarcated all castes from one another. Ultimately, all these practices have culminated in such a way that the patterns among various castes have been widened with the result that there has been communication vacuity and misunderstanding between the everyday person-to-person relations of India. This process went on unabated and it is still in force because there were no strong efforts on the part of the government to annihilate the caste system in any practical sense. Even though the sacred ideals of equality, fraternity, liberty, freedom and justice are there in written form, they are ignored to a large extent in contemporary society.

Inbreeding India

Another drawback of the caste system is that due to its nature of an inbreeding custom, a grave disadvantageous situation has occurred. The result is the intellectual regimens of all the people got affected unfavourably. For ages the members belonging to one caste have been procreating within their clan blood; thereby disallowing the inter-mixture of traits with that of other castes. Hence lack of hybrid breed vigor has resulted in the poor quality of the species and so there are downside consequences on the part of the families in every caste concerning their children's creative qualities, intellectual origins or instinctual physical attributes.

Ultimately, the situation has so evolved whereby the people are not in such a dominant position in terms of their brain power in comparison to their counterparts in some of the countries where much miscegenation has occurred. For example, when Columbus discovered America, India in its own standards was far ahead of the new world in terms of rich cultural heritage especially during the medieval period. But within 500 years of its racial melting pot existence, America grew in its economy and intellectual power to remarkable levels, whereas India struggling in the same standards with continuance of its casteist traditions, hardly making any headway in rational thought. Due to inbreeding within their own small sects, tribes and sub-castes, there were very few instances of people reaching a higher level, and the present situation of the country is not yet changed.

Whatever the government is doing about this issue, it has remained only a superficial effort. The very natural and rational criticalities of how the development of intellect and creativity occurs have not been looked into seriously. It has been due to ignorance or the deliberate arrogance of a few planners who are sitting at the helm of affairs in the government that the fate of Indian society is not encouragingly progressing.

Caste Fear Cost Dear

Casteist feelings in Indian society have also led to the inculcation of fear in people. The much revered ethic of *brotherhood* has been a rarity because of the feelings of caste animosity and the huge population of the country belonging to the backward and lower castes of literals is going unproductive because of lack of proper accessibility to means of knowledge economy and entrepreneurship. The few people, who are at the top, are from the laterals of the society and are also locked in the same unwitting situation because of their lack of a truly forward-looking bent of mind. All these consequences owe origination to the narrowed inbreeding and subsequent faulty socialising approaches. The caste fear and prejudice that were brought into the social system centuries ago resulted in such an unfortunate situation that the current Indian society has still been unable to recover.

There have also been violent shades associated with casteist phenomena. There were riots, tensions, disturbances and continued factions among the members of different castes in certain regions or in certain states and sometimes across the whole nation that trivialized the noble ideals of humanism, justice, freedom, equality, fraternity and liberty. And regarding the talent status of India, one can conclude on a disappointing note that there have been very negligible number of intellectuals in terms of sciences and art, whereas some countries having population much less than that of India have produced a large number of Nobel Laureates and great minds who have benefited the world.

Unspeakable Atrocities

India is known for various types of atrocities being committed against women and children. Juxtaposed to psycho-ethical values and underlying gender equality, the way the status of women in India has been assessed and maintained is something abnormal. In that sense, most of the offences committed do seem to spring from psychological deficiencies of the concerned accused persons. Again, it is to be noted that the subliminal deficiencies emerge from physiological conditions and ultimately they are tied up to innate instinctual characteristics of the individual. As human life is designed to survive on the support of food and sex, each individual strives to pull on life going through survival mechanisms. As long as food is not available, the individual craves and seeks to do whatever he or she wants by hook or crook to achieve it because food is necessary for self-survival.

On the other hand, every human being also needs to increase one's progeny. Hence for procreation, sex is an essential ingredient of human survival for the survival of the species. It is an instinctual requirement on the part of humans that sexual requirements are also to be given equal emphasis at *par* with food.

The situation in ancient India was such that earlier social systems took care of such instinctual libidinal needs by establishing certain institutions like the *devadasi* system, so that the vulnerable females do not fall prey to the ravenous eyes of sex-starved males like singles, widowers, divorcees, unmarried youth or separated ones such as those posted in far-flung areas away from families. But such a well-thought-out alterative system of the olden days are not in prevalence in current Indian society. Therefore, many unfortunate incidents have started occurring which has turned to a detrimental situation in the society, causing excess fear among the women and girls. The number of sex crimes has increased and there seems to be no decline despite stringent legal action against the perpetrators by the criminal justice system.

It is a fact that after the independence of India, the government brought out legislations through which *devadasi* system and the like were abolished, but alternatively, nothing in replacement was done, whereas in some Western societies, such aspects were taken care of. For example, there have been licensed brothels or some commercial sex centres which stand legalized at *par* with any professional business activity. Those who are registered or involved in such lawful activities became eligible for medical treatment and because of transparent and medical checkups, the people at large will not risk contracting diseases like STD or HIV infection etc.

Freedom or Feardom?

Unsurprisingly, the health scenario in India is also alarming in the sense that it is one among countries having high prevalence of HIV/

AIDS patients. This is because there is no legality attached to prostitution and commercial sex. The instinctual aspects of libidinal urge have been marginalized to more clandestine activities, however at the cost of one's health because it was due to fear of the police or fear of the state or it might be due to severe penalties. Apart from seeking fulfilment of their urges at the company of commercial prostitutes or in the underground brothels, the perpetrators also don't hesitate to offend the potential victims in pursuit of their sadistic adventures. Naturally, the prospective perpetrators look for the vulnerable of society like small children, lone or old women. Such instances have continued to occur undiminished across the whole country and in the recent past too. Though the government brought out legislation on various issues over time, one after the other, all they offer is symptom treatments, providing for more stringent punishments including that of death penalty from time to time. It seems that there was no decline in such offences. As a result, the womenfolk and the minor children in endangered circumstances feel threatened, thereby restricting themselves of their free movement, while attending to their professional activities or household chores.

Apart from these aspects, another crucial issue and blockade that has been spoiling the potentialities of the youth is that they are not focusing well enough on their studies or their work, as a result of which their productivity is down. When the youth, triggered with a passion for the fulfilment of their libido, find no ventilation to their urges and they naturally tend to look for their satiation by hook or crook in searching for clandestine brothels. Such avoidable wastage of energies on the part of young persons is resulting in huge losses in terms of human resource power. The prime reason for this kind of situation is attributable to the government which alone can rectify by studying the existing systems for practical interventions.

Fear of Roads

Unfortunately, India is the world capital for many problems. It is the capital not only of diabetic diseases at world level but also of cardiac issues, tuberculosis and leprosy. India is also the world capital for road accidents. If we go by the number of people getting killed on the roads because of motor vehicle accidents, the number is more than two lakhs per year. That is the largest number of casualties in comparison to that of other countries. Some statistical reports according to world bodies like WHO put the figure at further higher levels. The deadly number is nearing two and a half lakh deaths per year. Other than these casualties, the number of the injured and the crippled are much more. That way, whenever there is an accident there are many angles to probe. Every time, the police invariably comes into the picture along with the roads and buildings department officials, who face blame for whatever lapses that have been underlying as part of the causes for the accidents, whether pertaining to faulty road design or unrepaired roads or treacherous turns or ineffective enforcement and other human blunders.

The blame is also on the drivers of vehicles for their general noncompliance of traffic rules and for their ignorance about how to use vehicles and of road safety issues. Apart from that, the biggest issue that confronts the people as regards the occurrence of an accident is that nobody points out how responsible the government is. The police department, public works department, education department, municipal department and people themselves tend to fight amongst themselves, blaming each other for the causes or lapses that resulted in the occurrence of the untoward incidents on the road. Whose fault is this?

The government, if analyzed in a rationale manner, bears over-all responsibility because it being the highest body of coordination gives orders for the construction of the roadway as *per* the wishes of the people. The government has to acquire land for laying the road. Again, it has to allot funds for the execution of the project. The department concerned with planning and policy-making at apex level liaises with its sister departments, the public and voluntary organisations involved in traffic education, traffic management etc. But ultimately, one of the prime causes of road accidents is the lack of sufficient allocation of budget as a result of which requisite land for multi-lane broad roads could not be acquired or fly overs or subways that didn't materialise.

Moreover, non-recruitment of sufficient traffic men for road safety management also figures among the lapses. The one crucial reason is that of planning and the designing of the road in a scientific manner to avoid conflicts during the course of plying of the vehicles. If the road is built narrowly due to lack of sufficient funds, there is every possibility for head-on-collisions on the road. If the government allocates a larger budget and expands the area of land for multiple lanes, the road can be designed and constructed in such a way that there will be little or no scope for conflicts. All these engineering measures, including intelligent transport and traffic systems, do a lot towards preventing road accidents. Yet, people hardly find fault with the policies of the government and there is no public pressure to change. It is only the lower functionaries in the departments of police, municipality, roads and buildings, local administration, education etc. that end up becoming the targets for any public ire that surfaces.

State of Women's Status

The philosopher-monk Swami Vivekananda talked against the false glorification and over-romanticism of the past in India. Regardless, many espouse Indian history in boastful ways and even about the veneration of women's status. There were some scriptures that extolled the power of women in various myths and legends and such writings were passed on from generation-to-generation. However, coming to reality, the status of women in current India is, of course, improving much better than it was in previous times; but it is not yet up to the desired level as it should be by humane and international rights and standards.

The lot of women has been relegated to the unfortunate levels in the societal strata regarding education or their participation in normal regular public activities. More importantly, the so-called customs and traditions have pushed the women of interior rural regions to the level of complete subservience to the menfolk for their livelihood. Illiteracy, ignorance, superstitions, age-old practices, irrational beliefs, fatalistic bent of mind and the unfortunate continuance of the same systemic failures are still in currency inflicting inimical attacks on the dignity of women in a debilitating manner.

Though there has been some improvement in the conditions of women in urban centres, the traditional mind of the Indian citizen still needs to undergo a sea change. Again, when such maladies prevail in the society, the people tend to blame each other and turn largely against themselves than direct the source of the problem to the right powers who can make national and local changes in policy and actions.

The learned few will attribute the cause for this tendency to a significant number of people who have been adhering to age-old unfounded practices. The ignorant, illiterate rural folk blame the modernists with allegations like the modernists not paying respect to the rich traditions and customs of Indian culture. However, here also the relevant critical factor that it is going out of the memory of the public is the role of the government. The government still allows the continuance of practices of such irrational observances involving health hazards in many regions of the country. Sizeable funds are allocated by the government for such observances say for example for the promotion of unscientific traditions causing environmental pollution. So there is little effort on the part of the government to uphold the principles of rationality and scientific temper.

There is still a lot to do on the part of the government to raise the status of women by making them economically independent. Since they have not yet been entirely made aware of their potentiality regarding their education, their qualities, their creative abilities, and their innate strengths, most of womenfolk are still unable to realize the power of their productivity. Apart from the traditions and customs, the cultural practices are again making the women bound to unscientific modes of behaviour like restrictions on their free movement or social interactions with the menfolk. Most of them are not able to apply for jobs like their counterparts in the Western countries do. Hence, these unfortunate social conditions make half of the population of India unproductive, resulting in massive losses to the economy.

Inter-Caste Fears

Even now the casteist notions are highly prevalent in some regions of metros. One can overtly feel that casteism has been somewhat reduced in severity. However, at each rung of the social hierarchy including all sects and religions, casteist differentiation is felt across the country as a result of which the unity amongst people is still at stake. This goes on even though the forefathers of India had emphasized long ago the valued concept of *unity in diversity.* However, Dr. B. R. Ambedkar stressed that Indians must be Indians, firstly and lastly.

The results show that much has not yet been attained towards uniting the whole Indian community. Castes are numbering more than thousands and they stand as hurdles to national integration. It has resulted in the past also as well as in the current times in bloodshed and untoward phenomena like retaliatory and prolonged factions among the people. This kind of violent behaviour between the people by caste feelings has become a mummy's curse to the Indian concept of *Vasudhaivakutumbakam.* Today, all people are under suspicion to live in a family spirit as a consequence of which national fraternity is a distant dream in true sense. These are true pictures for the people in other parts of the world to look at in an appalling manner. Therefore, the image of the Indian culture is deemed to be an inconvenient truth.

Unending Unemployment

Say, there are one thousand jobs and let us suppose about one lakh people have applied for that. One thousand people will get jobs and the remaining 99,000 people will not get jobs. What will be the fate of these 99,000 people? The fate is that when they go home again, they face their parents, their relatives, and friends who will ridicule them saying that they have not fared well for the job interview or job examination. And the unlucky people also feel demoralized that they are not intelligent enough to face the examination, even though they had put in requisite hard work into preparation for the same.

Here, whatever the level of preparation on the part of all those one lakh candidates who had applied for jobs, it is a matter of common sense to understand that only one thousand people are going to get employment. The remaining 99,000 applicants have to return empty-handed. Again, let us suppose that the government had advertised for one lakh jobs because there are one lakh jobless persons. Therefore, depending upon the nature of the job description and as *per* the level of performance the candidates have shown in the examination, all can be adjusted to whatever post that they would deserve on the basis of performance rank, but ultimately the result would be that everybody is absorbed and there will be no such kind of situation where in the family members will reprimand the unfortunate, unsuccessful candidates. And there is also no possibility of depressive thinking on the part of the candidate since all could secure a job. Therefore for good or bad state of affairs, the government is directly responsible in paving the way for the progress or failures of the jobless youth.

Corruption as Cancer of Uncertainty

Let us analyse the state of corruption. In India, corruption thrives ubiquitously within financial, intellectual and moral domains. Transparency International puts India among the most corrupt countries in the world. The Corruption Perception Index for 2017 awarded 81st rank to India as one of the worst performers.

Corruption is an outcome of *fear* that in turn is due to uncertainty, as people feel that they are no longer secure and safe for survival in the case of any eventuality that may befall on them. Again, it is clearly visible that the feelings of financial uncertainty abound and social insecurity also prevails because social inequality is rampant, much like what existed in ancient India.

Because, fear of the unknown tends to take away self-confidence; for some literals it goes hand in hand with the fear of loss of power over survival essentials like food, sex, shelter, etc. Some laterals nurture the fear of loss of control over status, reputation, sophistication, etc. Driven by fear, is the attendant desire for power to control such things or relations that the persons of urgency of survival strive literally or laterally and succeed often by exploiting all available means for selfish gain. Such exploitation includes not only illicit financial gains but also intellectual, moral, spiritual and cultural transgressions.

It could be surmised that the root cause of corrupt behaviour emanates from fear at the individual as well as collective levels. It is the bounden responsibility of the government that effective measures are undertaken and implemented so as to alleviate fears in the minds of the people. The government, being the largest source of revenues and having all resources at hand to gather finances through whatever tax mechanisms they wish to go by, can take positive steps in this regard to see that everybody is secure socially, and that everybody's financial position is, more or less, certain in terms of universal basic income or other social security measures. Otherwise, even the laterals, comprising the rich and famous tend to fall for corrupt practices, unless they are intrinsically mature and ethical. Lopsided prioritisation in allocation of budget is causing uneven progress, with the result that the most vulnerable areas like health, jobs, education, pensions and environment are left with insufficient funds and the non-essentials at the moment like nuclear defence, space and the like are flooded with budget, which is far more than necessary. Judicious allocation of funds on the basis of vulnerability criteria can easily solve the problem of guaranteed income to all. Many developed European nations didn't go for nuclear arsenals or space satellites because their priorities are different and more humanistic.

One more reason that can be considered as a genetic factor for corruption is moral degradation. Former American President Herbert Hoover said, "Food will win the war." Americans emphasised the vital role of food in upkeeping the morale of forces fighting the First World War in Europe. In different terms, it can also be said that food will dictate ethics. Food being a vital source of survival, can affect morality of the individual by its absence or abundance.

The government again here has to handle the uncertainty element in such a way that uncertainty is transformed into reasonable levels of certainty. If certainty is not immediately feasible, the government has to bring the uncertainty element down to the level of risks. The risks are to be made calculable and need to be dealt with cautiously. If calculated risks are again managed in a better manner, as with fear, definitely the element of uncertainty can be resolved. Same way, insecurity can also be turned into security. For example, a rich man could also be made to feel that he does not need to worry about his survival in the eventuality of losses that might creep into business dealings or if something untoward happens due to natural calamities because the government has systematically provided ample compensatory measures and there will be hardly any move on his part to become unethical.

NOTES

1. See Fisher, R. M., Subba, D. & Kumar, B. M. (2018). *Fear, law and criminology: Critical issues in applying the philosophy of fearism.* Australia: Xlibris, pp. 76-77, 185.

CHAPTER 9

INDIAN FEARONOMICS

Cascading Effects of Caste

All measures to uphold the sacred ideal of unity and integrity of Indians fail when caste prejudices creep in between nearly all social interactions. Any enterprise, based on uneven foundations, is not bound to last long.

Many of the laterals, who own the agricultural and industrial ventures, speak about non-availability of farm hands or industrial labourers. It is surprising especially in the Indian scenario, which is popularly known across the world for cheap labour, that a workforce is not easily obtainable. The reason is primarily on account of lack of one-ness feelings on the literal labourers' part in relation to the lateral landlords or entrepreneurial owners. The apathetic attitude between the two towards each other is mutually fear-based and prejudiced. Inter-relationships are vitiated by the considerations influenced by hatred and aversion against each other, rather than trust, good will and sense of commitment to cooperate.

Deprived of land, capital and entrepreneurial activity for so long, the literals, when ventured to pursue knowledge as a means of power and economic production, miserably failed in the past. They were prohibited by the scriptures to acquire knowledge. Shambuka, a literal during the times of Lord Rama, went to the hills and sat in meditation to observe penance. According to religious texts, a literal was not allowed to perform such acts in those days. There was hue and cry not only among the laterals of the mortal world but also in the divine abode of Indralok. It was alleged that Shambuka's actions polluted the dharma, the order of the society. But the actual reason was that the laterals feared that Shambaka, a low caste literal would gain knowledge and become a challenge to their superiority; henceforth the laterals could not enjoy the monopoly over the resources all for themselves. Their outcry made Lord Rama to search for Shambuka in the far off mountains and ultimately kill him.

Another example pertains to Ekalavya, the tribal youth during the times of Mahabharata. He yearned to hone his archery skills under the tutelage of Drona, the royal teacher. Ekalavya was already an accomplished hunter, having been professionally self-trained in the interior hills and jungles. Drona did not accept him as his disciple. Being a lateral, Drona wanted only other laterals like Arjuna and Duryodhana to achieve excellence but not a literal like Ekalavya. Having personally assessed the autodidactical prowess of Ekalavya, Drona felt envious as well as prejudiced and hence asked him to sacrifice his right thumb as a token of gratitude for his audience. Ekalavya could not help but forego his thumb, not only making himself handicapped but also disabling him to teach archery to other literal youth.

Dump Yard of the Hungry

The stories of Shambuka and Ekalavya were culturally highlighted as a means of insidious propaganda to instill fear among the literals so they would not thereafter embark on learning more formally. Due to lack of knowledge in every aspect of socioeconomic and political life, the literals lost their thinking capacity to augment their learning faculties.

They could not read scriptures, so they were as unaware of these things as were the animals. Their illiteracy made them ignorant. As they could not write or read, their vocabulary was minimum, bare enough to survive in their little world of struggle for survival. One of the modern researchers Lera Boroditsky infers that words shape thought processes. Likewise, the literals in the past were hardly able to ponder on the plight they were passing through. Illiteracy and ignorance of language condemned the literals to remain in a near vegetative state intellectually. More or less, there is no change in the status of literals even in present days, except for a few improvements with the introduction of some benefits in education and employment through social legislations. Such gains were also limited to a small fraction of the literal population, because the number of educational seats and job vacancies reserved for them are also limited.

About one third of India's population is illiterate. They are all mostly literals. Apart from functional literacy, digital literacy among the literals is negligible. Due to lack of education, the Indian economy as a whole is a dumping yard for the starving people. Name sake growth of economy by 6% or 7% or for that matter –an economy touching 5 trillion dollar mark is a meaningless exercise to the one billion literals. There are only 26 million who are income tax payers among 1.30 billion Indian population in total. It means that around one billion people can't afford to make both ends meet comfortably and yet have to pay indirect taxes while procuring essential items. Such a lopsided economy if continued to proceed in the same manner, will only expedite socio-political ruination and a dismal future.

Impending Cataclysm

Poor educational levels of the literals have adversely affected the national economy. Whatever the goods produced for sales, the market could be found only in the laterals, leaving 70% of the total market potential, which makes that of the literals untapped. An illiterate literal has no need to read hence books or pens are not required. An ignorant literal has no idea to update his knowledge of current happenings; hence news channels are not a necessity. Apart from functional illiteracy, digital illiteracy is much more rampant among Indians. Though India boasts as one of the fastest growing mobile markets in the world, its digital literacy is only 10%. It lags behind in terms of internet connectivity. Hence, computers are simply irrelevant for 90% of the Indian population, which comprises most of the literals.

Policy makers hardly pay attention to such glaring indicators of a limping economy. They often undermine the pivotal linkage between functional and digital literacies. Knowing alphabet and numbers makes literacy functional that in turn becomes a means to enhance various skills including that of computer. Any skill development initiative without promoting and realizing functional literacy is not worthwhile. Because, it will affect inculcation of infotech skills negatively in rudimentary stage itself due to absence of functional literacy.

Lack of promotion in the literacy enhancement of literals weakened the economic foundations of India due to the simple fact that most of the population is unproductive and unskilled in the current days of knowledge–digital–attention economy model, which is sweeping across the world. As long as the literals are ignored in this respect, the socioeconomic entity of India remains endangered as the disgruntled literals tend to act like free radicals to the body politic of India at large.

As Stephen Hawking feared a great divide is ensuing between the haves and the have nots due to increased application of automation procedures. The same widening gap has long since existed in Indian society due to deprivation of means of livelihood on the part of literals. Automation will further add woes by usurping manual jobs hitherto held by them. On the other hand, the laterals, who own or invest in AI technology, will grow much richer. Hawking's idea of sharing the resultant wealth looks like a distant dream as the ethical inculcation and compassionate approach have never been heard of in the age old practices of inequalities and indignities that are still continuing in India. The lateral owners of automation firms would rarely allow corresponding high wages to their own literal workers.

Therefore, whatever the benefits that technology would bring in, will be cornered by the laterals. Same way, the advances in biotechnology and medical sciences would be solely at their own use. It is good that the laterals continue to progress but they should not simultaneously undermine the literals from coming up to higher standards of living.

History is replete with glaring examples of those events where in the progress of the haves was hampered due to the persistent backwardness of the have-nots. In 1944, the ILO Declaration of Philadelphia stated that, "Poverty anywhere is a threat to prosperity everywhere." On the similar lines, Martin Luther King Jr. stated in 1963, "Injustice anywhere is a threat to justice everywhere." Much earlier Karl Marx instigated the proletariat to unite in their struggle to win the world as they have nothing to lose.

If Yuval Noah Harari's predictions come true, the divide between the literals and the laterals will extend to many more areas like health, talent and creativity. The economic edge, which the laterals have been enjoying, would facilitate them to achieve the unimaginable. With unprecedented advances, the field of biotechnology will enable the affordables to prolong life span.

Highly specialised doctors can perform body transplants at exorbitant rates, which the rich laterals can only and easily bear. Already being accessible to AI, the laterals will further develop their infotech skills. More knowledge, more skills and more affordability will hone their creativity. Such opportunities seem to diminish for the literals, who lag behind further in the race of the third kind.

****

CHAPTER 10

THE LAW OF AMBEDKAR

Marx vs. Ambedkar

Of all fears that pervade the whole humanity, there is a unique one that Indians exclusively experience is caste based fear. Feudalistic fear was wiped out in Russia by Marxist-Leninist ideology. Class fears appear and disappear. Many political approaches ranging from capitalism to communism and from socialism to conservatism have reigned over different societies across the world but none seemed to find a cure for caste based fear in India.

When Karl Marx propounded communism, some nations adopted it and reaped positive results. But the same approach that had the opportunity to govern regional states in India, could not affect any change in the traditional social structure. Because, communism had its base on the principle of economic determinism. It did well in certain countries because the class structure that has been existing over there is nothing but economic based. But in India, caste structure is societal in nature. Economic determinism has little to do with it. Despite financial status, social mobility is not possible. Caste in India is characterised by societal determinism. It is here in this context that Dr. B. R. Ambedkar prioritised social equality over economic equality.

Economic equality may be the most sought after humanistic ideology for the rest of the world but not for India. Dr. B. R. Ambedkar's idea of reservations was aimed at achieving literal survival in a legally empowered manner. Associated with it was to educate and enlighten the downtrodden masses so as to unshackle them from the bondage of ignorance. Economic equality helps only survive but does not ensure life in essence. Life is a bigger canvas, encompassing liberty, freedom, fraternity, dignity and fearlessness which are embedded in social equality. It was the prime reason that Dr. B. R. Ambedkar emphasized on removal of societal inequities. This is the logic of Dr. B. R. Ambedkar's law, having the basis of scientific diagnosis of Indian societal malady. Let us, for example, take the chemical phenomenon of 'like dissolves like', where polar molecules dissolve in polar molecules. But in the caste ridden social system, there is no such easy feasibility or mobility on social ladder despite there is upward mobility on economic ladder, because social conditions and economic criteria are like polar and non -polar systems, that do not mix in normal circumstances. Hence, for social equality, something more in addition to economic equality is required. It involves the redistribution of social privileges in equitable terms, so as to make all Indians on equal footing in all parameters.

Churchill & Bergeron

Eradication of social privileges may amount to negative equality as envisaged by Kurt Vonnegut in his satirical story, *Harrison Bergeron*. A saying attributed to Winston Churchill reads, "you don't make the poor rich by making the rich poorer." Positive equality by raising the downtrodden on the social ladder to the level of the upper layer makes sense for an equal society.

But what is happening practically on policy making front is that it has no compatibility with societal diagnostics. The planners are agog with their economic models for treating societal illnesses. The recent amendment to Indian constitution, providing 10% quota in government employment and educational matters for economically poorer people will not abolish the caste system but deepen it. In his incisive column, Swaminathan S Anklesaria Aiyar observed in the (*Sunday Times of India*, January 13, 2019): "If the 50% ceiling (for reservation quota) is breached, why stop at

60%? Why not 75% or 90%? And why not have sub-quotas within each quota for sub-caste, gotra, and other social divide? This opens the door for ever-deeper social divisiveness?"

This hydra-like situation has arisen simply because of the fact that the government measures are not sufficient and are not the right medicines for the cure. One faulty measure leads to another blunder thereby aggravating the problem. Nissim Nicholas Taleb says, "complications lead to multiple chains of unanticipated effects. Because of opacity, an intervention leads to unforeseen consequences, followed by apologies about unforeseen aspect of the consequences, then to another intervention to correct the secondary effects leading to an explosive series of branching unforeseen responses, each one worse than the preceding one." [1]

Taxing to Eternity

As quoted by Benjamin Franklin, nothing is certain in this world except death and taxes. Fear of death (*thanatophopia*) haunts humans because survival makes them conscious, cautious and anxious on permanent basis. So do taxes as no one gets exemption from taxation. Whenever there is a budget session in parliament, everyone feels concerned about increases and the new entries in taxation laws. It also depends upon the magnitude and multitude of taxes as to whether there is threat to survival or not.

An anonymous author's tax poem reads,

Tax his coffin, tax his grave,
Tax the sod in which he lays.
Put these words upon his tomb,
'Taxes drove me to my doom!'
And when he's gone, do not relax,
We'll still be after the inheritance tax.

And the last stanza makes taxes a fearsome devil chasing from cradle to grave:

Taxes don't become botheration as long as they are requitable. Otherwise, they don the diabolical avatar if they are one-sided and remain unrequited in terms of social security measures. If common people feel pinched by the unrequited taxation, no amount of government's self-praise in terms of growth rate or upsurge in gross domestic product will matter. Marco Rubio said in the *Times of India* recently: "Ultimately, your economy has to be measured in the real eyes of real people, not simply in statistics that appear in newspapers about the unemployment rate and so forth." As regards solving unemployment, India has experienced worst phase in recent years as *per* some reports.

Politics of Inequality

Whereas survival is not much of a concern in developed nations, it is a serious issue in India whether it is in literal sense or otherwise. With increase in the degree of uncertainty of survival, there is a corresponding escalation in the intensity of the fear of the unknown.

Fear of the unknown abounds in India with the decreasing self-confidence on the part of the youth who have been rendered unemployed as well as unproductive. Losing self-confidence in turn triggers the fear of loss of power over things or relations. In order to continue holding that power to control things or relations, which is usually referred to as political power, different groups of people play different fiendish games that eventually prove to be nation's nemesis; because such games are mostly selfish oriented, devoid of altruistic motives.

Some of the precariat youth take to the game of guerrilla tactics, following the dictum of Mao Zedong – "political power grows out of the barrel of a gun." Terrorists, maoists, insurgents, militants and extremists fall in this line. There are no signs of de-escalation in their spread and intensity in the current Indian scenario.

Some conservatives having a fixated mindset resort to religious sentiments to garner public support in elections. Most of the self-projected leaders rely on caste equations for the purpose of maintaining and securing vote banks to form the government. Others go to the extent of spewing out the venomous feelings of regionalism, pitting one against the other in the same homogenous group. Separatism and social dynamics involving ethnolinguistic chauvinism are also not uncommon in many parts of the country. All these evil schemes of nefarious elements aim at the single objective of capturing political power by hook or crook at the cost of constitutional ethos of unity and fraternity. In the process, social inequality grows much deeper threatening the very foundations of national integrity.

The Law of Ambedkar

For social equality, Dr. B. R. Ambedkar's law can be applied at five levels of R's.

- Reservations
- Reconstruction
- Reconciliation
- Remedial marriages
- Radical reformation

The first R, that is reservations, the brainchild of Dr. B. R. Ambedkar, started operating during his times. This measure essentially aimed at creating an immediate survival assistance mechanism along with provision for education. As the government did not provide for ample jobs, the measure did not make requisite impact on the lives of the lower castes. Private sector, where the rule of reservations is not applicable, had hardly any benevolent attitude towards them.

Next is reconstruction. Means of production and common resources such as land, corpus capital, education, technical skills, entrepreneurial opportunities and partnership, which the downtrodden at the lowest rung of the society have been deprived of since ages, need to be restored to them. After the abolition of slavery in America, President Abraham Lincoln initiated various comprehensive programmes for the recon-struction of the lives of the blacks.

The objective of the reconciliation is that the lower castes must get integrated into the Indian community at large, in practical sense without prejudices, fears and negatives attitudes based on caste system. The perpetrators of prejudices and fears must accept their responsibility for what had happened since olden times because the objective of reconciliation would be to sincerely emotionalise them towards taking note of their violations for expression of remorse. After apartheid was dismantled in South Africa, the Truth and Reconciliation Commission was instituted with the motive of making the oppressors to realise their past mistakes but not to punish them.

Remedial marriages are the ones that are solemnised in a casteless manner. Dr. B. R. Ambedkar inferred that such marriages will expedite the annihilation of caste monster. Endogamous marriages, which have been perpetuating within respective castes must change over to remedial marriages between lower, backward and upper castes in various combinations, with legal back-up. Dr. B. R. Ambedkar felt that such marriages would break caste, creating the feelings of family oneness, the Vasudhaiva Kutumbakam. In Iraq, intermarriages between Sunnis and Shias were encouraged in order to build an inclusive nation.

The last R stands for radical reformation. According to Dr. B. R. Ambedkar, intercaste dining and intercaste marriages could eradicate caste system only to some extent but not completely. For a full-fledged social equality, he felt that the religious notions on which castes were founded, need to be destroyed. The 16th century's Martin Luther led Protestant Movement paved the way for reformation of Roman Catholic Church. Max Weber theorised that the Protestant interpretation of Bible on work ethic enabled the people to come out of the clutches of scriptural rigidity so as to promote the spirit of capitalism.

****

NOTES

1.   Taleb, N. N. (2012). *Antifragile: Things that gain from disorder.* New York: Random House.

PART 2
R. MICHAEL FISHER

Cultural Transformation, Vision, Consciousness Evolution

Thomas [Berry] spoke frequently of our broken relationship with Nature and the drift away from older traditional stories of creation [i.e., wisdom cosmologies]. These breaks followed from the inability of contemporary scientific, religious, and philosophical narratives to locate humans in a meaningful [and healthy] relationship with Earth's ecosystems and their evolution over time. Ironically, as Thomas observed, the break with Nature as well as with mythos, the storied magic of older cosmologies, occurred in the search for 'progress' and in the turn towards empirical reasoning as the exclusive guide to reality. The ways in which the drives toward economic progress and the reliance on reason alone have undermined the human spirit have only now become clear. [1]

The late Thomas Berry, a rare and wise geologian [2], was an eminent 'story-teller' of cosmic proportion. He has influenced many holistic-integral thinkers and followers, especially in the West. Everything important to human *meaning* is based in 'story' of some kind, and some stories guide us as individuals and as human societies, better than other stories. Today, we humans need a 'New Story' of the caliber that Thomas Berry offered humanity [3] and still offers. With gratitude, I am honored to be invited by B. Maria Kumar to share some views on India in light of his own views in Part 1. I see Kumar's 'Story' of India as compelling. It deserves attention. I offer my own 'Story' in response. May many of us tell our stories, in search of a functional and inspiring storying of a new India, and world, awaiting to be re-born.

Of many possible contexts and interpretational frames possible, the primary context in approach to the challenges of India and the notions of fear and prejudice, is from that of a *leadership, change and transformation theory, futures*, and a general *growth and development* orientation. Add to that, is my own expertise in *educational curriculum* and *research* on the nature and role of *fear* and *fearlessness* in terms of learning, since 1989. These contexts and specific topics in Part 2 are uniquely combined so as to be informative to the overall understanding of the incalcitrant problems India faces and the generic problems of development itself in a complex, fast changing and destabilizing world.

I aim in the following reflections to create an initial architecture for diagnosis and prescriptions of potentials and resistances—albeit, only generic, for which India may move ahead in its future and, to do so in relationship with the insidious *globalizing* forces shaping everything today. The *insidious* declaration is real and not a word I use lightly. One could easily call it 'evil' because the forces I and many other critical observers across disciplines see are forces of a self-destructive global system going into a rapid spiral of decline and decay. Potential total extinction of life on this planet at worst, and at best a deletion of a wonderful quality of life many of us privileged we have known in human history. 'Evil' stands for choices and actions, based on worldviews and values and beliefs (or stories), whereby human activity leads to the opposite of 'live' and thus, *evil* is *live* spelled backwards. The under-privileged have known this demise of quality of life for a much longer time, it is nothing new. For many of us more fortunate, if that is even the right word today, the wake-up of decline is starting to hurt and the future is looking rather closer to a nightmare, if one is honest, than a promise of prosperity.

The more I have studied the human dilemma, the growing alienation of the human *via* its culture(s) from Nature, it is obvious that economic ideology and ways of influencing everything are deeply dysfunctional in the long-term of planetary sustainability. The human-caused Global Warming catastrophe upon us is one that will continue and has happened largely because economic powers in the world, that is leaders who could have made a big positive difference, otherwise did act, disregarding scientific evidence for the Green House Effect and the Industrialization Era and its excessive exploitation of Nature and burning of fossil fuels. They had colluded in a 'Story' of forever greater 'Growth' with no limits. I studied this problem in the early 1970s as a student of ecology, environmental education and philosophy. I was 20 years old at the time, living in Canada, and it was not hard to predict the fate of humankind, and it was not a good one. No one knew exactly how long the great cascading crises would begin to maximize past a 'tipping point' but most knew, as I did, it would be in my life time, and my daughters and their children. But sadly humanity overall, coped and took to ignoring the potent symptoms and messages, example pollution build-up in the environment and our bodies, and thus the inevitable collapse of living systems and of social systems is real. It has overtly come to be noticed now by masses of citizens everywhere, especially in the past few years. And, there is no fact looming, more dangerous than any, that major powerful countries and leaders have ignored and delayed acting responsibly. The human course is now very precarious on many levels, not to forget to mention the potential for nuclear terrorism and wars of unimaginable negative consequences.

The climate and economic disasters that accompany our world have really begun to hail down on societies driven by profit, class status, and self-centered regard, while ignoring the legacy humans are leaving for future generations. This mass ignore-ance and arrogance I have called *fear patterning,* and an associated post-traumatic chronic dis-ease of culture itself on a grand scale. Only a very 'wounded' species that has forgot how to heal would try to cope and control nature to the degree our species has done so for a very long time, at least since evolution of culture came to a "point of departure" [4] from Natural laws some 10,000 years ago. Some critical contemporary scholars call it a "dominator culture" and worldview [5]" and/or I, and many others, prefer to call it a *"culture of fear"* [6], which I think is very appropriately labeled. I am *not* a culturalist and thus, I am not a romantic about the wonders of *culture,* to be clear; even though I am a life-long musician, writer, visual artist and designer. *Fear* bred within culture(s) for far too long unabated, is now, unfortunately, intensely controlling the planetary-human-industrial growth cycle—impacting all development everywhere.

I am *not* a romantic about the wonders of *human-made (industrial) growth—a growth that once in balance is now a massive cancerous growth.* I simply cannot write about developmental issues in India without this larger meta-context looming upon all the earth and its nations. I have to be a critic to be in integrity. But I am not here to write about that topic along with global warming in any depth in my response to Part 1 of this book. However, my lead to say what truths I need to say comes because of the inspiration from Kumar's truthing of his own kind, as someone of legitimate Indianess, of which I cannot not claim. Mostly, I am struck with the quote of the novelist cited by Kumar to begin Part 1, as Tharoor marks brilliantly a seemingly paradoxical, if not ironic twisted, thesis about India's history, culture and future. His words make me think twice.

Tharoor, an awakened literary writer with ethical passion for teaching says he uses "didactic [literary] works masquerading as entertainment" [7] and that speaks analogously to my understanding of Desh Subba's significant literary accomplishments in Nepal and beyond. Subba, the founder of the *philosophy of fearism*, is the person who brought Kumar and myself together around the topic of fear and development in India, even though it was Kumar who initiated this specific book project. Is it not surprising that all three of us as co-authors are independently deeply interested in writing as an art, literature, literary criticism, and the playful union of non-fiction *fiction* as intricate webs of means of teaching humans and hopefully of correcting our worst follies? I think it is no accident that the three of us have come to co-write at this very crucial and dangerous juncture in human history—and, the nucleus of our writing and teaching 'cell' is *fear(ism)*. I shall return to this later in Part 2 after I share more reflections on Part 1, and of course, Subba will return to why fearism as a new philosophy is key to his understanding and teaching in Part 3.

According to Tharoor, approximately five thousand years ago, India was at the top of the scale of impressive development in the world. He wrote,

> India, whose level of art, architecture, literature, and philosophy, made it perhaps the most developed country on earth....I see cultural reassertion (the reassertion of a pluralist Indian culture) as a vital part of the enormous challenges confronting a country like India—[and] as vital to economic development. We are all familiar with the notion that 'man does not live by bread alone.' In India, I would agree that music, dance, art, and the telling of stories are indispensable to our ability to cope with the human condition....Without culture, development becomes mere materialism, a set of figures on GNP tables, a subject for economists and planners rather than a matter of people [i.e., "their freedom to create"]. And if people are to develop, it is unthinkable that they would develop without culture...without stories. [8]

My own experience and critique is that "culture" is a two-edged sword, it can enhance human existence and development and intelligence on the one-edge of its capability and it can also inhibit. The latter it accomplishes, for example, by taboos, in which the development of intelligence is restricted by forcing cultural-codes of conformism upon the soul, and thus delimiting the freedom to create that Tharoor, and myself and Kumar and Subba find so precious to the human experience. When a "culture of fear" reigns then everything good about culture is cut down with the other-edge of the sword. Decay of civilization is inevitable, that is unless the society can change its old stories that have led to fear taking it over to such an extent as India has experienced, but also many other nations.

So what is this called for *"pluralist India"* as the modern novelist Tharoor praises as the way to go? It is a complex topic I can only briefly articulate in my opening thoughts in Part 2. Yet, surely "pluralism" is a conception that the modernist thinker treasures and holds as a virtue of accomplishment and progress, as it underlies democracy, freedom of the individual, universal human rights, and so on; and, pluralism supports an idea of where there is no one and only "belief" system or class, or caste system, that should dominate all others, at least in the ideal sense of the term. Kumar has well- articulated the disaster of the unique caste system in India in Part 1. He argues, it has been and still is a disaster for the majority but perhaps not for the elite upper castes. Yet, I will argue below from an integral systems perspective, that if one part falls then the whole of society will fall—eventually—and, all will both stall and become crippled, and eventually the entire fabric of the society or civilization will fail. History has shown that civilizations, empires and nations, like species, will potentially fail and some go extinct.

Now, to return briefly to pluralist India as a notion needing more clarification. I call my own holistic-integral perspective of fearanalysis [9] a form of *post-pluralism*. Which, simply means, I embrace, critique and re-assess the good and bad of modern pluralism and any notion of a pluralist India as the developmental solution or a sure 'fix' to a culture's or nation's challenges. Turning to the integral philosopher Ken Wilber, pluralism and post-pluralism are two stages, respectively in modern and postmodern eras, as natural developmental stages on the continuum of evolutionary progression of consciousness itself.

Wilber's definition of *pluralism*, based on a universal theory of consciousness, includes identifying the stage(s) of organizational systems that evolved before pluralism in order to understand what is going on evolutionarily, and what pluralism has grown from as its prior developmental foundations. The structure-stages of humanity have evolved from *archaic, magic, mythic, rational, pluralistic, integral*—at least, as described by Jean Gebser's survey of cultural evolution and Wilber relies on that in part in his spectrum schema [10], and he extends to post-integral stages as well. For our purpose, lets simplify by focusing only on mythic stage and the major shift of consciousness/culture that came with changing life-conditions and brain development to finally reach rational stage. Note, not all places, cultures, or nations have made this shift where most of its populations are now rational-centered developmentally. In fact, a good majority percentage of the planet has not reached this (modern) rationalist stage as their center of gravity for organizing, policies, and operations. This is not a moral judgmental assessment, says Wilber, it is merely a developmental reality and all nations or individuals have to go through one stage at a time, each stage preparing the ground for the evolution of the next emergence, the next transformation to a whole other modality of consciousness, culture and organization of reality. The self-identity structure also shifts with these cultural shifts. The rational (e.g., science and the Renaissance of W. Enlightenment in 16th-17th centuries) is a very potent shift and the Age of Reason, more or less, was being hailed by those accessing reason/rational mode as the 'answer' to the problems of the mythic stage. The mythic stage is of course not willing to give up its dominance in a culture or even in the way an individual or group thinks and perceives the world—yet, as Wilber and other developmentalists and evolutionists argue, the shift is more or less inevitable, unless the resistance and conditions are such that they can forestall the shift and progression—which, sometimes is the case. Sometimes, says Wilber, there is simply not the need to progress to the next stage of development, and things will be fine. However, in a complex globalizing world like we have had especially since the Industrial Revolution onward, there are rapid pressures to change, transform and adapt new intelligence capabilities almost everywhere on the planet because of the interconnectivity of all places, influences coming from afar to even the remotest of cultures. The danger of the 'new' form of consciousness emerging is to become dissociated and arrogant to the point where it can believe everything that has evolved before it is just 'old' and 'useless' if not harmful. The danger of the 'old' form is to believe it is already the highest stage of development and there cannot imaginably being anything better. Both these are narrowed ideological perspectives and create a rigidity in evolution along the full-spectrum.

This is why Wilber's theory of development (map) is so important for all people, especially leaders and planners to understand so they can have an attitude of *both* acceptance of the developmental dynamics of change *and* transformation, of interpretations of reality, and see ways to intervene and help the flow move along the spectral progression but do so with respect for the prior levels or stages of evolution. Each stage has its own wisdom. And, each stage has its own 'shadow' pathologies. My own work as a cultural therapist (see later below) works with this 'big picture' view of cultures as representative of something beyond their own bloodlines, beliefs, geographies, politics, identifies—and, that is the relationship of *consciousness itself* and its differentiations; because any culture will have many people at different developmental levels, and any culture may be dominated by any one or two levels of consciousness; what empirical evidence shows is that most cultures of the world are *not* yet up to rational, never mind pluralistic. Yet, having this vision of the higher reaches of human potential and cultural evolutionary potential then one can better guide, with great vision, advancement to the next level—and, ultimately every higher level of consciousness (especially, past rational stage) has less and less fear-based structuring. That's a much more complex fear management systems theory that I have discussed at length elsewhere [11] and it is not included in Part 2 *per se* other than to indicated the mapping and theory behind the thinking I utilize here.

Now, with that simplified bit of Wilber's theory, there is the importance to focus on defining *pluralistic* stage *per se*. In North America societies for about the past 40 years, this stage represents the "leading edge" with significance impacting some 10% of the population [12], some say maybe 20% but it is still relatively minor in proportion—often recognized by people who are "green" values oriented with a sense of caring about the whole sustainability of planet earth and its ecosystems. Cognitively (re:

consciousness capacity), the big step here beyond *rational* stage is the ability to stand back from one's own culture, rather objectively, and,

> [T]ake a critical stance toward the idea of truth [reality which] has other important implications. Individuals at this stage often have a much deeper recognition [awareness and awakeness] of the culturally constructed nature [and relativity] of their beliefs. Because every belief is true only in a certain context, the role of class, culture, and media forces are strongly considered [and biases noticed]. [13]

You get a feel for the rather rebellious "no" quality of postmodernism, as it often (unfortunately) rejects the modernist *and* pre-modernist traditions and values, beliefs and ways of knowing reality. So, with this in mind we have to ask what would a pluralist India look like (a la Tharoor)? It would be a less *ethnocentric* mind-set or worldview and more *worldcentric*—seeing truly and valuing truly advancement of consciousness—that is, expansion of consciousness, required to live globally well today. No longer can its mythical or even rationalist thinking be held as adequate or even as 'the best' there is. If and when one's world opens up in the postmodern all is not great either—one has to also see there can be great insecurity that comes with this postmodern pluralism, albeit, that is another topic for another book.

However, all the discussion about *fear* (and sometimes fearlessness) in this book by all of us co-authors is indicative that we are pluralistic and somewhat post-pluralistic thinkers—as we know there is an existential crisis often involved with these major transformations of consciousness—individually, organizationally, and culturally. Yet, clearly one has to think about 'culture' as a unit of analysis and change—and, that's a complex scale to work with. That said, I believe it is a workable scale and most of what I say in Part 2 is more or less linked to this pluralist and post-pluralist perspective, which challenges "cultures" to not merely cling in fear to their already familiar security systems to the point that they inhibit growth and lose the ability to adapt—and, to move toward true freedom.

The rest of the world, and some specific countries analogous to India, have many similar problems in development—that is, in arriving at a healthy, sane, just and sustainable way of living, not just within their own country but in living with their neighbors on this planet. The scope of which I envision sustainability, is one not unlike the way of the ancient Indigenous peoples who for 99% of human history lived relatively successfully and undestructively, because their guiding holistic worldview included a sensitivity to the sacred authentic relationship with all other beings, through living in harmony with the laws of Nature [14], in what today eco-reform movements have been calling the permacultural (r)evolution [15]. Modern people have a lot of wisdom to learn from this Indigenous worldview and our ancestors at their best. And this can be done through what Four Arrows and others offer as Indigenizing education and societies everywhere [16]. I personally have been involved in part with this work and highly recommend it for future planners of modern and postmodern societies everywhere. Yet, this would be a topic better for elsewhere, in order to do it justice, rather trying to squeeze it into Part 2.

For my part, I have in mind the application of a type of *cultural therapy* [17] for India, of which readers can make up their own minds as to how well I present such a therapeutic intervention—that is, simply a *fearanalysis*. It seems to me that this book *India, a Nation of Fear and Prejudice*, requires us to at least give credence to the proposition that *fear* may indeed be a major context for understanding India and for understanding the powerful forces that reproduce fear, and how we can intervene, yes, as a cultural therapy, in order to move the nation (and world) toward a healthy *culture of fearlessness*, leaving behind as much as possible the contemporary rule of a *culture of fear*. Neither Kumar, nor I have total blame on the Indian citizens and their leaders for their state of affairs nor for their fear and prejudice that goes with it. This is a point that needs to be repeated. India has, like so many countries, been traumatized and manipulated by colonialists from the West, not the least of which Britain is culpable of having wrought massive oppression to India for many years, even though, as Kumar argues, there have been some gains to India's progress from the Western intervention into their nation. Reparation of a once colonized nation, ideally involves many participants (including past colonizers), and, yes, India will have to take lead responsibility to initiate such a coalition or reformation and transformation. It also will require allies who will not only judge it's progress but compassionately be/with its struggles to build and re-build a better nation.

Part 1, by B. Maria Kumar, furnishes the lived-experience of a person born and raised, and who has worked his whole career, in India. He knows the ins and outs of how love and fear, trust and mistrust, justice and injustice travel through the veins of India's life, body and history. My own lived-experience is from North America, and thus I'll bring some different views to the problems and solutions that India may find valuable—especially, to leaders, designers and developers of India's future. As a cultural therapist (and *fearologist* [18]), I offer insights from three decades of research on the nature and role of fear (and fearlessness) in human affairs. I have given a lot of attention and professional service to individuals, couples, families, communities and organizations in a therapeutic mode of working. The patterns of health and pathology are very similar across these scales of human behavior and systems.

As a researcher, I am steeped in the literatures on fear from the West and the East, and have argued for a total revision of the ways we tend to imagine fear (and thus fearlessness) [19]. As a 'boomer' generation youth, I was heavily influenced by the flux of Eastern philosophy (much that came from India, especially ancient philosophies and spiritualities) into North America in the 1960s-80s. Upon reflection today, I have questions about how those Eastern philosophies were appropriated and commodified in the West, often in not very healthy ways, and equally I wonder if a similar distortion has occurred in the West's offerings to the East? In Part 2, I keep this international interchange in mind and acknowledge there is great challenge and caution required in any importing and exporting of knowledges and wisdom, be it East-West or North-South. The local area of importation of ideas or technologies must be in charge of and determinant in their own future. My basic principle of appropriate development work [20] is that I have no intention of superiority as I offer my views as a Westerner today on India.

In moving into this particular case study of India, fearologically, I am well aware of the maturity in India's philosophical and spiritual roots when it comes to understanding the *'gift of fearlessness'* (*abhaya dāna* traditions) [21]; perhaps, I will be able to embellish these traditions with a contemporary holistic-integral perspective and draw from the hybridization of ancient and new forms of knowledge and wisdom, compassion and understanding—in order to point to a "free India" and vision of a "fearless India" [22] as a movement from beyond the grips of its most devastating forces of dependency—such forces traceable, I will suggest, as has Kumar suggested earlier, to the deepest barrier of human progress—that is, *fear*. I mean the *Fear Problem* [23] and its excesses, and thus, how to improve *fear management*.

I'll return throughout this essay to explicate briefly these new terms I have used, and the contextual frames of fearanalysis itself, so readers have some sense of my rationale, positioning and strategies in diagnosis and interventions. There's no need for readers unfamiliar with my work to understand all the new terms *per se*, but they will give you a source to search out in my writings if you wish to. My goal is to attempt to make them understandable in their context of use, and make their meaning self-evident and simple but not overly simple. A theoretical and philosophical attitude is important in my fearological work and it is my strength. That can turn some readers off quickly. I am well aware that anyone who spends some time studying the problems of India has, along with their critiques, a deeper interest to improve things. They want practical and actionable solutions now. Yet, I stated earlier, the futurist perspective is my emphasis even while appreciating solutions are needed now. To be clear of my intention, I am not going to write out a guide-book of solutions here. I am, as I said, going to offer a scaffolding, an architecture of social evolutionary change for what has been described as "Conscious [cultural] Evolution" [24]; and I will be doing so because that is what I can best do because I have not lived in India.

And only the native Indian people in India are best suited to practical and actionable solutions. They merely need some guidance, new perspectives, and maybe insights that bring them to change themselves as they come to address the problems of their nation. In that sense, this approach of mine is one of transformative learning [25]. Change has to come in a radical form no doubt, and it will be both 'internal' (e.g., mind) and 'external' (e.g., systems) for without that integration there will likely only be insufficient and superficial changes. India's problems are complex and "wicked problems" [26] that require deep analysis and patience, as Albert Einstein once said: "If I had an hour to solve a problem I'd spend

55 minutes thinking about the problem and 5 minutes thinking about solutions." We have to be careful not to jump prematurely to solutions in desperation or as driven by fear that closes down perspectives and creates reductionism in forms of consciousness and rigid analysis. Without a (r) evolution of the ways humans feel, perceive, think and act, there's the troubling tendency to try to solve problems with the same 'mind set' (and values) that created the problems in the first place (*a la* Einstein). Kumar has his own pet-peeve on "irrational mindsets" (i.e., irrational fear-based thinking and acting as part of leadership corruption) in India which are prevalent and damaging. I'll expand herein somewhat beyond only the binary concern of rational vs. irrational, as is most common in the *fear imaginary* [27] when people are trying to understand and manage fear. My own career follows the Einsteinian principle and I generally spend 90% of my time on fearanalysis of problems and 10% on solutions. I ask how any solution offered increases or decreases "artificial fear" (i.e., excess and toxic forms of culturally-modified '*fear*') [28].

One of my biggest realizations and critiques is when someone or some system attempts reform but does so using fear as the major motivator for the change. Some call this a type of fearmongering, and other's critique it as a dynamic in the making of a "culture of fear" or "climate of fear" [29]. Worst is, they are not even aware of doing this. I'll return to this problem and point ways of how to assess when excess fear is the motivation to trying to solve problems that are mainly caused by excess fear in the first place. This will be talked about under the name of "fear-based" [30] operations. *Fear-based* is defined in Part 2 as the dynamic motivational imperative of a living system (individual or collective) whereby over 50% of the drive is based on fear, be it conscious fear or unconscious fear, be it rational fear or irrational fear (cf. Kumar's *quantum of fear* concept [31]). This notion is distinct from, and only somewhat related to, *fear-focused* in this essay, where the latter is merely referring to an approach of analysis where fear is given the primary focus as a factor, a context, and even a philosophy (e.g., *fearism* [32]). The type of fearanalysis I am doing is designed to be fear-focused but not fear-based. In some ways, the latter is a type of pathological patterning. There's no point in getting into this further for the purposes of this overview but it is an important distinction.

I follow on the foot-steps of Kumar who has pointed out some gains and strengths but most importantly the failings of India's progress of development on many grounds; but the one potent cause he comes back to over and over in Part 1 is *fear*. He identifies several problems in India, past and present, across sectors of the society and cultural landscape, all related to fear:

- poverty and classism, caste system, *via* some stories and myths serve as "a means of propaganda to instill fear among the literals [i.e., disenfranchised]"
- the apathetic attitude between workers and owners "is mutually fear based"
- the thinking and behavior of many is "corruption...an outcome of fear"
- the scenario related to HIV/AIDS and sexuality and their high cost on health is "due to fear of the police or fear of the state"
- institutionalization of religion(s) seem riddled with an irrational "fear of god... giving way to fear of rituals or fear of religiousity"
- differences (relation to the Other) causes great wastages of time, money and labor and ultimately lead to unproductive "fear of conflicts"
- the hierarchical accumulation of power by elites (e.g., legislator literals) prevents a strong democracy and skewed policy-making "due to fear and domination" of the elites
- if more of the majority were better educated, especially in the past history, "they could have managed their fears more rationally" and been more productive and empowered citizens
- state laws, including the national level through laws of central government, have "proved to be causing fear"
- insecurity is bred in many *via* social inequalities and "the tyrannical rulings of the elite minority... who manoeuvre through various fear mechanisms"

These are some, not all, of the ways the *force of fear* pervades Indian society and the nation's development in the last few centuries in particular, according to Kumar. These make common sense to me, and likely a lot of people will agree. Yet, there will be many who disagree with this assessment and/or they will give explanations for the troubles of India other than by the *fear factor*. I will at times address these forces in my own way and attempt to dialogue with potential resistances to the claims made by Kumar—and, especially his emphasis on what I call Kumar's preliminary fearanalysis. I wish to acknowledge Kumar for his brave trajectory in taking on this topic and his naming the fear problem in India as it manifests, and that he does this in his own unique and pragmatic ways. His perspective of police officer as career but also as a life-long learner and writer, make his overall passionate analysis and views compelling. I find his work freshly enthusiastic, even if very critical at times. I may not agree with all his points, yet, that is not the point of my response in Part 2.

For example, to name an entire nation *"a nation of fear"* is a strong all-encompassing label—albeit, it is in comparison to the label of *"culture of fear,"* that may need to be revised; but that's not a barrier I find delimiting of my own thinking well about the future of India. I am on his side as ally. He is well aware there is a naming of the *fear context* required in his country, at all levels, and especially at leadership levels throughout all sectors of society. He laments but also inspires because he is optimistic this fear can be rationally recognized as a catalyst and moved—it can be transformed. I too am an advocate of the transformation of fear [33], *via* learning, philosophical worldview analysis, and therapeutic processes as well as economic, political and sociocultural change that includes the spiritual dimension. He is not shy to espouse a succinct "target" for India's development which includes *"fearlessness"* right up there with liberty and happiness. All countries deserve this. But the struggles will be immense in some cases, and Kumar, a historian in his own right, snoops out the 'old' entrenched ways that keep India from fully growing up. His historical and mythological [34] sensibility also make him a very patient observer of the human condition, and patience is a virtue I detect in his positive work for change, for renewal, transformation and healing.

'Big Picture': Future Leadership, Development & Fear

In an optimistic but realistic recent development book (anthology), *Alternative Futures: India Unshackled* [35], asks, as one reviewer suggested:

> Can a radically different and progressive future India emerge, overcoming the systemic injustices—economic, ecological, political, social, cultural—of today? Any such seemingly utopian vision to become feasible must show that it is workable and reachable.... [from accounts in this book] It points to different experiences in India that already embody the values and actual practices that are needed for such functionality. [36]

I too have a type of utopian vision, a "fearless India" on my mind. And, I agree, we must show, sooner or later, feasibility. However, feasibility can be very restrictive when privileged above all knowledge pursuits, and especially, when trying to bring about transformation, healing and creative possibilities that are often invisible in nature—like a shift in consciousness, for example. The good news, it looks like there are already many parts and players, more or less, doing the right things, with the right values to make India a great nation, if not utopia but it seems that such practices still need to be more systematic and in more places. Another reviewer wrote,

> To enact radical socio-ecological transformations [in India], we first need to imagine them. This is what this book brilliantly does, it decolonizes our imaginary. [37]

Of course, this expanding our imaginary, decolonizing our fear-based minds and souls is essential to healthy organizations and nations. Yet, I was curious in this book, with its radical and empirical results from India, that the word "fear" only appeared 11 times in the book and with no deep exploration at all. The words "fearless" and "fearlessness" were non-existent. One of the first parts of a fearanalysis of a text, is to look at the inclusions and exclusions of words—especially, fear-words that I am interested in. I'm surprised fearlessness is not being brought forth amongst the many authors in this book on unshackling India. Similarly, in a scholarly essay on the history of India, social and religious reform and Indian Renaissance from the early decades of the 19th century, the author and cited authors within make no reference to fear or fearlessness, even though Indian-born poet Rabindranath Tagore was quoted as speaking well about Raja Rammohan Roy (propagator of modern Western education and a new national consciousness in India's Renaissance) [38]. I was curious the author of this history article did not mention Tagore's "Where the Mind is Without Fear" as a pre-independence poem from the great Nobel Laureate. Fear is not central to their historical and social analysis of the problems in India, not even close to an insightful approach compared to Kumar's offering in Part 1.

The remaining comments and research summary in this section are generic, rather than specifically related to knowledge about India or research coming out of India, thought it ought to be still applicable to India.

cdiagnose the ills from the past, into the present, and then try to correct what one can for a better future. However, my own approach is always to maintain a vision of the future before being swamped (often depressed) in only details, problems and crises in the present and with their incalcitrant roots from the past. Change can seem so slow at the cultural level. This creative visionary approach involves a kind of 'objective' view, a futures view or what some call a transpersonal or even transcultural or transhuman perspective. It's a 'Big Picture' view. In a sense, it is an "It" (third-person) perspective for viewing the state of a nation (or anything). Changing one's perspective, changes reality, at some level.

It's from the point of view of Evolution itself, I ask readers to entertain momentarily. It is from the point of view of Order-in-Chaos itself, where there is never just chaos and crisis, but there is a restructuring of a 'new' order (quantum leap perhaps) from the 'old' order. It is not a bad thing that crises arise. Without a fear-based lens, we have to reframe how we imagine the universe operates and our worldly existence. Our ego and ethnic perspectives and identities are not the most important or only perspective to take. Both mythology and science, art and philosophy and spirituality have a lot to offer, each in their own ways to this understanding. I've called this a holistic-integral approach—and, when applied to fear management, everything shifts, as does the nature of fear itself. But, I'll come to that later.

This reframing of reality and our role in it is what I meant earlier by practicing here in this essay a form of cultural therapy that places us in a position of seeking Conscious [cultural] Evolution, that is, being total participant in it—that is, reconfiguring ourselves within "the participative nature of the universe" [39] and the Laws of Nature that accompany it. Culture and Nature have to learn to get along in close intimate balance for things to work well for either. Thus, relationship interconnectivity means everything important—first priority—in this new way of living and developing to our highest potentials. In other words, we make our future, rather than be of the fates of our development and evolution. Fates tend to make us feel victims and that can lead to a lot of despair and disempowerment and apathy—and fear-based living. In this victim way of perceiving we often will try to "dominate" (*via* violence) everything around us to secure ourselves. No, we have alternatives; rather, we can see ourselves as the *spirit* of evolution itself [40]; albeit, always a part-in-a-larger whole Spirit of Life. The new leadership for the 21st century, as many leadership gurus and research studies show, has to be of a radically different paradigm and perspective, leaving behind the unsustainable (highly polluting, fear-based, violent) mechanical views and approaches to management in general. I won't review that vast literature on new leadership here. India's leaders and others ought to be making themselves continuously participants in educating themselves and doing research on 'new ways' of governance, leadership and learning.

My focus is more on some of the new leaders and their understanding of fear, and to explore very briefly the recognition already arising in leadership and development studies. In speaking of the new leadership literacies required for the 21st century in general, one contemporary business and organizational author [41] takes a futures perspective and assumes:

> The future will be a world of disruption *and* a world of disruptive opportunity. Leaders will need to travel to alternative [imagined] futures. Leaders will need voluntary fear exposure, not only to learn how to live with fear but

>also to learn how to flip that fear into opportunity. [they
>need to risk to learn]

Risking and exposing one's self to fear voluntarily, is a way of participating in the universe of order-in-chaos and living in/with change—not a victim to it. It is a way of maturing one's fear management strategies and expanding a vocabulary and experiential higher Fear Quotient of Defense Intelligence. The interest in *fear* is evolutionarily (conscious or unconscious), an interest in "defense" (i.e., fear management) on the part of living organisms [42]. This is a very important principle of fearwork, of which I see as exercising the fear-muscles, so to speak. It's like building a better fear-immune system, but not by avoidance of fear—because fear is seen as only bad or a contagious disease [43]. No, there is a reframing here, and of seeing a dialectic development of fear/fearlessness [44] as part of the universe-in-action, of the spirit of evolution and as a potential opportunity. Many call this, for example in the philosophy of fearism (*a la* Subba *et al.*), as being more positive in imagining fear. Some, in the West have called this (somewhat erroneously) the "gift of fear" [45]—the point being, there is something important we can learn from fear. Of course, this is all a far cry from touching into the depths of the larger Fear Problem I frame in my own work, and which I'll speak about later. On the surface, yes, fear can be positive, but we also have to look at a more complex reality of the total Fear Problem below the surface.

Proceeding with this brief survey, there's futures scholars who have identified "six pillars" for how to build "futures thinking for transforming" organizations and any other level of a system. It is interesting to see in the six pillars of questions the author asks, that two questions directly address the fear topic: "(2) Which future are you afraid of?... (4) What are some alternatives to your predicted or feared future?" [46] This pillar guides leaders and designers in nations to not take the problem of fear lightly in investigating what is going on for the people, including leaders. Fear is a very important factor, past, present and future. As indicated in this essay, I say we have to go beyond the *fear factor* analysis to something like a *fear as context* analysis, the latter more comprehensive—a point I'll bring up later around the topic of India and the "culture of fear" phenomena.

Margaret Wheatley, a contemporary wise woman and organizational development (O.D.) consultant in the West, has written and taught extensively on development, human potential, and transformation. More than any other in the business and O.D. world, from what I have researched, Wheatley moves fear from only a *factor* to a *context* in analysis. With her influence from Buddhism especially [47], she also approaches fear/ fearlessness as a unit of analysis, that is, a dialectical relationship where we cannot really understand one phenomenon without the other. In one of her outstanding speeches "Eight Fearless Questions" she focuses on "authentic leadership" and what that means in a 21st century context. She presents a "Call to Fearlessness" [48]. She calls for new leadership around the world (excerpt: from her Berkana Institute (1992-) website):

> ... we need leaders who know how to nourish and rely on the innate creativity, freedom, generosity, and caring of people. We need leaders who are life-affirming rather than life-destroying. Unless we quickly figure out how to nurture and support this new leadership, we can't hope for peaceful change [anywhere]. We will, instead, be confronted by increasing anarchy and social and ecological meltdowns. [49]

In pursuit of authentic leadership, Wheatley has demanded, in a gentle and compassionate feminine way, that leaders of all kinds ask themselves to consider the following (excerpt: one of the "Eight Fearless Questions"]:

> *Are you choosing names that demand fearlessness?* You're a coach. You're an executive. You're a consultant. You're a teacher. You're a minister. You're a hospital administrator. You're a civil servant. Are those names demanding fearlessness of us? I don't know what would create fearlessness, but I think this is a very important question. [50]

I'll end this brief overview with noting that a 2007 article, with an interview of Wheatley, by an organizational business development person [51], discusses intimately how "fearlessness" is more important than developing only courage in organizations and systems. The two of them talk about how they noticed that in spite of great gains in humane sensitivity and courageous skills of leadership development for decades with entrepreneurs in the USA, and especially in New York, once 9/11, 2001 hit and the tragedy flowed throughout the culture and business community, most of the highly qualified/trained leaders in top corporations more or less panicked and reverted back to their old "cut throat" survival tactics that they operated on before Wheatley had trained them to develop a higher moral consciousness in business. Lamenting this reality of regression under duress, that is, under fear, both these people discuss that something went wrong in that teaching Wheatley was doing. They point out that "fearlessness" ought to be the way to go as "the last organizational change strategy" that offers authentic change and transformation—true reform. This ought to signal as well how governments, like India, need to be assessing their own leadership and change strategies.

The point of the two in dialogue is: gained *courage* (by itself) is neither developmentally mature enough for understanding the holistic nature and role of fear, neither is it adequate alone to lay down a firm enough ethical basis for evolutionary advance of consciousness essential to authentic (new paradigm) leadership; especially, this proved true in crises and a context of a "culture of fear" environment, like 9/11 exacerbated in the extreme. India's leaders, and others, ought to take heed of this lesson, which in my experience with people in general is *regression* [52], a descent pattern from our higher functioning to lower functioning, quite consistent with typical or 'norm' human behavior. However, just because it is the 'norm' does not mean that we cannot do better than the 'norm.' I does not mean that we cannot learn regression-preventative strategies. For example, later in this essay I'll offer the basic recommendations for a process of fear-vaccine(s) that can build resilience to reduction of human behavior and motivations to fear-based ways.

When it comes to the 'best' fear management/education to offer in development work in underdeveloped or developing countries (e.g., *via* philosophy of fearlessness and fearism, see Fisher and Subba [53]), the point of this section has been to show that humanity needs a new progressive *fear education*, analogous to when many countries under a renaissance of modernization realized they needed a new universal *sex education*, for example. I believe India has deep roots of wisdom to draw on in improving its contemporary and future fear education for the people, so let's turn to that historical and philosophical opportunity.

Sourcing the Great Fearlessness in India

General Context of Analysis & Methodology

As I read Kumar's analysis, much of India's history can be summarized as a battle of "The Fearful vs. The Fearsome." This is both intriguing as a summary analysis and deeply disturbing. Some may argue against such a summary as being overly pessimistic and psychological—that is, a reductionism of many complex factors to only the affective and/or emotional register [54].

And, as that is no doubt a reasonable argument to make contra Kumar's analysis, indeed one has to be cautious of any such over-simplified reductionism, there is a legitimate and empirical case to be made that it is high time that historical, cultural, economic and political analyses begins to give serious equal importance to the value of *affect* (along with cognitive) as a major shaping force, and not merely rational, moral and materialistic and economic factors as explanations for why a society is the way it is and has been. This is a significant, near revolutionary, postmodern "affective turn" in thought [55], of which the entire emergence of psychology, emotionology, fearology (and fearanalysis), etc. has been part of. The heavy focus on *hope* and *courage* in analyses of history and societies, although it touches on the affective side of human motivation and shaping development, is being revised for there are scholars who now think *fear* is much more important in shaping human reality. And by this some say "fear is an idea" not merely a primitive emotion, and thus has great power of influence in shaping societies/politics [56]. McManus argued, going back to Spinoza's philosophical approach and emphasis on the affective and emotional dimensions of reality, there is a good case to be made that, for example,

> Contemporary politics... is shaped by the amplification of fearful affects, and the multiplication of sites at which fearful agentic orientation and futures are produced. The political [historical] landscape is scarred by the cultivation, intensification, mobilization and calibration of fear.... [57]

> "Fear... is the most useful key to understanding today's society. [58]

Understanding today's societies and our past under a lens that focuses on the nature and role of fear (*via* a "fearist perspective" as Subba calls it) is the very foundational focus of a philosophy of fearism and fearlessness by Desh Subba and myself [59]—and is relevant here because our methodological orientation has somewhat influenced Kumar's analysis.

Point being, any futures, developmental and leadership focus on a country (e.g., India) has to take this affective turn of thought and analysis seriously, if they really want to understand deep motivation and organizational structuration of themselves and their histories. In this sense, Kumar's analysis of India becomes more relevant re: a history of the "Fearful vs. Fearsome." I want to keep this awareness in the back of my mind and I trust readers will do so as well.

Let's proceed with a fearanalysis going back briefly in time and the evolution of the imaginary, ideas and wisdom in India. Two underlying questions, not necessarily that will be fully answered here, based on that summary analysis is: (a) how did such a state of affairs *via* the 'rule of fear' become so dominating in India's history and, (b) how has India tried to manage such a 'rule of fear' in ways that are both inadequate and at times exemplary of best practices and even emancipatory? There are vast lessons to be learned in such an overview.

A core presumption in my own fearwork is that people are really only interested in *fear* because they ultimately want to manage fear better; and, in some cases (unfortunately), the intent may be to have more control over fear and (mis-)use that to manipulate others. I have challenged the latter motivation and set out to create a design for curriculum on fear management/education that will be emancipatory [60]—that is, it approaches fear from a *fearless standpoint* [61] that is ideally authentically liberating. Of course, this is not what human societies and history has generally done.

In doing so, I am convinced that *fearlessness* works dialectically with *fear*, therefore on a philosophical dimension fear/fearlessness is a common unit of analysis I use. You can't have one without the other, they co-evolve and act upon each other. With that in mind, even if it may be a little hard to grasp for some readers, I offer a dictum that universally applies to all humans (and more-than-humans): *"When fear arises, there will be fearlessness"* [62]. This dictum asserts that fear is many things, with no one definition absolute that everyone will agree upon; but what is more important than a fixed definition is the fluid and dynamic functioning of fear and fearlessness that comes with fear pattern and defense strategies; this is built-in to at least a few billion years of evolution of organic living systems. We are made to fear *and* be outside or beyond the grip of fear. We regulate fear so that it doesn't accumulate and become so excessive and toxic that it can harm and even kill life forces in the extreme. Various evolved mechanisms help us achieve 'balance' and 'harmony' (i.e., equilibrium) as a living system. I have taken this a step further with my own theorizing.

Fearlessness, at its evolutionary and biological level, is a self/system regulation process. The good news is, while fear is arising, fearlessness is there to help us manage and transform fear, no matter what. Problem is we don't always recognize or focus on fearlessness. At least, that's a theory. And, to be sure, I am no idealist in a pure sense that I believe the arising fearlessness (which takes several different forms) is a panacea to solve everything. I once wrote,

> To focus on fearlessness and its many forms... is not wise if such focus denies or takes flight from the fear-based historical, economic, sociopolitical and cultural context in which most of humanity is living today.... fear and fearlessness are dialectical conceptions and phenomena, neither of which can be understood well without knowing the other [63].

My objective, as Fearlessness (R)evolution or Fearlessness Movement, or Fearlessness Project, to bring a new and improved global fear management/education about has included a critique of the *disguises of fear*, even in forms of love, courage, strength, hope and so on [64]. Disguises as lies have also infiltrated fearlessness to create bravado and pseudo- "fearless" expressions, especially as commodified and branded in the West in the last few decades [65]. I have argued elsewhere, and I won't repeat the arguments here, that if we could improve our understanding of fearlessness, and mature its manifestations in our individual and collective life, then fearlessness could be a universal ethical guidance principle and a replacement for "hope" [66]. So, let me say, I offer India fearlessness and forego offering it hope. Hope, unfortunately, from my critical fearological view, is too permeated by irrational fear. I am not a hopemonger, cheerleader and/or coach, as I am not a fearmonger. Let's see what it is that I can offer that is different *via* a fearanalysis.

Fearlessness: The Indian Way of True Education

I am immediately confronted as I move into investigative mode, with a question based on my research of Indian philosophical/spiritual and ethical thought: How is it that a *"nation of fear and prejudice"* has emerged (at least, as Kumar has named it)? I ask that question not because of my intimate experience living in India or any other nation in the Eastern world. My question arises because of my global research on the topic of fear and fearlessness. And, right off the top of my head, I can think of some amazing literature and quotes I have encountered from India and/or near India as source. They have inspired me and no doubt many around the world for eons.

From my perspective as a fearologist, amazing literature that speaks wisdom and compassion and guides humanity to become fully humane and just, is a literature of teachings which offer the individual and communal sphere to follow a path from *fear to fearlessness*. "We always seek a fearless path, and our civilisation[s] have developed [relatively] continuously along this path," according to Desh Subba, founder of philosophy of fearism [67]. I am speaking first of the very ancient text of the *Bhagavad Gita*, and Vedic traditions. Fearlessness is the first great virtue—the virtue of virtues. If it is not well achieved, the *Gita* pronounces, the other virtues will not develop in healthy forms [68]. These originary philosophical and spiritual writings much later became "religion" (e.g., Hinduism) and were institutionalized—the latter, with their own unique set of problems and dependency formations that delimit too often the human potential. Religionism, as in a "cult" formation is likely oppressive, even if the best mystical truths of religion are emancipatory. So, ideologies can be found in all forms of cultural manifestations, including science, philosophy, populist expressions, mythic folkways, and yes, in religions too. Ideologies, are in my view, always fear-based, more or less.

So, let's return to the spiritual and philosophical thought, which is generally not ideological and thus not fear-based. I will focus on the Indian thought here which guides us (and India) to understanding fear and fearlessness, and practically guides us as humans to better manage fear using the 'best' knowledge available. The philosophy I am interested in particularly is a philosophy of resistance to the norms, resistance to the *status quo* and to the unjust, prejudice and fear-based ways. According to Bushan & Garfield, philosophy during the Indian Renaissance emerged with a "renaissance gesture" even under British colonial rule. Thinking of resistance in a less overt form, they claim, "Philosophy—both public and academic—was central to the formation of India as we know it." [69] The very core philosophical renaissance spirit, which Mahatma Gandhi utilized was productive, if not instrumental, in giving strength to India's peoples and institutions to counter British Imperialism and finally move to independence. During this battle philosophy and spirituality made efforts to "reach to the past for the materials to be used for the construction of the future," whereby Vedanta, Sufism, classical sources and Indian philosophy overall "flourished under colonial conditions" [70]. Without going into all the details and history, beyond the scope of this Part 2 fearanalysis, suffice it to say, that fearlessness as the virtue of virtues (*Gita*) was more or less implicit in this resistance movement against the fear inculcation of British colonial rule. And, arguably, was also resistant to fear-based earlier religious-cultic tendencies in the mythic-magical consciousness of the ancient history of India that Kumar critiques. From a philosophical tradition (East-West), exoteric religion has a reputation, in part, as being a major cause of conflict and fear and/or equally being a symptom of fear-based consciousness [71].

A product of the Indian Renaissance, Narendra Nath Dutta, better known as Swami Vivekananda (1863-1902), was a disciple of Sri Ramakrishna, and "proclaimed the essential oneness of all religions" while criticizing caste-systems, most religious rituals, ceremonies and such that were part of cultural superstitions and taboos long shown to be of little benefit to contemporary India at the time. "Vivekananda's main role was that of a social reformer rather than a religious leader. He propagated Ramakrishna's [progressive] message of peace and brotherhood.... He believed that is was the social responsibility of the better placed [privileged] people to take care of the downtrodden" [72]. Certainly such a philosophy fits in many ways with Kumar's own recommendations, and underneath the intervention is the awakening to the insidious nature of excess fear that promotes dis-unity [73] and dis-harmony, past and present, amongst the nation.

Swami Vivekananda spoke of the future a good deal and encouraged especially the youth of India: "Be moral. Be brave, Be a heart-whole man [sic]" [74] Like several other great spiritually-based (nondual) philosophers and sages, Vivekananda taught fearlessness [75]. "Strength and fearlessness are the two prime [eternal] virtues... which are markers of health of a human being... and society. Every crime, [and anti-social, inhuman act]" as he taught, "is the outcome of lack of true strength and fearlessness"—India requires "fearless youth" who can shape a peaceful and happy human society of the future." As Vivekananda travelled around India as a prophet, he was very aware of how the peoples were suppressed in freedom, both external and internal, and "were in a stranglehold of fear, and worst of all they were paralysed, utterly resigned to their fate" in vast numbers. Vivekananda's recurring message: "Arise, awake and stop not till the goal is reached. Fearlessness! Fearlessness!" [76].

Would it not be a stunning contrast to a "culture of fear" if today sages of all kinds were guides to governments, businesses, educational leaders, etc., so that a higher referent of ethical fearlessness could pervade a society from the top-down, but also be heard amongst the lesser privileged ones, who also could find the basic inspiration to live beyond fear-based ways? The fearologist also points to this potential shift, and offers alternatives of which a life of fearlessness is undeniable in its natural usefulness on many levels of individual and societal health. Later, I'll discuss the insidious generic resistance to fearlessness and how it may be overcome.

Somewhat in the footsteps of the teachings above but in another era of challenges for India, Mahatma Gandhi, a great and controversial leader, proved that a *philosophy of fearlessness* (my term) is essential to quality life but also to just resistance movements and liberation. He called this the *Satyagraha* movement—non-violence. Gandhi wrote,

> The votary of non-violence [*ahimsa* as central to *Satyagraha*] has to cultivate the capacity for sacrifice [without revenge] of the highest type in order to be free from fear.... [S]He who has not overcome all fear cannot practice *ahimsa* to perfection. [77]

In limited forms, this Gandhian (r)evolution and movement has spread around the world and influenced other great leaders, e.g., Martin Luther King, Jr. in the civil rights movement. A colleague, Four Arrows, writing/ teaching from an Indigenous worldview (*contra* oppressive Dominant, Western worldview), wrote,

> [O]ne thing that stands out that not many understand is... that many people believe being Fearless is pathological. I believe Socrates *via* Plato said, more or less, "fearlessness is foolishness." The only philosopher I can remember who disagrees is Gandhi. He thought it was necessary for truth-seeking. That it is an essential practice in Indigenous cultures and reveals one of the great contrasts between Dominant and Indigenous worldviews.... I believe that courage is a necessary step between Fear and Fearlessness. Courage, emotion that honors truth, and "doing right," takes energy like most emotions [and one can burn out], but Fearlessness is the full-tilt action that assumes whatever happens is also that which is the right thing. There is no distress when one is in Fearless action. [78]

Four Arrows locates the origin and imperative of fearlessness *via* a "deep trust in the universe" [79], in primal human (i.e., Indigenous) cultures universally, or nearly so. More accurately, it is located in their Indigenous worldview [80]. This Indigenous reading of primal cultures is often quite different than one made through the Dominant worldview (Western) lens of Modernism, the latter, in which primal cultures are often interpreted as overly superstitious and filled with fears. It is assumed that being highly developed as a technological civilization (e.g., modernism) is less fear-based, which Four Arrows' Indigenous perspective has challenged and equally Desh Subba has challenged from a fearist perspective [81]. The point here is not to elaborate debate on the anthropological, sociological or psychological interpretations of ancient societies and tribal cultures re: fear and its management, but to imagine that there are potentials for finding insights to fearlessness within them that often have been neglected in modernist interpretations. They likely have a source-root of primal understanding and ways of practicing fearlessness that have since been largely lost because of modern scientific and technological 'progress' and its very different values, beliefs and customs. The point is that we would be wise to integrate, as Gandhi did, the ancient wisdom traditions *and* the more modern as we seek to interpret fear/fearlessness dynamics.

Vinobā Bhave (1895-1982), a prophetic-educator and honored pupil of Mahatma Gandhi, wrote, "The goal of education must be freedom from fear.... Until education is really based on fearlessness there is no hope of any [transformational] change in society" [82]. The Indian philosopher J. Krishnamurti, had echoed that sentiment when he wrote at the end of Bhave's life,

> Without an integrated understanding of life, our individual and collective problems will only deepen and extend. The purpose of education is not to produce mere scholars, technicians and job hunters, but integrated men and women who are free of fear; for only between such human beings can there be enduring peace. It is in the understanding of ourselves that fear comes to an end....What is the good of learning if in the process of living we are destroying ourselves? As we are having a series of devastating wars, one right after another, there is obviously something radically wrong with the way we bring up our children. I

think most of us are aware of this, but we do not know how
to deal with it. [83]

The wisdom of such teachings above, are only a few examples of a larger sample of works one could draw upon in order to embellish a particular wisdom branch in Indian thought. Fearlessness is not a strange concept in India, and it turns out that it is not a strange concept elsewhere in the Eastern world in particular. Following an ancient cultural imperative, the *gift of fearlessness* (*abhaya dãna*) tradition of the ages provides a common root source of proper socialization, education and overall ethical development within Hinduism, Buddhism, Jainism (at least), has been well researched [84]. *Fear* is therefore recognized in this tradition, especially when it moves from the natural survival response to a culturally-conditioned chronic, artificial, habitual and self-serving response, as a danger to the social-ethical fabric of a culture, tribe or nation. Under fear's rule, the higher consciousness potentials of the spiritual self are reduced to lower ego-impulsive gratifications—that is, a deficit motivation over a healthy growth motivation (*a la* Maslow). A natural 'gift' of Life-flow that is pre-given to all living things equally (e.g., the Sun and Earth, Water, etc.) is interfered with, distorted, and truncated, by the injury of fear in excess—and, ego needs of the self tend to flourish in such an existence. Love and trust are greatly compromised. From a gifting economy of sharing [85], to recognition of the *commons* as part of public efficacy onward to authentic democracy, the gift of fearlessness tradition works at not increasing fear unnecessarily. It is the opposite of and contradiction to any normalizing of fear—that is, based in fear-mongering and a *culture of fear* dynamic.

One wonders when and where today in India one can see and hear leaders, development designers, policy-makers, futurists, visionaries or others involved in law and order, making remindful speeches and mindful additions of fearlessness in their work for the betterment of all? It ought not be neglected. It is basic civic education curricula. I am in particular honored to have had extensive dialogue and co-writing collaborations with B. Maria Kumar, where his philosophy fits very nicely with the gift of fearlessness. He recently wrote, "It is the responsibility of police to facilitate public peace and order in the society so that all the individuals enjoy their lives freely and fearlessly [86].

Development as Cultural Therapy & Its Resistance

Changing in a big way has to begin with a change in our understanding of fear itself and that involves a change in consciousness.

—Fisher & Subba [87]

Don't fear fearlessness.

—His Holiness the 14th Dalai Lama [88]

God is fearlessness.

—Mahatma Gandhi [89]

As a critical integral fearologist, as a post-postmodern thinker, it behooves me to be speaking 'truth to power' as I enter in the latter sections of Part 2. Let's enter into the finer attunements of this architecture I envision for a "fearless India" and "fearless children" as a goal for the next generations to come. I envision also a "Fearless Age," as Desh Subba has spoken [90] of because we will need something extreme to motivate us beyond merely fear-based survival strategies and a dubious (out-of-date) worldview that accompanies that minimum of human potential. We are reaching for something much higher (like a utopia), yet grounded in survival realities too—some call this an Indigenous worldview, primal worldview, emancipatory worldview, it matters not by name what we call it but we have to make radical change in our ways of relating to the cosmos itself [91]. Yes, this is 'Big Picture' thinking I am calling for here. Remember, my aim is not to provide fixed solutions and advice, but more to provide an architecture of potentialities from the higher consciousness of a fearlessness perspective.

There is no way I can offer anything new or useful or liberational to India or to an individual if I am not thinking, writing and speaking beyond the grips of fear itself and the 'Fear' Matrix that I have been raised in and that most all peoples are raised in. A an unhealthy matrix of a system-regime of excess fear, of fearmongering, a "culture of fear," which controls people—yes, it is a good sociological term to imagine what this oppressive sticky architecture is that we are all, more or less, embedded in—as one sociologist called it "Fear's Empire" [92]. This, ought to be the first great acknowledgement for any possible true (r)evolution in the field of human/ national development initiative(s). Everyone, poor or rich, ought to be taught and ought to share what they experience living in Fear's Empire. There are alternatives but that's the hard work to figure out how to lead an ethical life that is *not* ruled by Fear's Empire. My work is all about that and there's the basic premise that Fear's Empire is constructed, bit by bit, throughout history and by all people who live by its rules, be they consciously doing so or unconscious. We are all responsible for it, no one is to blame alone for this situation our human species has got itself into. That said, we can still be critical at what points in our communities and nations the worst polluters of 'fear' are to be found. We can point out and correct where the biggest resistances to fearlessness are. We have our homework cut out for us.

Thus, *fear/fearlessness* takes on even greater importance than most would imagine. Fear and fearlessness have also conceptually taken on a greater imaginary of expansion in our times. I suggest to not assume we already understand everything there is about fear and fearlessness. There is no one definition either for these terms and phenomena that can be pinned down and agreed upon by everyone [93]. Both Desh Subba and myself have stretched the imaginary, with Subba creating 21 definitions/meanings for *fear* and I with finding 15+ definitions/ meanings for *fearlessness* [94]. Our significant education to building a critical literacy for a "fearless society" (and India) has got to put a radical revisionist *fear management/education* in the foreground of priorities, for everyone.

I have earlier shown that some development and leadership thought has already caught on to the idea that *fear* is an important phenomenon, if not a critical factor and organizing force for human potential and the growth and development of a nation. Most often they recognize fear as a major barrier suppressing human achievement, the very conclusion that Kumar makes about India in Part 1. Few frame *fear as context* (or meta-context) as I do in my work. Adopting this latter perspective requires a lot of thought and study and may not likely be the place to start a development plan but it also ought not be ignored. However, I have both assumed and somewhat argued that what is currently available in development, planning and organizational literature is not a significant body of research, knowledge or awareness that is available yet—not enough has the *force of fear* been taken seriously by leaders, planners and developers overall. Myself and Desh Subba have provided the first article to focus on a "fearist perspective" based on our philosophies of fearlessness and fearism, respectively. We argued for taking fear as central to development. We made the case for a "new consciousness" for a "whole education" has to be at the forefront of development initiatives. We wrote,

> ... a whole education must be based on the right to grow
> and develop in freedom from fear as well as being free of a
> basic fear of freedom that is inculcated in oppressive [i.e.,
> fear-based] societies. Fear, when not understood in its full
> complexity, and thus, not managed well individually and/
> or collectively, leads to the source of all other oppressive
> ism's like classism, racism, sexism and so on. [95]

There is no point developing a nation *via* reform, if the same *fear-based* consciousness, and unsustainable ways of thinking, and actions are motivating and designing the so-called 'better' advancements called "progress." Albert Camus, the great existential philosopher, wrote poignantly and poetically in 1946 of the indictment that humanity has to face in terms of its knowledge production and education over the past 300+ years:

> The 17the century was the century of mathematics;
> the 18th century that of physics;
> the 19th century of biology; and
> the 20th century is the *century of fear* .... [96]
> [and the 21st century is turning out to be the century of
> terror]

"Progress" now has to be questioned in this post-Camusian world, a post-WW-II imaginary, and sense of a precarious postmodern future that is not looking very bright the way things are going. I pointed this out earlier with Albert Einstein's cautionary and I pointed out earlier that the great philosophical sages of India, in particular, have already also made this a priority as they advanced the fearlessness education and ethical imperative for a progressive India. This is such an important resource for India today. Schools and socialization have to be redesigned at the core curriculum to fit a 21ˢᵗ century the youth are going to have to live in. As well, India can draw upon other nations' philosophers and educators of fearlessness and draw from experiences of fighting through oppressive colonization (e.g., see Nelson Mandela in S. Africa, and Martin Luther King Jr., and today Marianne Williamson's 2020 run for president of the USA based on "love" over "fear" [97]). Any good leadership, development expertise, and permacultural planning ought to return to the roots (including Nature's laws), and integrate the best cultural wisdom of the past, including the best victories and practices of the Indigenous primal peoples, and Renaissance of India, and go from there—ensuring that Fear's Empire is *not* re-built in merely 'new wine skins' in merely new forms and surfaces. Short-term crisis management alone will not do! Otherwise, the same basic problems will reoccur. The great depths of the dominating and dysfunctional worldview of economic predatory capitalism (i.e., Westernism globalization and its colonialist pathologies), that is, a fear-based worldview has to be transformed as part of the development process in India. I ask India *not* to blindly import the West's insidious *fear dis-ease* as the cost for modernization! Rather, import, if anything, something like other soft technologies of fearlessness, as I have been documenting from the work of Four Arrows [100], as one example, whereby a de-hypnotizing of the people under Fear's Empire is a real possibility.

I particularly love this quote (above) by the Dalai Lama, when he was talking with groups of Westerners on one of his speaking tours. It resonates with my own experiences as a fearlessness teacher. There are serious implications in *fearing fear* (as F. D. Roosevelt spoke of [101]) and worse implications for *fearing fearlessness* and how that has likely spread into the wider world *via* colonization and W. Enlightenment Reason held so highly by the West [102]. Anyways, I wonder how this specific cautionary of the Dalai Lama's teaching on fear and fearlessness would relate to India? My guess is (with some evidence provided earlier), the Indian people are much more comfortable and understand an ethical philosophy of fearlessness (i.e., *abhaya*) as a virtue—and primary virtue of all virtues. Now, whether they fear it at some level may be an issue that I'll explore at some point later, below. Hint: oppressed and fearful humans often, like an animal kept in a cage all its life, are often fearful of freedom itself when the cage door is finally opened.

I aim in the following reflections to create an initial architecture for diagnosis and prescriptions of potential and resistance—albeit, only generic, for which India may move ahead in its future and, to do so in relationship with the insidious globalizing forces shaping everything today. The rest of the world, and some specific countries analogous to India, have many similar problems in development—that is, in arriving at a healthy, sane, just and sustainable way of living on this planet. The scope of which I envision sustainability, is one not unlike the way of the ancient Indigenous peoples who for 99% of human history lived relatively successfully, because their guiding holistic worldview included a sensitivity to the sacred authentic relationship with all other beings, through living in harmony with the laws of Nature.

As I (or anyone for that matter) attempts to build an emancipatory development architecture for *"India, a Nation of Fear and Prejudice"* (*a la* Kumar), the architecture has to focus on good leadership and a healthy and sustainable vision of the future, with a strong emphasis on emotion (affect) and its relationship to sociality and community and the 'good life.' Ultimately, the economic structure and politics ruling in India have to also be included. This is what Kumar lays grounds for in his Chapter 10 of Part 1, where he argues for a new "social equity" beyond mere economics and one that has to deconstruct the caste system in India. The task is enormous. I can only touch on a few surfaces and some depths in this fearanalysis. I briefly explored why a "Nation of Fear" has arisen and linked it to the Dominant (Western) worldview that was exported and imported by India— and, not all by its own free will. *Fear* is capable, in its worst excesses, of polluting all parts of a society without barriers. Fear can be imposed, of which colonization is one major form. I investigated especially the fear/ fearlessness dialectic in the past, when, as I showed earlier, the history of India is one with great wisdom re: the nature and role of fear and the virtue of all virtues "fearlessness" having been recognized, taught and remaining in the cultural, philosophical and spiritual fabric of the people and institutions (perhaps) of this great nation. Mahatma Gandhi's quote above being symbolic of this wisdom he gained from the ancestors and passed on to the future of India, and the rest of the world—especially as he linked non-violent resistance against the colonizer with fearlessness.

Unfortunately, fear and fearlessness are not typically part of everyday conversations, not in India or any other country is my guess. Other things get more attention. It is not likely a big surprise that virtually everyone in India, or any developing nation will identify and agree that "things need to change" and likewise, "things ought to be improved." After that general agreement, we then are faced with all the different ways that people perceive what it is that needs to change (and priorities), and their scale of application from micro to macro may also differ—if not be conflicted. Everyone does not agree on what is "good" change or "progressive," and that's where big conflicts (politics) often lies. This disagreement can be potent and even hostile while creating an atmosphere of insecurity and fear, including *fear of conflict* (as Kumar pointed out)—that is, it creates often a stalemate amongst the various leaders and their followers.

Little real productive action forward may be the result or often changes are created in a society by the elites without the agreement of a population affected by them. Terrorist activities can grow out of this despair of feeling one has 'no voice' in the affairs of their nation [84]. Elites can easily say, and there is some partial truth to it, that the weaker citizens are just not educated enough to play a part in decisions, in democracy, and that is left as that. It becomes a norm way of believing, thinking and operating. It can become the hidden, all-powerful shaping, rule.

The powerless, so to speak, are then often left with believing no one wants to hear them anyways. The *fearsome* (i.e., strong, elite or laterals as Kumar says) rule the *fearful* (the weak, marginal and literals, as Kumar says, barely surviving day to day). With all of what these two major groupings of people in India have in common, fearologically speaking, is "fear"—each in a different relationship to it (perhaps), but each managing fear nonetheless in their own ways. There is something very interesting about this fact. It may be an important *bridge* to connecting the two groups and aligning along some 'new' catalytic trajectory of possibility for them to join together in a campaign of reform and transformation? I'll return to this point of *fear* as common psychological and social ground, and another aspect of interest from Kumar's Part 1 (Emergence of Body Politic), where he declared in Indian society from the start, "all were fearful of natural phenomena like thunders, lightning... earthquakes."

Progressive development, from a fearological view (i.e., my own position), is going to have to be itself a cultural therapy and a *therapia* from a new paradigm (see below) not the old traditional and habitual, not the patriarchal contemporary ruling *paradigm of fear*. We'll need a new governance and cultural foundation based on a *paradigm of fearlessness*. And, it will have to be acknowledged that such a therapeutic intervention will be criticized ruthlessly, if not viciously attacked, and largely it will be ignored (through denial as a psychological defense). To minimize these resistances to a proposed progressive development architecture and plan is going to have to involve great attention to what is commonly called "fear of change" ideas. At least, that's the common discourse and imaginary around fear that exists. So many times have we heard this statement repeated, "people fear change" that it has become a truism. It is the norm belief, whether we are conscious of it or not and at the same time it easily can become a self-fulfilling prophecy that involves that most important context (and factor)—*fear*. The essence of Fear's Empire is built on this glue of an insidious disempowering self-fulfilling premise.

Great cultural and spiritual leaders, as well as grass-roots leaders, are going to be important in any transformation of India from a culture of fear to a culture of fearlessness. I recommend a unified message: *People don't fear change, they fear being changed by forces outside their control!* I assert with that message that the Fisherian dictum: *Where arises, so then does fearlessness.* We are made of this spirit of fearlessness and it will grow as we pay attention to it rather than overly pay attention reactively and habitually to all the symptoms and effects of fear. At least, this is one way I envision leaders re-thinking through the old adages about change and assuming "fear of change" is the ubiquitous reason things don't progress well and thereby elites have to control and force the change because they perceive "the people" (majority) are afraid of change. No, this paternalism has to end its self-fulfilling prophecy, and as such I believe there is one very powerful strategy awaiting in the wings, already well cooking in the pot, but yet fully untapped in India. I am speaking of the resurgence, if not insurgence, of progressive women's movements in India. But first, let me address another avenue for the citizens of India and their leaders—and, that is to begin to educate themselves on the universal and constitutional reformations and transformations going on in some parts of the modernist and postmodernist world in regard to the nature and role of fear that is, and that ought to be.

Legal Humanitarian Grounds for a "Fearless Society"

> Either in ancient India or modern India, the people belonging to the lower castes could not realize their full potential because of various reasons, one of which mainly is fear....They were fearful to such an extent that they could not think of imagining a good life....Though there has been a trend to show that a little improvement took place because of modernization and education..."
>
> – B. Maria Kumar, Part 1

> Life [beyond economic survival/equity] is a bigger canvas, encompassing liberty, freedom, fraternity, dignity and fearlessness which are embedded in social equality.
>
> – B. Maria Kumar, Part 1

If there has ever been a universal problem, a kind of paradox yet unsolved in humanity (in India), it has got to be the dynamic of *freedom from fear* <---> *fear of freedom*. This is a continuum of which any one individual (or society) struggles. On the far right of this equation is the ever common problem of oppressed peoples, rich or poor, is that they actually don't want freedom and its full responsibility—they are yet mature enough to be self-actualized and self-authoring of their lives. They want others to control their lives, even if they complain and rebel. It's a kind of paradoxical and enigmatic relationship with authority, their self-concept and self-esteem and their need to conform. As well, environmental conditions and traumatic histories can influence this orientation of "fear of freedom" as a typological positioning adopted with conscious and unconscious knowing. Integral therapists call this positioning "preconventional" in its most immature forms and "conventional" in its more matured forms [103]; once one matures further along the spectrum of consciousness and development towards a positioning of "freedom from fear" as most important as a life-orientation, then we are moving into the higher levels of human potential called "postconventional" [104]. The importance of this maturing imperative, and developing a policy of governance that works continually to shift the center of gravity of an individual and/or a society along the spectrum, is the critical advance of being able to take more and more perspectives on in the perceptual field and thinking (cognitive) capacity, in which developmental research correlates with advancing moral and existential (i.e., fearlessness) capacities—thus, in the end an ethical fearlessness emerges (more or less), beyond the 'grip of fear,' that guides behaviors, design and planning, organizations and overall health of sociality itself.

The maturation dynamic or spectrum I am pointing out here ought to be front-and-center in any leaders' minds, even if they themselves have not reached the higher levels of consciousness and self-actualization. The 'map' is well drawn by integral theory and integral therapies and in developmental psychology generally. It is also found in the hierarchical perennial philosophies around the world, especially in the East. Some would call this a spiritual framework of human potential. This is basic guidance for humanity's growth and development and it is not limited by or distorted by (at least, very little) by egocentric, ethnocentric, or religious ideologies or simple cultural myths and beliefs or taboos. The basis is scientific, which is a point that Kumar continually raises in his work over the years, is that we require scientific-rational approaches to development and improvement in India.

There is a vast, often empirical, literature from social sciences to philosophy and spirituality, that have indicated the paradoxical relationship people have to freedom. On the one hand we can be inspired perhaps by the great Indian sages and other world leaders who recognize fearlessness as just that—an escape from fear—that is, they teach "freedom from fear" [105]. On the other hand, there is an equally vast literature showing "fear of freedom" is by far the more common norm, which Erich Fromm, the psychiatrist, famously uncovered as so problematic in acting as a barrier to human health and development [106]. A good cultural therapy for India, for example, requires a sensitivity to this paradoxical dynamic in both diagnoses made and prescriptions offered to the maladies of Indian society, past and present.

My view is that a nation ought to govern itself by perspectives and principles and virtues of the higher orders of consciousness and development, with ethical guidance, even if the vast majority of the leaders and peoples generally are nowhere near that higher level/stage of development in their actual practices. I think leaders of all political stripes and kinds, lower or higher classes, make a big mistake when they reduce their vision of human potential to only the immediate "needs" of the lowest common and obvious order of reality of the day-to-day struggles. It is not that leaders are to ignore daily-bread-survival struggles, but the analysis and interventions must be deeper, a point Kumar makes in his analysis as well. Fear/fearlessness dynamics, for Kumar, Subba and myself, are an essential part of that package of liberties required for all humans, no matter what their daily plight. 'Humans do not live by bread alone' is the common wisdom notion that many have heard of and of which is relevant to what my argument is all about. Every human needs higher perspectives on the meaning of life beyond survival needs, impulse-gratifications and basics, at least that is the evolutionary *paradigm of fearlessness* [107] that I purport in Part 2.

India, like any nation, can draw upon the already grooved workings of a higher social and cultural evolution in some developed nations—where there has been recognition of something more than survival, something as basic human rights. The explicit policies, laws, constitutional guarantees related to what I am speaking about have already appeared. Let me briefly overview some of them.

"Freedom from fear and want" is the foundational principle and human right that began the thinking of the former U. S. President F. D. Roosevelt's 1940s "Four Freedoms," essential to development logic and ethics. F. D. R. delivered this formulation of worldwide social and political objectives in his State of the Union Message to Congress on January 6, 1941. In 1946, after establishing the United Nations, Eleanor Roosevelt (his wife), the United States ambassador to the UN, was selected to head the newly formed Commission on Human Rights to determine the constituents of humankind's inalienable freedoms. According to Clements, "She and other members of the commission were determined to write a document that

would live and last, a document that would protect and empower men and women [and children], irrespective of color, creed or culture. Their goal was to establish a universal framework for all beings to realize their highest potential and live in freedom and dignity [despite their economic status]. Thus on December 10, 1948 the Universal Declaration of Human Rights was adopted by the UN General Assembly stating that 'freedom from fear' was [hu]mankind's highest aspiration" [108].

It is not surprising that a woman's (and feminist) sensibility to truly caring about people, Eleanor Roosevelt was a spear-head advocate for the UN 1948 declaration and it likewise is not surprising to me that another woman, an internationally recognized ethical philosopher, at the turn of the millenium, came forward to publish 10 "Central Human Capabilities" as a universal checklist for human societies to assess themselves and utilize as a guide for their future policy making, their new laws, and their overall improved governance practices. It adds a nuanced sensitivity to the UN document on human rights. Nussbaum in this declaration has given *fear* its due recognition in #5 capability that should be nourished and honored by nations and any organization—she wrote, *"Emotions*- Being able to have attachments to things and people outside ourselves; to love those who love and care for us, to grieve at their absence; in general, to love, to grieve, to experience longing, gratitude, and justified anger. Not having one's emotional development blighted by fear and anxiety" [109]. Nussbaum, rare amongst Western contemporary philosophers, has pursued her study and publishing on the critical and insidious pathological role of fear in society, and especially in the USA [110]. She proposes "love" as the answer, a similar tactic (albeit quite different from) as seen recently by Marianne Williamson in her 2020 presidential campaign in the USA [111]. Love is of course important (see below), and I also want to note that it is not enough—fearlessness, and its imperative teaching towards a better "fear education" [112] is essential to the actualization of Love vs. Fear (*a la* Williamson [113]—that is, in the growth and development of a culture of fear into a culture of fearlessness. India can learn from the West's progress on this front—albeit, the reverse is also true.

A Feminine Logic Challenging Fear/Fearlessness

To change society, to free ourselves from the 'grip of fear,' that is, to transform it at the roots and not merely reform its surfaces, we must imagine and think radically different ways about the world we live in (reality), who we are, and what is the cosmos itself—all in terms of a 'new story' as I suggested at the beginning of Part 2. Listen to some women's voices and imaginaries required today:

> We must realize that market exchange is not natural, real or necessary. It is an invention of patriarchy. The illusion that some religions find life to be is created by the disalignment of our behavior, and constructions of reality, with the deeper logic of nature. Women are more "natural" because they are in alignment with this logic while patriarchy is an aberration and an illusion. Our disalignment and refusal to practice and value this deeper logic creates our unhappiness and our problems.
>
> – Genevieve Vaughan [114]

> There is an underground of people in ... who are seeking higher wisdom. We are rich and poor, progressive and conservative, young and old. And what we share at this moment is deep concern—concern about the direction in which our country is headed, the assaults on our democratic foundations, and the erosion of our human values.... Our task is to generate a massive wave of energy, fueled and navigated by we the people, so powerful as to override all threats to our democracy. Where fear has been harnessed for political purposes, our task is to harness love.
>
> – Marianne Williamson [115]

> What is essential is not to develop new doctrines or dogmas, or to define a new, coherent political schema but, to suggest a new imaginative attitude, one that can

be radical and subversive which will be able to change the logic of our development. Perhaps as the poet says we should now break the routine, do an extravagant action that would change the course of history. What is essential is to go beyond the politics of violence and exclusion of our times and to find new political imaginations. An imaginary where people of the margins, of the global South are subjects of our own history, writing our own cultural narratives, offering new universals, imagining a world in more life enhancing terms, constructing a new radical imaginary. We must seek new imaginaries from the South: the South not only as third world, as the civilizations of Asia, the Arab world, Africa, Latin America; but the South as the voices and movements of peoples, wherever these movements exist. The South as the visions and wisdoms of women.

– Corrine Kumar [116]

When I think of the complex maladies of India today, the gains the country has made and the restrictions and failures it experiences (see Kumar Part 1), there is no doubt in my mind, any cultural therapia has to go to the core of how Indians see themselves and the cosmos itself. This includes relating to how Indians have seen themselves historically, including reconnecting today with the 'ancestors' and accessing that ancestry on many dimensions, including the arational healing modalities [117]. Rational planning and policy is not enough on its own, especially when religious cultural history is so alive and deep and ancient in India and will likely be for some time. Modernism is not a solution on its own. An integrative and holistic-integral approach, including a feminine and/ or feminist approach is required.

Sure, there are traditional and contemporary philosophies, religions, spiritualities, there are social sciences and economic sciences, and organizational and management theories to guide India's development. But you can bet that almost all of those are male-led sources. They are visions from the patriarchy itself. I think Krishna Kumar's recent lecture on "Education and Girlhood" in India is exemplar on the topic of how girl (female) problems are not going to be solved by boys and men, fathers and uncles, grandfathers necessarily. As a feminist researcher and activist, Krishna Kumar notes that there will only be a real improvement in the education of girlhood in an emancipatory (non-fear-based) way when India's leaders take in and critically reflect on what she called "the psychological split in the state's mind" and "the state's difficulty in engaging with culture"—especially, but not only, around sex and gender [118]. In B. Maria Kumar's analysis of India, especially re: sexuality and the HIV crises related to the intractable caste problem unique to India, he says the choice is "Freedom or Feardom." I agree with both the Kumars' analysis on this point. I've learned in studying for the writing of this essay (Part 2) that the political state, especially as it modernizes and tries to remain secular, has a great problem of how to manage the religious-cultural traditions that truly operate on the ground, in the everyday, and influence the lives of people, regardless of the state's laws and principles of modernization. And, yet, truly we have to look at "fear" in the state itself and how it is afraid of the religions, and the religions are afraid of the state. This is the classic conflict of premodern and modern priorities and agendas—whereby nations have to figure out how to find harmony in this division—because some major parts of the nation ("split") want modernism, the other wants traditionalism. You can also find this tears countries apart in similar ways re: dominating efforts of staunch nationalism, internationalism and/or localism mindsets. No small problem.

If I were India's leaders, the place where I would look for fearlessness is in the women's (and girls') awakenings and resistance and emancipatory movements. These are 50+% of your population and recently we are seeing powerful signs of unrest in India amongst its female populations (especially—but also precarity amongst its youth [119]), for example a few recent events:

a) "Women's Wall" – 3 million females, a chain of 620 km in Kerala State in India was an amazing signal of resistance and protest as a calling for equality and social justice (Jan. 1, 2019)

b) #IWillGoOut – a group of women in New Dehli supporting the Women's March in 2018, Washington, DC, resisting the current growing trend of fascist like governments trying to turn back any progressive gains in women's rights around the world

c) Gender-based resistance, led by women for women in Kashmir's 2016 uprising [120]

d) Vandana Shiva, author, scientist, warrior, mother—leader of #seefreedom movement is having a major impact in India and around the world in the battle to control natural seeds and prevent them getting trademarked by corporations and polluted by GMO's [121]

And it is also the case, from my research, that a lot of these types of movements do not talk directly about, theorize about, fear and promote fearlessness within the typical academic or male-dominated ways of rationalist discourse. No, they operate more from their bodies, their femaleness and motherness, their deep sensitivity to living as a "creation" making being, whereas males are so often conditioned away from this and become "destructive" making-beings—leading wars and violence disproportionately. Of course, women and men (adults) are responsible for their actions and their nations' actions and the point is not to make this a divisive argument on my part for the need to pay more attention to women, the feminine, feminists, etc. I merely am suggesting that societies, like India, will do well to listen to their women and females, and their relationship to fear (and fearlessness). It may be a whole new imaginary of fear that will be discovered by nourishing the feminine perspective—and, feminine perspectives—that can integrate perhaps with masculine ones. We are out of balance, is all I am saying. I could not find the female philosophers of fearlessness very easily in India's canon literatures. However, you'll see that I draw upon women in this essay (e.g., Margaret Wheatley, Marianne Williamson, in the West) and I look forward to having more dialogues with women, from around the world, on the topic of fear and development. India's leaders would do well to build a matrixial, non-paranoic psychodynamic into their fabric of social life—a movement that Bracha L. Ettinger [122] has been doing for decades. Citations to start off this section (above) are from the "gift economy" and that is linked to the "gift of fearlessness" tradition, and Indigenous worldview, and these are essential paths to follow and gain insights from, as the fear-based capitalism that has become so predatorial must be challenged and transformed. We need matriarchal principles of non-violent economies based on the "gift" and thus, based on "life" (see Kumar's Life concept beyond mere survival). But these are topics of details beyond the scope of this essay, I merely am adding them into the architecture of fearlessness I have gathered here. Let me end this section with a teaching story (fiction) of the *gift imaginary* (of fearlessness) powerfully embodied in female wisdom and compassion, where notions of "victim" (e.g., the poor) are, using a different logic than 'normal,' turned around upside down and re-imagined in terms of value and empowerment:

> Let me tell you a story: a story of women, of their creative survival, a story of timeless care, a story of the gift imaginary. it is a story from Tagore on the Riches of the Poor.

> Once upon a long ago and of yesterday it was a time of darkness; it was also a time of famine that was devastating the land of Shravasti people gathered; poor people, hungry people: Lord Buddha looking at everybody and asked his disciples who will feed these people? who will care for them? who will feed these hungry people? he looked at Ratnaka the banker, waiting for an answer: Ratnaka, looked down and said but much more than all the wealth I have would be needed to feed these hungry people Buddha than turned to Jaysen, who was the chief of the King's army: Jaysen said very quickly of course my Lord I would give you my life but there is not enough food in my house. then, it was the turn of Dharampal who possessed large pastures sighed and said the god of the wind has dried out our fields and I do not know how I shall even pay the king's taxes.

> The people listened, and were so hungry: Supriya, the beggar's daughter was in the gathering, listening too as she raised her hand, she stood up and said I will nourish these people: I will care for the people everybody turned to

look at Supriya: how would she they thought do this? How will she, a beggar's daughter with no material wealth, how would she accomplish her wish? but how will you do this, they chorused: Supriya gentle and strong looked at the gathering and said It is true that I am the poorest among you, but therein is my strength, my treasure, my affluence, because I will find all this at each of your doors.

Supriya's words and actions come from another logic: she refuses the logic of property, profit, patriarchy; inviting us to another ethic of care, of concern, of connectedness. She sees the poor as a community of people with dignity in a relational way, not as individual separate units; and speaks for the many all over the world who are challenging the totalitarism logic of the master imaginary and trying to re-find and re-build communities, regenerating people's knowledges and cosmovisions, reviving the dream for us all. [123]

Fear Management/Education (FME)

Throughout Part 2, a mostly implicit architecture and *paradigm of fearlessness* is offered as a perspective—as part of a radical revisionist worldview—and, as a means to "see" in and through the surfaces of India's challenges and problems and to see its strengths. In general, I have agreed with Kumar's preliminary fearanalysis. I am learning still from Kumar's Part 1 with its conclusion that "fear" is source problem in India and has been for a long time historically; and at the same time, I don't want to totalize my thinking and imagination such that I construct fear as only a problem for human societies or nations. Therefore, it's not wise to only label India a "nation of fear," I have argued elsewhere that our basic *fearuality* (like sexuality) is *not* just a problem; rather, it is also inherently part of the essence of what makes us a living system and a human being developing towards maturity [124].

Such a 'balanced' positive (and negative) perspective on fear is core to the newly emerging philosophy of fearism (*a la* Subba), of which Kumar and myself have drawn inspiration from, in part, in our analyses of India. My own philosophy of fearlessness branch of fearism takes the position that *where there is fear, then also there is fearlessness arising.* This is a simple but complex understanding and theoretical frame that fits the paradigm of fearlessness, unique to my own fearanalysis. Thus, I repeat, I cannot accept that India is a nation of fear literally because it is equally a nation of fearlessness. The question is, how are we going to help people perceive this and move towards the latter as a goal of maturing nationhood—maturing humanity, and arguably as the only sane way to build a sustainable and healthy society.

This brings me to the conclusion of my reflections here. My reading is that fear management/education (FME) is the solution to the deepest core problems of India and what it is facing today and into tomorrow. FME has to be part of a holistic analysis and solution plan. The skeletal architecture for this holistic analysis is indicated in this essay Part 2, and no doubt one could integrate the Part 1 and Part 3 of my colleagues in this book in order to make an even better analysis and set of solutions. Because of limited time and space to invest in this book project, I have had to focus on certain aspects, as I mentioned, leadership, development and futures, with my own specialization of study of fear/fearlessness. I am interested in any organization or nation (or even an individual)—to find freedom as part of their developmental path and that is a freedom from the limitations of the worst excesses of fear—and, from the context of a "culture of fear"—to move toward a "culture of fearlessness" as ideal—which, is ultimately, and metaphysically in my view, a way to Love. Is this what a politician in India would be interested in? Well, not typically, I admit. But I give evidence and make suggestions of the link between a culture of fearlessness (and 'gift of fearlessness' tradition), a gifting imaginary and economy, and a woman's (and/or feminine) perspective on leadership and how best to care for a people's and a planetary ecology.

My own view, again for brevity sake, is that a better (holistic) FME is required as central to any plan to salvage and to grow a better India (and world). If as Kumar (Part 1) is correct, that a major source of fearfulness, in all India's population, is rooted in historical sources of a fear of Nature (see his Chapter 1 "All were fearful of natural phenomena")—then, it behooves me as a fearologist to probe into this great source of fearfulness, and the assumptions that go with Kumar's claim. My point, is not to construct a critique of Kumar's claim as that is not my purpose in this essay, it is rather to respond to what Kumar has raised. In this response, I have to ask if a possible solution to the fear problems of India lies in this common ground of fearing Nature and all the various defense systems (e.g., magical, mythical and rational thinking) that evolved around that basic primal fear. I have to ask if there is no other alternative to the FME that has evolved? I have to ask if there is more than one interpretation of this common primal fear? What is interesting to me is that it is (hypothetically) *the common ground* which unites all peoples in fearfulness they carry and have carried for millenia. Fear is the unifier—not love. This gets very interesting and complicated but I'll be brief in my conclusions to make some sense of the great potential for designing and planning reform and transformation upon the common ground of the people of India, from past to present. I realize this is generalizing all people, and that is a problem, but for practical purposes I believe there is something worthwhile in such a generalization.

I hypothesize and imagine, that if the common ground of *fear* is basically the same for the rich and poor, the religious and secular, and higher caste and lower caste persons, then FME interventions would tap into that common ground. This is the bridge between the 'gaps.' It is a kind of equalizing force—that is, if it is facilitated carefully and wisely.

And FME would offer a better education on fear *for all* that shows that just because this common fear was managed in some particular ways in the past, the future does not have to be dictated by the past ways of managing fear. And, that the managing of fear in the past, for better or worse, was based on the knowledge and experience available at the time. So, there is no need to criticize the past ways in a sense, other than to discern that today and in the future there will be a better FME knowledges and practices available to draw upon, as priority, and that FME is state-sponsored for the very emancipation from the past mis-guided ways of managing fear and less than complete forms of understanding fear.

Thus, one could present a great case of a renewal on how to manage fear in India, and it could be stretched out to be a campaign nationally that seeks to develop the 'best practices' in FME anywhere in the world—that is, to become a 21st century exemplar for leading the rest of the world in how to manage fear! The analogy is like that of a country taking on the CO_2 crises of excess that causes most of global warming and mass destruction—and, thus, similar the Fear crises of excess (e.g., fearmongering and culture of fear) could be also reduced and/or eliminated with target dates. Would this be truly inspiring and unite a country so divided as is India—and, divided arguably by "fear(s)" as Kumar points out?

India could and ought to encourage women to lead this initiative for all the reasons I mentioned earlier and to do so by integrating the best of the fearlessness teachings and ethics of the great Indian sages and educators, and also by inquiring into the new Fear Studies and work related to the philosophy of fearism. These combinations have never been systematically tried and built in to a curriculum and design plan for development, that I know of. Why not start it in India? There is no doubt in my mind that fear of Nature spills over to be a fear of Women—as both Nature and Women are 'Creators' and of the greatness we fear as Marianne Williamson has written and taught about in her leadership campaign (see above).

I see Culture as the 'child' of Nature. I think we need to see this for what it is, a great universal truth (and healing)—and that Culture mimics Nature; but also does its own creating in its own ways which inevitably go beyond Nature, in a certain ways but are always linked to Nature. However, Culture with such freedom and creativity also often 'forgets' to follow some of the most important laws of Nature and when it does this things will go badly awry—and human societies will decay and go extinct because they depend on Nature as 'Mother.' She is source of Life. Due to woundedness, trauma, and fear-based patterns that arise from coping and not healing sufficiently, humanity gets twisted and skewed from its connectivity with Nature. Then Culture turns against Nature—that is what fear ultimately will do when it is not managed and transformed well. History of India, like the history of humanity, tends to show this pattern of development. Conscious cultural evolution and development of the human potential can change this type of error and mis-direction of Culture.

Thus, in my transformative 'Big Picture' view I am painting there is a role for the Spiritual. The triad Natural-Cultural-Spiritual has to be integrated to stay "whole" and "good" for all—humans and other-than-humans on this planet. In a type of social permaculture, and as in any good cultural therapy, as I have said, there is some dimension of a required Spiritual correction of the Cultural when it gets off-track from Nature too far. So, going beyond religions and ethnocentric interests alone, I have presented a path to an integral-holistic cosmology here briefly at the end of the essay—as a way to understand the dynamics of what humans are contending with and it also is a design basis for how to analyze and plan interventions into the cultural dis-eases of India. If there was a plan of FME universalized for India, with a triadic cosmology as I suggested, then the FME offered would be of the highest calibre and no doubt would have dramatic positive impacts on the nation, and the world. At least, that's my 'Big Picture' view and approach in Part 2.

Of course, there will be resistance to this corrective of FME I am suggesting. Postmodernism itself tends to deny 'grand narratives' and 'universal' truths. There is the fear-based vested interests of the powerful (elites, especially) that will not want to unwind their control and management systems of governance that mis-use fear against the weaker. There will be many forces of Fear's Empire that will fight being dismantled. So, expect that. No need to be naive here about the kind of change I am insisting with FME. A 'team' and a coalition of leaders in India and beyond India, are needed to 'hold the vision' I am speaking about. They need to do their homework, their education on fear and fearlessness, and do their healing around their fears that such changes would be terrifying to a nation so used to (if not addicted) to fear for so long. Thus, a cultural therapy of fearlessness, seems the way to go. It will have to start with those who are leaders already who connect with this proposal. Then, on the ground where the people are in the majority, the FME can be spread, slowly, radically when necessary, but done with sensitivity and done with passion and commitment. It will be one large experimental operation.

My most basic reminder in this (r)evolution of fear/fearlessness is that we will feel fear and thoughts will create fear—as we move to challenge Fear's Empire of controls. The main thing is to remember, *when fear arises, so then does fearlessness.* The only problem comes when we only pay attention to the arising fear (and its symptoms) and forget to notice and enhance and grow the fearlessness (and its symptoms) arising. That is the shift of perception. It takes guidance, skill development and practice. I'd be glad to help this FME (r)evolution and I know many others would too.

I close with a quote from my Indigenous-based colleague Four Arrows, as he works tirelessly to reclaim the 'old' traditional ways of the Indigenous worldview that all current nations have as a resource in their past. Four Arrows wrote, of the 12 basic components of the Indigenous worldview, "A fearless trust in the universe [i.e., Natural] comes from a continual cultivation of courage and generosity... [in contrast, whereas fear avoidance and a focus on materialistic gain largely defines the underlying motivations in dominant worldview oriented cultures" [125].

****

NOTES

1. Excerpt from http://thomasberry.org/life-and-thought/about-thomas-berry/story-as-functional-cosmology

2. For more information see https://en.wikipedia.org/wiki/Thomas_Berry

3. Berry, T. (1978). *The new story. Teilhard Studies, No. 1* (Winter). American Teilhard Association.

4. Four Arrows (*aka* Jacobs, D. T.) (2016). *Point of departure: Returning to a more authentic worldview for education and survival.* Charlotte, NC: Information Age Publishing.

5. Eisler, R. (1987). *The chalice and the blade: Our history.* San Francisco, CA: Harper & Row.

6. Fisher, R. M. (2014). Educating for Sustainability & Well-being in a Risk Society & Culture of Fear. Paper/Round Table at 3rd Interdisciplinary Conference on Educating for Sustainability and Well-being, University of Manitoba, Winnipeg. http://www.eswbrg.org/uploads/1/2/8/9/12899389/sust_well_fisher.pdf

7. Quote from Tharoor, S. (2012). *Bookless in Baghdad: Reflections on writing and writers.* New York: Skyhorse Publishing, n.p.

8. Ibid., n.p.

9. See, for e.g., Fisher, R. M. (2016). Invoking fearanalysis: A new methodology applied to wicked problems and paradigm shifts in the Anthropocene. A CSIIE Yellow Paper, DIFS-15. Carbondale, IL: Center for Spiritual Inquiry & Integral Education. https://prism.ucalgary.ca/handle/1880/110038?show=full

10.   Taken from Jean Gebser's stages, see Wilber (2006), pp. 89, 92. Wilber, K. (2006). *Integral spirituality: A startling new role for religion in the modern and postmodern world*. Boston, MA: Integral Books/Shambhala.

11.   See Fisher, R. M. (2010). *The world's fearlessness teachings: A critical integral approach to fear management/education for the 21st century*. Lanham, MD: University Press of America.

12.   Quoted from Forman (2010), p. 134. Forman, M. (2010). *A guide to integral psychotherapy*. Albany, NY: State University of New York Press.

13.   Ibid., p. 135.

14.   Ibid., see Four Arrows (2016).

15.   Holmgren, D. (2002/15). *Permaculture: Principles and pathways beyond sustainability—revised*. Retrieved from https://us.permacultureprinciples.com/product/principles-and-pathways/

16.   Four Arrows (aka Jacobs, D. T.) (with England-Aytes, K., Cajete, G., Fisher, R. M., Mann, B. A., McGaa, E. & Sorensen, M.) (2013). *Teaching truly: A curriculum to Indigenize mainstream education*. New York: Peter Lang.

17.   See Kumar, B. M., & Fisher, R. M. (2019). Mythical seductions and diversions: A dialogue, with fear. *International Journal of Fear Studies, 1*(1), 45-56. I am not restricting my image/ practice of *cultural therapy* to current uses in psychology (i.e., "relational/ cultural therapy" with its emphasis on ethnic aspects added to traditional psychotherapy practice) but am extending the notion (as ontopsychocultural *therapia*) to diagnosis and treatment of the "Dominant worldview" (see Four Arrows, 2016) and the deepest unconscious functioning of what O'Sullivan (1999) labeled the modern Western "entrancement... as a profound cultural pathology" (p. 3) that has left us moderns "in possession of a damaged planet" (Berry, 1999, p. xi) and left us with a disconcerting number of *"sociopathic leaders"* in powerful positions (e.g., Perry, 2015). I believe, in part, India, as a once fully colonized (i.e., Westernized) nation, is infected deeply by this dominant and dysfunctional worldview and continues to be due to globalization processes led by the Western dominant economic nations and conglomerate elite

businesses and oligarchies of capitalist predatory commerce. I will not further elaborate the *therapia* herein as that is beyond the scope of this essay (cf. Wilber, 1995, p. 73). However, what my naming this indicates is that culture, once it 'turns' and becomes a "culture of fear" (Fisher, 2006, pp. 51, 56-57; Furedi, 2007) the best way to work with this dynamic is to name it as *pathological*—in which others have called it "Fear's Empire" (Barber, 2003) or "Culture of Empire" (Korten, 2005, p. 54) where "Fear is Empire's friend" (p. 34). Four Arrows (2016) argues, the base of this disastrous turn (e.g., "point of departure" in developmental history of humanity) is based on "mass hypnosis and negative trance-based learning," (p. 27), a topic I'll return to later in this essay on the role of CAT-FAW/N de-hypnotizing technology, critical emancipatory education and the role of a pedagogy of fearlessness. Barber, B. (2003). *Fear's empire: War, terrorism, and democracy.* NY: W. W. Norton; Korten, D. C. (2005). *The great turning: From empire to earth community.* San Francisco, CA: Berrett-Koehler; O'Sullivan, E. (1999). *Transformative learning: Educational vision for the 21ˢᵗ century.* NY: Zed Books; Berry, T. (1999). Foreword in O'Sullivan (1999); Fisher, R. M. (2006). Invoking 'Fear' Studies. *Journal of Curriculum Theorizing, 22*(4), 39-71; Furedi, F. (2007). The only thing we have to fear is the 'culture of fear' itself. Spiked, 4 April, retrieved from http://www.spiked-online.com/index.php?/site/article/3053/; Perry, C. (2015). The 'dark traits' of sociopathic leaders: Could they be a threat to universities? *Australian Universities Review, 57*(1), 17-25; Wilber, K. (1995). *Sex, ecology and spirituality: The spirit of evolution (vol. 1).* Boston, MA: Shambhala.

18.	*Fearologist*- [beyond popular internet definitions] is "one who self-identifies as a specialist in the systematic study of fearology [i.e., the study of the interrelationship of fear and life]" (Fisher & Subba, 2016, p. 158). Fisher, R. M., & Subba, D. (2016). *Philosophy of fearism: A first East-West dialogue.* Australia: Xlibris.

19.	My study of *fear* has always been transdisciplinary and holistic-integral, which involves integrating knowledge from all parts of the world, in order to create a synthesis of knowledge globally to help solve the global Fear Problem (e.g., Fisher, 2010). Fisher, R.

M. (2010). *The world's fearlessness teachings: A critical integral approach to fear management/education for the 21st century*. Lanham, MD: University Press of America.

20.   I am referring to a movement of development thinking coined by E. F. Schumacher from the 1970s that is very useful to principles of good international relations and applications of appropriate technology from country to country, especially the so-called First World countries to others; see https://en.wikipedia.org/wiki/Appropriate_technology

21.   I acknowledge this tradition is likely way more complex than I can ever understand as a Westerner. I will however, apply what I have learned from religious scholars of *abhaya dāna* later in this essay. Let it be said, that many Westerners (e.g., De Becker, 1997) have advanced a secular pragmatic notion of "gift of fear" (part of what I call the fear-positivism movement), of which, in my view is rather skewed because of the general ignore-ance by these authors of the Eastern ancient sacred tradition of *abhaya dāna* and lack of a history of the Fearlessness Movement (Fisher, 2007). De Becker, G. (1997). *The gift of fear: Survival signals that protect us from violence*. NY: Bantam; Fisher, R. M. (2007). History of the Fearlessness Movement: An introduction. Technical Paper No. 22. Vancouver, BC: In Search of Fearlessness Research Institute.

22.   I acknowledge use of "fearless" in this instance is generic and non-technical—and, not my preference but it is easier to use in English language. I critique over-utilization, without theorizing, all uses of "fearless." The point I am making, is beyond this technical matter however, and one ought to examine my work on what it may mean to envision and work towards a "fearless society" (e.g., Fisher, 2000) and "fearless children" (e.g., Fisher, 2010, Chapter 4). Fisher, R. M. (2000). The movement towards a fearless society: A powerful contradiction to violence. Technical Paper No. 10. Vancouver, BC: In Search of Fearlessness Research Institute.

23.   "Fear Problem" is a very large embracing complex concept, beyond the scope of this essay; suffice it to say a simple definition includes: "a synthesis of all the diverse problems that may be associated with fear (usually in regard to its excess); applied to individual and

collective experience; applies to the epistemological challenges of knowing fear (and 'fear'); see also 'Fear' Project, 'Fear' Matrix [Fisher's other concepts]" (Fisher & Subba, 2016, p. 156). I have referred to this as a "wicked problem" (Fisher, Subba, Kumar, 2018, p. 164). Fisher, R. M., Subba, D., & Kumar, B. M. (2018). *Fear, law and criminology: Critical issues in applying the philosophy of fearism.* Australia: Xlibris.

24. See Barnesmoore (2016), p. 112 and Barnesmoore (2017). Barnesmoore, L. (2016). Conscious vs Mechanical evolution: Transcending biocentrist social ontologies. *Environment and Social Psychology 1*(2), 104-14; Barnesmoore, L. (2017). Conscious evolution, social development and environmental justice. *Environment and Social Psychology, 2*(1), 11-25.

25. There are many definitions and contested meanings of transformative learning and education; for purposes here, I'll basically follow Mezirow's definition: "Transformative learning is the expansion of consciousness through the transformation of basic worldview and specific capacities of the self; transformative learning is facilitated through consciously directed processes such as appreciatively accessing and receiving the symbolic contents of the unconscious and critically analyzing underlying premises" (Mezirow, 1995, p. 50). Mezirow, J. (1995). Transformation theory of adult learning. In M. R. Welton (Ed.), *In defense of the lifeworld* (pp. 39–70). NY: State University of New York Press.

26. See "wicked problems" and the need to give complex attention to their detailed definition before jumping into solutions (e.g., Fisher & Subba, 2016, pp. 149, 164). No more important is this than when dealing with the wicked Fear Problem itself (Fisher, Subba & Kumar, 2018, p. 164).

27. *Fear imaginary-* (coined by Fisher) "refers to the contents of imaginations, and also the ways we are allowed or not by systems to imagine the nature and role of fear and ourselves in relation to fear" (Fisher & Subba, 2016, p. 156). One's individual (or a collective nation's) imaginary of fear is an important construct to analyze critically in any fear management analysis, because there may taboos (i.e., fear of fear itself) controlling the imagining of fear

and its role; dialectically, this will also influence the imaginary of fearlessness.

28.	To avoid overly technical precision, and using a lot of space here, I'll by pass the distinctions I make between fear, 'fear' and "artificial" (or "unwarranted" or "irrational" and "culturally-modified") fear—but suffice it to say the latter forms are what cause most of the problems with fear and its management. See Fisher & Subba (2016) for further technical clarifications re: fear (p. 155) and 'fear' (p.156).

29.	There is a vast literature, across disciplines on these two terms, and some authors use them interchangeably, unfortunately. "Culture of fear" is the most technically precise term and the one I prefer. For a quick summary see Wikipedia https://en.wikipedia.org/wiki/Culture_of_fear. However, note, my own research (e.g., Fisher, 2004) makes a much more extensive synthesis of this construct and phenomena than most others. My simplistic definition is *culture of fear* is a dynamic where in trying to manage fear, more fear is created not less. Fisher, R. M. (2004). *Capitalizing on fear: A baseline study on the culture of fear for leaders.* Minneapolis, MN: Intellectual Architects, Ltd.

30.	Fisher, R. M. (2013). The problem of defining the concept of "fear-based." Technical Paper No. 48. Carbondale, IL: In Search of Fearlessness Research Institute.

31.	See Kumar's view on "quantum of fear" and "Fear Quotient" and "Fear Intelligence" in Fisher, Subba & Kumar (2018), pp. 76-78, 81, 85, 87.

32.	See Subba (2014) and Fisher & Subba (2016), p. 157.

33.	See Fisher, R. M. (2016). Transformation of Fear: A critical look in educational philosophy and contexts. Technical Paper No. 63. Carbondale, IL: In Search of Fearlessness Research Institute.

34.	See Kumar, B. M., & Fisher, R. M. (2019). Mythical diversions and seductions: A dialogue, with fear. *International Journal of Fear Studies 1*(1), 45-57.

35.	A. Kathari & K. J. Joy (Eds.) (2017). *Alternative futures: India unshackled.* Authors Upfront.

36.	Excerpt from (front matter) book Commendations, Achin Vanaik, Retired professor of International Relations and Global Politics, University of Delhi.

37.	Excerpt from (front matter) book Commendations, Frederico Demaria, Editor, *De-Growth: A Vocabulary For a New Era.*

38.	Aggarwal, M. (n.d.). The religious and social reform of India—The Indian Renaissance! Retrieved from http://www.historydiscussion.net/history-of-india/religious-and-social-reform-of-india-the-indian-renaissance/1637

39.	See, Wheatley, M. J. (1999). *Leadership and the new science: Discovering order in a chaotic world.* San Francisco, CA: Berrett-Koehler, Chapter Four.

40.	A major part of this "spirit," which will surface later in this essay, is what I call the "spirit of fearlessness."

41.	Johansen, B. (2017). *The new leadership literacies: Thriving in a future of extreme disruption and distributed everything.* San Francisco, CA: Berrett-Koehler, p. 146.

42.	"Growth and defense operations and design are primal drives [cf. *freedom vs. fear* dual-motivation theory (Pyszczynski, Greenberg & Arndt, 2011; and/or Love-force vs. Fear-force meta-motivations (Fisher, 2018, pp. 3, 8, 14, 47); and/or growth vs. deficit motivated values of Maslow, 1966] of survival and beyond" (Fisher, 2018, p. 16). Fisher, R. M. (2018). *Fearless engagement of Four Arrows: The true story of an Indigenous-based social transformer.* NY: Peter Lang. Pyszczynski, T., Greenberg, J., & Arndt, J. (2011). Freedom vs. fear revisited: An integrative analysis of the dynamics of the defense and growth of self. In M. Leary and J. Tangney (Eds.), *Handbook of self and identity* (pp. 378-404). (2nd ed.). NY: Guilford; Maslow, A. (1966). *The psychology of science: A reconnaissance.* NY: Harper & Row.

43.	Debasish Mridha, MD. said: "Fear is a disease of the mind we inherit from society." And White (2016) wrote, "Fear is a disease" and, many others have done so as well if one looks at the Internet. Retrieved from https://www.quotes.net/authors/Debasish+Mridha%2C+M.D. White, A. (2016). Voices from

Standing Rock: Fear is a Disease. Retrieved from https://yr.media/news/voices-from-standing-rock-fear-is-a-disease/

44. In Fisher (2010), this dialectic is constructed as a universal principle and/or dictum: *"When fear arises, there will be fearlessness"* (p. xxviii). This represents a kind of basic spirit of resiliency and self/system regulation—of which, I'll return to later in this essay.

45. See end note 6 (De Becker, 1997).

46. Inayatullah (2007, p. 7). Inayatullah, S. (2007). Six pillars: Futures thinking for transforming. *Foresight, 10*(1), 4-21.

47. A large influence on Wheatley is the eminent spiritual Buddhist nun Pema Chödrön, the later who is author of several popular books on fear and fearlessness.

48. Wheatley, M. (2006). Eight fearless questions," excerpt from "A Call to Fearlessness for Gentle Leaders," address at the Shambhala Institute Core Program, Halifax, N.S., June 2006. Published in *Fieldnotes*, September/October 2006 by The Shambhala Institute for Authentic Leadership. Retrieved from http://www.shambhalainstitute.org/contact.html

49. Excerpt retrieved November 13, 2008 from http://www.berkana.org/index.php?option=com_content&task=section&Itemid=136

50. In Fisher (2010, p. 266) are the other seven questions and I note that she challenges the notion of *hope* and how it may not be the best way to go for future leaders on the path of fearlessness. For example, she asked (question 6): "Can we work beyond hope and fear?" by which she meant the way that fear/hope are constructed religiously, psychologically and politically by systems, as part of a fear-mongering agenda of control and manipulation of people and their fears and hopes, especially manipulated by authoritarian-style elite-based leadership regimes, not authentic leadership. I have argued that fearlessness no longer requires hope and ought to replace any dependency on it—but that is complex, because there is likely a development of consciousness consideration to such a replacement if it is to be effective. This is a topic beyond the scope of this essay, but it is analogous to the argument made that courage is not enough as well to bring about a sturdy resiliency and ethical-integrity, especially when in crisis.

51.   Kleiner, A. (interview of M. J. Wheatley), Fearlessness: The last organizational change strategy. Retrieved from http://www.strategy-business.com/li/leadingideas/li00044?pg=1

52.   *Regression*, and/or what the integral philosopher Ken Wilber calls *retro-regression* are important topics that would require more space to do justice to than I have here. Point being, development from one stage (or level) to another is a slippery slope—that is, it can slip ahead and slip back; progressive "advancements" then, as many developmental theorists have shown in psychology (e.g., Jean Piaget), are never only in a straight line ahead to maturity. Many factors are involved in progress. At the same time, healthy integration (or integrative development) biologically, psychologically, sociologically and otherwise, can really help with strengthening a shift to a new level of consciousness, for example. That's why I suggest a holistic-integral approach to development and then added to that, I recommend that we understand fear and its impact, and ways of managing fear and educating about fear, within a holistic-integral framework as well. Fear and its impacts (as well as fearlessness that arises with it) contribute enormously to susceptibility re: developmental backsliding, that is regression (and dissociation). This latter process is fundamental to identifying pathologies (e.g., neuroses) in development and in organizations on any scale, micro to macro. When a worldview is pathological, then a cultural and philosophical *therapia* is essential for correction. Recently, I have been arguing for a "fearlessness psychology" as a new type of psychology of a whole different order to bring to the task of therapy and *therapia*. See Fisher, R. M. (2019). A new psychology: Fearlessness psychology. Retrieved from https://fearlessnessmovement.ning.com/blog/a-new-psychology-fearlessness-psychology

53.   I'll return later in this essay on the topic of Education, to the points raised by Desh Subba and myself on development education in countries like Nepal, etc. (Fisher & Subba, 2016a). Fisher, R. M., & Subba, D. (2016a). The true gift of education for development: A fearist perspective. *Participation: A Nepalese Journal of Participatory Development, 17* (December), 23-29.

54. For e.g., the labeling of "culture of fear" has been challenged by anthropologists like Margold (1999) as being too reductionistic of culture itself. Margold, J. A. (1999). From "cultures of fear and terror" to the normalization of violence. *Critique of Anthropology, 19*(1), 63-88.

55. For e.g., Hoggett, P., & Thompson, S. (Eds.) (2012). *Politics and the emotions: The affective turn in contemporary political studies.* NY: Continuum International Publishing Group; Athena, A., Pthiti, H. & Kostas, Y. (2012). Towards a new epistemology: The "affective turn." *Historien, 8,* 5-16. See also Fisher (2010), pp. xxxiii, 7, 65, 134 etc. on the role of the affective dimension. Another aspect of this challenge, from Spinoza through Nietzsche through postmodern criticism in contemporary times, has been the related realization that humans are not as rational overall in functioning as they like to see themselves in the modern era. For example, see Barrett, W. (1958/90). *Irrational man: A study in existential philosophy.* NY: Anchor Books/Doubleday.

56. Robin, C. (2004). *Fear: The political history of an idea.* NY: Oxford University Press.

57. McManus (2011, p.1). McManus, M. (2011). Hope, fear, and the politics of affective agency. *Theory and Event, 14*(4), 1-33.

58. Jeffries (2013, p. 333). Jeffries, F. (2013). Fear disarmed. *Perspectives on Global Development and Technology, 12,* 332-39.

59. Fisher & Subba (2016, p. 157); specifically see "fearist perspective" defined in Subba (2014, p. 11) and elaborated in application re: development in Fisher & Subba (2016a).

60. See for e.g., Fisher (2010).

61. Using a universal *spectrum* (theory) of the development of consciousness (*a la* Ken Wilber) and my own research on *fear management systems theory*, there is an arguable case that 10 generic fear management systems exist that have provided humanity overall with adequate adaptation for both defense and growth and reaching a higher potential (Fisher, 2010). The highest stage/level of fear management systems (FMS-9) is what I call "Fearless" and that has served as a strategic referent point for a deeper, truer and healthier perspective on the entire study of fear (and 'fear')—that

is, I have adopted a *"fearless standpoint theory"* not unlike, and analogously to, "standpoint feminism" (theory), the latter as a counter-hegemonic strategy of critique of pathological patriarchy and its theories on just about everything. My fearless standpoint is theoretically 'outside' (transcendent to) the 'Fear' Matrix and thus it is useful for leadership today (Fisher, 2003). See Fisher, R. M. (2008). Fearless standpoint theory: Origins of FMS-9 in Ken Wilber's work. Technical Paper No. 31. Carbondale, IL: In Search of Fearlessness Research Institute. Fisher, R. M. (2003). Fearless leadership In and Out of the 'Fear' Matrix. Unpublished dissertation. Vancouver, BC: The University of British Columbia.

62.   Fisher (2010), p. xxviii. Part of the basis of this self/system regulation thought and research behind the dictum is discussed under the evolution of "inherent Defense life strategy and Intelligences)...that have evolved in the domains of the Natural, Cultural and possibly even in the Spiritual" (p. 32).

63.   Fisher (2010), p. xii.

64.   See e.g., Overstreet (1951/71, Chapter Seven). Overstreet, B. W. (1951/71). *Understanding fear in ourselves and others*. NY: Harper & Row.

65.   See e.g., Fisher, R. M. (2016). Problem of branding "fearlessness" in Education and leadership. Technical Paper No. 59. Carbondale, IL: In Search of Fearlessness Research Institute.

66.   See e.g., Fisher (2010), pp. xxix, 40, 178, 240.

67.   Subba (2014), p. 273.

68.   In context of the *Gita*, Hindu spiritual teacher Sai Baba Gita teaches, "Of all the great virtues, fearlessness occupies the place of primary importance. It is the ideal virtue." (cited in Fisher, 2010, p. 180).

69.   Bushan & Garfield (2017, p. 3). Bushan, N., & Garfield, J. L. (2017). *Minds without fear: Philosophy in the Indian Renaissance*. NY: Oxford University Press.

70.   Ibid., pp. 5-6.

71.   The rationalist-pragmatic philosophy of fearism (*a la* Subba) tends to reinforce this, as Subba (2014) cited Bertrand Russell: "Religion is based on fear and the fear is the father of cruelty....both religion and cruelty begin with fear" (p. 265). I am not myself making

such a claim outright as it would involve a more nuanced and long argument to sort through the meaning of Russell's position, albeit, it is commonly held and no doubt has a lot of partial truth to it.

72. Retrieved from http://www.historydiscussion.net/history-of-india/ religious-and-social-reform-of-india-the-indian-renaissance/1637

73. A similar philosophical argument, in the African context, is made by Eneyo, M. (2018). *Philosophy of fear.* Australia: Xlibris; Eneyo, M. (2019). *Philosophy of unity: Love as an ultimate unifier.* Australia: Xlibris.

74. Vivekananda cited in Ruhela, S. P. (1997). *Quotations from India.* M.D. Publications PVT, Ltd., p. 9.

75. Cited in Fisher (2010), p. 124.

76. Cited [paraphrased] in Tathagatananda, Swami (2016). *Fear not, be strong: Vivekananda's message of strength and fearlessness.* Uttarakhand, India: Advaita Ashrama, n.p.

77. Cited with discussion in Fisher (2010, p. 161). Original citation of Gandhi in Bondurant, J. V. (1965). *Conquest of violence: The Gandhian philosophy of conflict.* Berkeley, CA: University of California Press, p. 29.

78. Four Arrows' excerpt in Fisher, R. M. (2018). *Fearless engagement of Four Arrows: The true story of an Indigenous-based social transformer.* NY: Peter Lang, p. 37.

79. See Four Arrows (aka Jacobs, D. T.) (2016), pp. 61, 7.

80. Ibid., pp. 7, 27, 60-61.

81. A similar perspective to Four Arrows' is found in Subba (2014), p. 233.

82. Bhave, V. (1996). The intimate and the ultimate. [excerpt from] M. Hern [Ed.], *Deschooling our lives.* Stoney Creek, CT: New Society Publishers. Retrieved from http://www.learningnet-india.org/Ini/ data/publications/revive/vol1/v1-6b8.php

83. Krishnamurti, J. (1981). *Education and the significance of life.* NY: Harper & Row, p. 15.

84. See e.g., Heim, M. (2004). *Theories of the gift in South Asia: Hindu, Buddhist, and Jain reflections on dãna.* NY: Routledge; Hibbets, M. (1999). Saving them from yourself: An inquiry into the South Asian gift of fearlessness. *Journal of Religious Ethics, 27,* 437-62.

85.	See https://en.wikipedia.org/wiki/Gift_economy

86.	Fisher, Subba & Kumar (2018), p. xix.

87.	Fisher & Subba (2016a), p. 26.

88.	Cited in Ferguson, M. (2005). *Aquarius now: Radical common sense and reclaiming our personal sovereignty.* Boston, MA: Weiser Books, p. 154.

89.	Cited in Rao, K. L. S. (1978). *Mahatma Gandhi and comparative religion.* India: Motilala Banarsidass, p. 69.

90.	"The stage [in human evolution] of fears is fearlessness," (Subba, 2014, p. 45). "Fearless Age" is described by Subba (pp. 45-46) as a historical rendering of the evolution of society and fear together, and what the possibilities are after (and if) we make it through the contemporary "Extreme Fear Age" (pp. 44-45).

91.	It is unfortunate I cannot give more background on the critical theory and thinking behind doing a worldview analysis, which is fundamental to everything in Part 2. However, I can refer readers to the excellent summary analysis by Four Arrows (2016), pp. 6-7 where he contrasts the Indigenous (original, primal) worldview vs. Dominant (Western) worldview. This is a great guidepost reference for any revisioning of the hegemonic worldview that leaders in India may utilize at any time and place. While I appreciate the complexity of India and that many worldviews (i.e., sub-worldviews, belief/value systems and cosmologies) may exist—it is still worthwhile to attempt to understand generic worldviews *via* the Four Arrows' binary distinction.

92.	Barber, B. (2003). *Fear's empire: War, terrorism, and democracy.* NY: W. W. Norton.

93.	Fisher & Subba (2016), p. 53.

94.	See Subba (2014), pp. 13-19 and Fisher (2010), p. 151.

95.	Fisher & Subba (2016a), p. 23.

96.	Cited in Ibid., p. 26.

97.	Remember FDR's famous warning as president of the USA in his 1933 inaugural speech: "All we have to fear is fear itself...". Church (2004) wrote of this speech, "What the new president did was to utter the hitherto unspoken word that lurked in everyone's heart—*fear*.... No other presidential address matches Roosevelt's... in directness and immediacy of its impact" (p. 4). Church, F. (2004). *Freedom from fear: Finding the courage to act, love, and be.* NY: St. Martin's Press. Note, this powerful phrase of FDR's has a long history in the West "traced to Montaigne, Lord Willington, Henry David Thoreau and Francis Bacon (among others)" (Fisher, 2010, p. 271). In many ways, the current 2020 US presidential candidate, Marianne Williamson, is sounding very similar to FDR.

98. Fisher, R. M. (2019). New ethical leadership: Marianne Williamson. Retrieved from https://www.youtube.com/watch?v=EjyENboIzxc

99. See Fisher, R. M. (2015). What is the West's problem with fearlessness? Technical Paper No. 53. Carbondale, IL: In Search of Fearlessness Research Institute.

100. See for e.g., Fisher (2018). See also https://fearlessnessmovement.ning. com/blog/de-hypnotizing-technology-of-cat-fawn-by-four-arrows

101. Extensive dialogues have been carried out on the philosophy of fearism/fearlessness and the nature and role of terrorism (see, e.g., Fisher, Subba & Kumar, 2018; and Kalu et al. (2018), pp. 109-23 in Fisher, Subba & Kumar, 2018; and see "re-thinking" terrorism p. xxxiii. Kalu, O. A. (2018). The terrorism dialogue. In R. M. Fisher, D. Subba & B. M. Kumar, *Fear, Law and criminology: Critical issues in applying the philosophy of fearism.* Australia: Xlibris.

102. Ingersoll (2010), an integral therapist, noted "If we are in a period of intense transformation, the map provided by ego [self-system] development theory can give us a sense of our next stop on the journey [our future possibilities]" (p. 103). The preconventional levels: Impulsive, Opportunist—depending the nation, on average in the USA this is 10% of adults. The conventional levels: Expert, Diplomat, Achiever, on average in the USA 80% of adults (see Ingersoll, 2010, pp. 103-12 for details). Ingersoll, R. E. (2010). The self-system and ego development. In R. E. Ingersoll & D. M. Zeitler, *Integral psychotherapy: Inside out/outside in* (pp. 77-119). Albany, NY: State University of New York Press.

103. *True fearlessness* as a center of gravity developmentally appears full-blown at about stage 7-8, out of a possible nine stages identified on the spectrum of consciousness by integral therapists and theorists (e.g., Ken Wilber, R. E. Ingersoll, etc.). Postconventional four levels:

Pluralist, Strategist, Magician, Unitive, and these are on average less than 10% of the adult population (see Ingersoll, 2010, pp. 112-19 for details).

104. E.g., "The League for Fearlessness" (1931-) had an agenda "To Free The World From Fear" (see Fisher, 2010, p. 172), a famous Nobel Peace Prize Laureate 1991 speech by Aung San Suu Kyi, Burmese (Myanmar) political opposition leader, was entitled "Freedom from Fear" (see Fisher, 2010, pp. 13-14). See also Pyszczynski, Greenberg & Arndt (2011).

105. See, e.g., Fromm, E. (1941). *The fear of freedom*. NY: Farrar & Rinehart.

106. Recently I am calling this specifically a new *"fearlessness psychology"* (Fisher, 2019).

107. "Paradigm of fearlessness" refers to an entirely different way to organize, research, and create discourses—from a position and awareness, and valuation, where fear (i.e., 'fear'-based) thinking is not dominating; see Fisher & Subba (2016), pp. 14, 62, 93, 125, 147, 148.

108. Excerpt from Clements, A. (1999). "Editorial," *Spirit in Action: WorldDharma Monthly Newsletter, Vol. 1.*

109. Cited in Goodin, R. E., & Parker, D. (2000). "Introduction: Symposium on Martha Nussbaum's political philosophy." *Ethics, 111,* 6-7.

110. I have also critiqued her largely Aristotelian conceptualization of fear and fear management. E.g., see Nussbaum, M. (2019). *The monarchy of fear: A philosopher looks at our political crisis.* NY: Simon & Schuster.

111. Fisher, R. M. (2019a). Psychological problem in America: New politics of love (and fear). Retrieved from https://fearlessnessmovement.ning.com/blog/psychological-problem-in-america-new-politics-of-love-and-fear

112. Williamson and her followers of *A Course in Miracles* would only likely ever want to support a "love education" but not a "fear education." That's a mistake, from a fearological perspective. A fearism critique of Williamson's philosophy and politics begins in Fisher & Subba (2016), pp. xxxi-xlvi.

113. See interview "How to Choose Love Instead of Fear" with Marianne Williamson. Retrieved from https://www.youtube.com/watch?v=J4fNmVgLhxM

114. Vaughan, Genevieve. (2017). 36 steps toward a gift economy. *MagoWork* e-magazine. Retrieved from https://www.magoism.net/2017/09/essay-36-steps-toward-gift-economy-genevieve-vaughan/

115. Retrieved from https://www.marianne2020.com/

116. Kumar, Corinne (n.d.). Supryia and the revisioning of a dream: Toward a new political [gift] economy. In G. Vaughan (Ed.), *Women and the gift economy: A radically different world view is possible.* Retrieved from http://gift-economy.com/women-and-the-gift-economy/

117. For e.g., from the ancient Yoruba Tradition and/or modern psychotherapy, there are new models and practices for systemic healing in/with our *ancestors* that are very powerful and have a lot of potential for today's societies that have become so fragmented and lost a lot of their historical continuity to their best sides, and especially this has been lost with extensive wars, and other cultural traumas; see for e.g., Foor, D. (2017). *Ancestral medicine: Rituals for personal and family healing.* Rochester, VT: Bear & Co.

118. Kumar, Krishna (2017). Education and girlhood. Retrieved from http://www.cwds.ac.in/wp-content/uploads/2017/01/24-JP-Naik-Lecture.pdf

119. See Kumar, B. M., & Sushmita, B. S. (2018). *The youth don't cry: A critical commentary on the youth about their fears and hopes amidst adversities and opportunities.* Bhopal, India: Indra Publishing House.

120. See Kazi, S. (2018). Gender as a site of protest: Women's resistance in Kashmir's 2016 uprising. *International Feminist Journal of Politics, 20*(4), 651-53.

121. See http://www.vandanashiva.com/

122. See e.g., a recent interview with Ettinger. Retrieved from https://lareviewofbooks.org/article/feel-worlds-pain-beauty/#!

123. Kumar (n.d.).

124. I coined this term *"fearuality- the total dynamics, interrelations and development of one's relationship to fear (analogous with sexuality or spirituality)"* (Fisher & Subba, 2016, p. 158). See more details in

Fisher, R. M. (2013). *Fearuality: Introduction to a theoretical and conceptual breakthrough*. Technical Paper No. 50. Carbondale, IL: In Search of Fearlessness Research Institute.

125.   Cited in Four Arrows (2016), p. 7. The Indigenous worldview, more so than the predominant worldview of the Western world and most of modernism, is holistic-integral, is based on matriarchal systems of values, and is Nature-based (ecological) and has proven through time to be sustainable with the Natural world better than most cultures that don't follow the Indigenous 'traditional' ways. In that sense, what is often called "primitive" is actually the more "advanced" than current societies based on fear rather than trust in the universe—that is, a type of inherent and essential evolutionary fearlessness.

****

PART 3
DESH SUBBA

Fearism

Some Short-hand Meanings Used:

RPB= Ruling class, Priests and Business class

EBCP= Excommunication, Banishment, Confinement and Physical
    Violence

D3= Danger, Difficult and Dirty

Lower castes= Untouchables, in ancient India, now legally called as
        Scheduled Castes.

Harijan= is an untouchable, as referred to by Mahatma Gandhi.

Bapu ji: an affectionate usage of address to Mahatma Gandhi

Philosophy of Fearism is an emerging philosophy of the world. It looks at a holistic way of life. It is universal in application. It deals with states, societies, politics and citizens' lives, past, present and future. Where it is necessary, we can theorize and apply a philosophy of fearism with its focus on the primary role of fear in shaping everything in living systems.

Despite universal principles, applications of fearism ought to be contextualized and customized depending on local politics, social relations and economic background. The context of South America, North America, Africa and Asia, for example, have unique qualities to be translated through a fearist perspective [1]. Geographically and politically fearism varies. The assumed pillar of life of fearism, either in political, cultural, religious, economic or psychological domains is *fear*; nobody can ignore this fact, if they are truly honest about reality.

Central to all fear(ism) is the fundamental fear of *Thanatos* (simply, an existential fear of death or mortality). Scientists are trying their best to cryopreserve the human race because of this fear. At the social level, to protect life from death, we are motivated towards development, inventions, and creativity through culture, politics and economy. Politicians adapt to this threat to life collectively *via* diverse means such as dictatorial regimes, democracies, republics, monarchies and/or socialistic political systems. Fear drives the form of economies and societies equally. Monopolistic politics of over-domination and control is not acceptable to all and for that reason a good deal of disagreement occurs and may take the form of wars, protests, revolutions, enemies and killings. Fear is central to all these adaptations and outcomes—for better or for worse.

Today, I wish to inquire into India, one of the most ancient and rich cultures on the planet. It has diversity in so many domains, like languages and religions and is the second most populated country of the world. India has had a long journey of civilization-making and creative adaptations like building educational systems, ethics, politics, and philosophical and religious dialectic systems. Today, this great nation's leaders and others (like Maria B. Kumar) are asking the question: "Why is India still backward in development?" We need to inquire into the deepest root causes.

The Oracle of Delphi has once said that Socrates was the wisest man in Athens. Socrates himself didn't believe it and tried to prove it wrong. He asked many people to prove it to be wrong. He became unsuccessful. Poets, politicians and authors, for example, countered by saying they were the wisest; but Socrates knew that they knew nothing enough to be wisest. And for some, even though they knew nothing enough to be wisest, they still said they were the wisest. "In comparison with them, I don't know anything, but I honestly say I don't know. In this context, I am definitely the wisest of all of them," Socrates said.

This example can be suitable for India in reminding us of the tenuousness of knowing all. Socrates' wisdom was that of humbleness and admission of not knowing as much as one may want to think and brag about. Our knowing faces a great vastness and mystery—India. India is rich in culture, history, geography and religion. The world knows India is the richest country of the world but still we are put to the task of asking the questions in the Agora. One day India will enlighten us as Socrates.

India is a Musk Deer carrying scent glands. Perfume of deer has good smell for the world and we may ask: Where is this good smell is coming from? Indeed, it comes from the body but being explored outside. India doesn't know the source of perfume. India is a 'Socrates and Musk Deer' country. Many people say, "India is doing a lot of development like science, technology, infrastructure, roads etc." However, beneath that, the real important core of the country is never growing up: the poverty level and ignorance of the masses (masses mostly belong to lower castes). It is a curse like *Ashwatthama* carrying wounds forever. *Ashwatthama* was the hero of Mahabharata. India shows the practical way of life. This system is a big headache of the nation. Mahatma Gandhi, Dr. B. R. Ambedkar, with great difficulty, and some other leaders tried to sweep away this dangerous plague. Yet change is slow. Some powerful people remain sitting on the throne above the downtrodden—they never wished to clean society and bring about transformation. As a consequence, they not only took society backwards, but the whole nation became the victim of plague.

India's woes have been continuing for thousands of years. Before colonialism and British Empire, there were a handful of people who were rich; high officials or kings. Their property was based on the blood and sweat of poor people's exploited labor, including low castes. Mass of the people were without land and property. As a result they had not enough crops to sustain themselves. They always slept with hunger, and meanwhile the rich were enjoying and celebrating many parties and festivals. Among all these were *fear games* based on domination and control. The situation never changed for the lower castes much for all these centuries. They paid a lot of blood and sweat in freedom, independence and democracy and yet some deep-rooted problems of inequity remained. When the West was in the grip of the Dark Ages, modernism and postmodernism, the East was not exceptional. The Indian continent was encountering the same kind of dark life. Dark life of lower castes was never improved either with British rule or the independence movements and eventual regaining of Indian rule.

The changing weather of colonialism was flowing all over the world. The grand British sun was setting finally. In India, the British flag went down and the Indian flag rose. India became independent, a republic, a democracy whatever we say; but the lower castes never experienced due enjoyment, brotherhood, respect and freedom. Their slave life was under the Indian flag now. The boot was changed. Old British boot was replaced by nationalist (Ruling castes, Priests and Business castes = RPB).

History and politics were written by and in the name of high-caste Indians. Unfortunately, untouchables were again untouchable. No persons had advocated seriously for them except *Baba Saheb*. They were assigned menial work a long-time before. The curse of only menial tasks is still on their forehead. It was transferred from generation to generation. They wanted to be free. They did many struggles but the RPB was using them, using their fear, to keep them servants. The lower castes were always suppressed under the boot of fear. Once they came out from the fear boot, and only then, will they possibly enjoy real life. That will be real independence and a new starting point for most Indians. It will be a green light for fast development. So far, that glorious day never comes in their life.

Too many people are taking benefits from use of and/or showing a *fear gun* and other people are losing everything under the fear gun (i.e., weaponizing of fear) [2]. It is the bad luck of a beautiful country, India. Even today, oppressors don't want to open that shackle which tied up so many for such a long time before. Political leaders with RPB are pretending that the country is running smoothly and the lower castes are joining the main stream, but it is an illusion and deception of the worst kind.

In the round table conference in London, before the independence of India, Gandhi said, "I am representing *Harijan* community of India," In that conference, Dr. B. R. Ambedkar was also present. He immediately protested Gandhi and said, "how can the *Bapuji*, represent us?"

Dr. B. R. Ambedkar was right. No need to represent the lower castes, just make them free from cultural prison. If RPB represent them, they always keep the bonus of exploitation. Constitution draft committee of the United States is the best example. Majority of draft committee members were males. They reserved patriarchal powers when they drafted constitution. Until many years there were no equal rights for women in the United States and this continues to today.

One day Lala Lajpat Rai, leader of Indian congress met *Baba Saheb* in London, during the freedom movement against British rule. Rai requested Dr. B. R. Ambedkar to join the Congress Party. Dr. B. R. Ambedkar replied to him," it is no difference either rule by British or by Indian RPB, torture is same. If we help to make country independent, still we will be tortured by forward caste Indians. We are facing multiple oppressors. So, I am fighting for my untouchable people." (Dr. B. R. Ambedkar was the chairman of Indian Constitution drafting Committee. He is also addressed as *Baba Saheb*.) He was correct. Still in independent India, lower castes are suppressed by upper castes to a considerable extent.

Dr. B. R. Ambedkar was always fighting for low caste people during and after British rule. He was bargaining with Indian government for reserved seats. There was a big dispute between government and Dr. Ambedkar. Leaders of the congress including Nehru tried to convince Dr. Ambedkar to step down. Both parties were in a stand-off. No one was ready to step down. High tension was seen. Dr. Ambedkar was not going to sacrifice the rights of lower castes. Tension was raising and Gandhi used his *Brahmaastra* of fasting. Dr. Ambedkar didn't care. Health of Gandhi was worsening. The whole nation was worried about the health of Gandhi, then again congress leaders requested to *Baba Saheb* to step down and compromise. *Baba Saheb* stepped a bit down and solved the problem. If Dr. Ambedkar's demand was accepted, justice would have been restored to lower castes.

"Man is born free and everywhere he is in chains," wrote Jean Jacque Rousseau in the 18th century. This quotation is for the world. If normal people are everywhere in chains, then we can estimate how many chains the lower castes have. How difficult it is to live for them? Upper castes became successful only because of playing and manipulating unfairly the fear game.

To enable the lower castes to join the main stream, government formed Mandal Commission (MC) in India in 1979. It was like the tusk of an elephant not the teeth. For some time lower castes need reservations because tame tiger and wild tiger cannot do competition. MC faced a huge protest, it was difficult to implement. High castes feared that backward people are taking their jobs? These were happening because of a high percentage unemployment and poverty. If unemployment rate is low and citizens have good income, these problems are automatically solved. High and low division comes from survival like 'survival of the fittest' theory of the thinking of ideology of Darwinianism. In natural state; strong kills the weak. In human state the clever becomes cheater, cheats the poor and weak. If lower castes become strong, genius and rich, they will be difficult to be dominated.

Some feminists argue, "During the time of British rule, women were in double colonization" [3]. This is the issue of feminism generally in postcolonial analysis but lower caste women have more oppressors than upper caste women. They had to face British, RPB women, and male dominations—in what is a triple colonization. This remains unsatisfactorily dealt with in Indian society today. Fear is in extreme for girls and women because of this condition of culture.

Introduction: Philosophy of Fearism's Wikipedia

His mother and father moved from a rural peasant hilly village Fakhumba, Taplejung District to Dharan in 1963. Desh was born in 1965 at Dharan. Dharan is a small city of eastern Nepal. It was established in 1898 by Rana regime. Now it became sub metropolitan city of province 1, Nepal. Taplejung district is on the border of India and China. Third highest mountain of the world Kanchanjangha Himal is in this district.

Born [1965] in <u>Dharan</u>, <u>Eastern Nepal</u>, Subba lives with his family in <u>Hong Kong</u>, he is a philosopher, <u>author</u> and poet. His book *Philosophy of Fearism* (published by <u>Xlibris,</u> 2014) brought his work out onto the international stage and created a following of an increased proportion. This philosophy portrays fear as major part of life. According to Subba, *life is conducted, guided and controlled by fear.* He argues for a basic and essential utility of fear, while acknowledging negative impacts of fear as well. He has developed a unique practice of *dephilosophy* of philosophy [4] and has co-written with others, including Fisher and Kumar. His philosophy is practical and social in orientation to improve humankind, and this is shaped by his early life-experiences in the rural setting of Nepal.

His father left him when he was eleven days old and never returned back from Assam, India. It is also described on the back cover of his first English book *Philosophy of Fearism* (2014). His mother Tilmati Limbu was brave, courageous and hard working. She had knowledge of many types of craftwork. She cared for her children as a good mother. He had three sisters. One daughter was from his father and two sisters from a step- father. After left Kubir Jung, his mother married again but the step-father had already a wife and some kids in a rural village Taplejung, near Kanchanjunga Himal. His step- father had a pension but he gave it to his first family. All burdens were taken by his mother. Life was very hard.

She had no farm land to cultivate, no job, no income and no pension even though her husband was double ex-army. His father was Indian and and a British Gurkha soldier but with incomplete service. He had served three years in Indian army and seven years in British. He was not eligible to have a pension. His mother was a village woman with no education, so she couldn't find a good job. She helped neighbours, relatives and others in menial works. She got sometimes some crops as wages, and little money. When she couldn't earn anything, they had to sleep hungry. People hesitated to lend them debt because they had no source for repay back.

God had given Tilmati some craftsmanship, knitting work, handloom work and she produce domestic alcohol, which she fed children. She had overcome her shyness, shame, and losing face. She took her children one place to another place like nomadic people. She had nothing but she never lost her hope and never tired from life.

At age of eleven she admitted Desh in a local government school. He started to learn English alphabet at the age of fifteen. He had to go through many hardships to educate himself beyond the usual levels of literacy in the country-side. Tilmati Limbu, inspires him daily to continue on to reach his highest potential. Desh is still remembers those days. His family was fully under care of his great mother. His father was careless, irresponsible and non-social. His mother told him she was sometimes violated at home and beaten.

His formal higher education includes a Master in Business Administration, while his most accomplished activities, beyond being a husband and father of children, is his writing like *Philosophy of Fearism* and published novels (in Nepali) *Doshi Karm* 2050 B.S, *Apman* 2052 B.S., *Sahid* 2056 B.S., *Aadibashi* 2064 B.S. The latter novel *Aadibashi*, recently published in English is entitled *The Tribesman's Journey to Fearless*, a novel based on philosophy of fearism. He has won several book awards for these works and he travels the world regularly speaking to diverse audiences about fearism, literature, literary criticism and what is happening in the world and how we can better manage its problems. He is the leading fearism spokesperson in the East, and co-founder of the Fearism Study Center (2009-) in Dharan, Nepal. Involved in organization: Hong Kong Nepalese Literary Academy [5].

Philosophy of Fearism explores all the colorful aspects of life. No one has previously viewed the structure of society from the point of fearism. We can interpret the state, society and philosophy itself through the ages via this new lens. Classical philosophies mostly focus on political philosophies—states, societies, virtues, justice etc. In fact neither politics nor states run without undertaking direct actions with fear. As a critic, Subba believes we are far behind in our thinking because we left out major thoughts about life as lacking acknowledgement of the central importance of fear in shaping power. States, politics, religions, caste systems, medieval era, modernism, postmodernism and post-postmodernism depends on fear. The motivational driver of fear, for good and bad, has stung the vehicle of progress. The fear driver has been driving family, society and states since the dawn of civilization.

Fearism Activities in India

Philosophy of Fearism has had an active publishing, educational and promotional agenda in (especially, N. E.) India for some years. Although several articles and books have been written on this philosophy, theoretically and practically, many in the East are not written in English [6]. Fisher & Subba (2016) summarized some of the events of fearism of which the Indian locations and applications included at least the following:

a) "Fearism and Intercultural Discourse," an international program in Dharan, with 55 participants from eight states of N. E. India [7]

b) Rana Kafle, from Assam, India, speaks of how "All people from different languages, castes/ethnicities, and religions comprehend [the premises of fearism]... [and] adopt this philosophy" [8]; he knows because he teaches many people in India in villages and towns, exposing them to the work of Subba; he has published several of his own literary works with a basis in philosophy of fearism (in Nepalese, Assamis language and Hindi); he leads and coordinates a team throughout N. E. India creating a grassroots adult education programming [9] (see also Appendix 1); in July 2013 Rana Kafle conducted a Fearism educational tour himself in N.E. India and Myanmar; according to Bordolol (2018), "Kafle grew up to be a man of influence in many ways in his area and in the state.... Kafle emerged as a multifaceted personality, a resourceful philosopher, social worker, educationist, literature and cultural activist. His noted achievement was in promoting the "Indigenous Cultures of Assam" as a cinematographer, when his achievement was highlighted in one hundred "Indigenous Cultural Programmes" in the NE region through Doordarshan" [10];

c) Desh Subba has lectured in India, and gained many endorsements from academics, professionals and lay people over the years; he has offered a journal summary of his main tour in 2016 [11]

Gradually begins the new prospect to review traditional values. We are looking at prejudice: vis-à-vis the castes. Most fearologists agree that caste prejudice is possible because of fear. The so-called RPB in order to give them authenticity used ghastly arrangements such as legends, and fabricated fables. French Marxist Louis Althusser says," Ideology cannot only consider the field of false and illusion of ruling class. It has real affects. It affects the daily life of people". These were only the front face. Underneath of these faces was apprehension. Apprehensive was made of EBCP (i.e., excommunication, banishment, confinement, physical violence or even death). These icebergs are unveiled now by the critique of Fearism.

Common masses are the backbone of India. In the present world, service business is taking second place. Then how can menial workers be treated under the slave type of system? Most of the developed countries started to pay highly for D3 (danger, difficult and dirty) work. Upper castes warn, threaten and ostracize them to do menial work. Fear is the more powerful tool for them to use on workers. Even today it is very active. Suppose somebody is a scientist from low caste in United States. He has high honor in USA. When he comes back in his village in India, he doesn't dare to enter any temple, houses of other upper castes. The villagers follow the tradition, not education degrees. Due to fear of scold or banishment he stays away. Together with Dr. Ambedkar, many villagers embraced Buddhism. Such kind of caste and untouchable system was not in Buddhism, which believed in equality and humanism. Buddhism has racial harmony. The first step of light in society is social harmony. India is on its way, still requiring this because it is not fully awakened.

Insecurity Feeling in Tiny Things

Indian government is like the proverb: 'once chase a dog with the brand, it is always afraid when thunders in the sky.' The government is suspicious because terrorists always intimidate. For security purposes, the nation puts surveillance and harsh controls strictly on the public. Terrorists always emerge from public. Maybe there are many reasons—among them, poverty, scarcity, domination, prejudice, and unfairness are the main reasons. Terrorism involves activities of fearmongering and enforcement, between government and terrorist—there is production of excess fear and mistrust. Government fears the terrorist and terrorist fears the government. Mostly, the root of terrorism is injustice, unfair and domination. In *Fear, Law and Criminology* book the authors (Fisher, Kumar and Subba) discussed this [12].

A decade before, Nepal had a civil war. Some of the Western countries defined it as terrorism. If they were defeated by government they would have been permanently labeled as terrorists, but they came in agreement. History is always in favor of winners. Some of the leaders are still under red notice. When we go back to see the root of this war, first communist party posed 52 points to government; these points were about basic needs of people. Government ignored it. During that time, Maoist party was not declared. Maoists didn't have a single rifle. Government became irresponsible. Behavior of government, ego of Maoists and many problems of the country were the cause of civil war. Emergence of war, civil war and terrorism are almost the same. If people have enough food, facilities, standard of life, there are less chances to provoke terrorism. Children always demand, protest and do some naughty activities. Government is a parent; it must be responsible towards people. Instead of doing some good, government created insecurity, and a panic-based environment. It produced tension and suspicion. In this situation, country became a sandwich. Those Maoists were born in the soil and womb of mother Nepal. They were not migrants or imported from other countries. Life was very hard at that time. Many Nepalese went abroad to find secure life. Lower castes of society of Nepal had hard times. It was the duty of the nation to look after them. Security of life was at bottom. When the life of RPB had difficulty masses had harder. So, they stayed in high alert. These kinds of environments made common masses suffer most.

Government in the name of anti-terrorist operations tortured the public. Public could not get justice. Even to take a phone card, government makes many rules, *Aadhar* Card. It is not a problem to take phone card in any country of the world. Only it is in India. Terrorists are all over the world and they are threat to the world. Controlling some communication is not the solution of terrorist activities. Nowadays communication is common. Unfortunately, activities of the government make things more fearful for the public. It is the duty of government that in panic conditions, government must keep calm. Peace is possible if the government keeps law and order. Law and order controls panic. Law means fear. On the contrary, Indian government is indirectly making more panic. It shows weakness of security system. Many security checking points order public to close shops by evening. It shows government is unable to provide security to public. When the situation goes out of control, nominal things make people feel insecure and because of insecure situation they are afraid to walk, invest, and visit. As a result, the country loses tourists and investors. Even in the parcel, postal items have difficulty to pass customs. When people realize such difficulties, they avoid importing and exporting. Then, it decreases tax revenue. For tourists government set up much security check points. It harassed the general public and tourists. They are not willing to visit next time. To give good environment, government's first priority should be a sound system. A sound environment, not fear-based, produces sound systems.

In India, there is lack of quality security systems: only a handful of people enjoy night life. Nature has given us to enjoy day and night life. Developed countries can enjoy 24 hours but developing countries are missing it. Its main reason is insecurity. If forward castes of India are missing then we can guess the conditions of common people? Most international cities started 24 hours life. In 1990s, Hong Kong had 17 hours life. Average working hours were 12 hours. Businesses and customers increased and after 2000 it became 24 hours. Multinational companies McDonalds, KFC, departmental stores were earlier open till midnight, later changed to 24 hours. Its main reason was shortage of time. 12 hours was not enough for them. Government is providing full security. Public transport is available 24 hours. In the street, a man or woman feels secure. They had no fear. If any accident occurred, immediately police arrives. When the public realizes that there is protection, they are enthusiastic at any time to work. Only good security system appoints double shift employment. In a single shift there is single employment, double shift entails double jobs, more sales, increased revenue tax.

People are still scared to go out at night in India. It is very risky to go out. They are afraid in mind; and cannot enjoy parties. Mind is pinched by unknown threat (by fear).

Political Weakness: Addiction to Power

Fear brings out the best and worst in human beings.
– R. W. Dozier, Jr. [13]

Politician are the worst barrier of India; 95% of the leaders are corrupted and addicted to power. Whatever happens to the country, they don't want to detach from the power. It is their elitist blunder that at any cost they want to hold any ministerial post. They never see back what mistakes they have done. There is no culture of handing over the power or resigning if anything wrong happens in their ministry. They consider the public as a gathering of the foolish.

As a result of this elitist arrogance, the country is put in relative immobility. Many states of India have racial, communal and cultural disputes. In the name of identity, small groups of people start to demand things. In the beginning, they have small demands, later that grows and changes into severe headaches of the nation, particularly in the north east states. Manipur, Mizoram, Nagaland, Assam, Meghalaya, West Bengal, Arunachal Pradesh and Bihar are the major red-light states. Every state has conflicts, but major racial problems are in the north east. For the racial sake, they abduct, kidnap and sometimes massacre their enemies. These groups use road blocks, demonstrate, and strike to draw government's attention. Central government or state government plays the dumb audience role. They calculate their vote. If they solve the problem what happens to their political career? If oppositions are doing these, they do their best to trap them. Sometimes they set up dragnet to trap opposition. Problems of these demands are not big and unsolved, but government's green signal is absent. They never think of such kinds of misbehaviour and unfortunately, that sets India backwards in the development race.

Recognition from Indian Scholars:

"Fear is the founder of human emotion," declared Bikram Bir Thapa, Indian Literary Academy Winner, India [14]. Fearists are the first thinkers to dwell about these states re: fear and social life as well as life of mind. Philosophy of fearism (Subba) is unique, a philosophical thinking beyond Hinduism and an original philosophy "apart from Buddhism in Nepal.... It's a new dimension to the world," according to Dr. Tanka Nath Khatiwada, Presidency College, Head of Hindi Department, Imphal, Manipur, India [15]. Western philosophy of Thomas Hobbes, Jean-Jacques Rousseau and John Locke spoke of the ideal state, each had their own analysis, but I think particularly western political thinker's philosophy is not applicable in the context of India because they never think on the base of fear and its construction within the base of India's lower caste and race dynamics. We fearologists are the first systematic thinkers to think on the basis of fear, that is, a fearist perspective, so we can see caste systems, racial discrimination and crime all happening under the *fear gun*. According to Prof. Dr. Streamlet Dkhar, *Khashi* Language Department, Nehu University, India,

> Fearism is a new concept [*a la* Subba]; it is utilized to keep the cultural dominance and the matrix of superiority intact [*sic*. under control].... Identification of the practice of fearism would take us [as a nation of India] to deeper layers of psychological impact.... when one has realized there was [still is, fear being used destructively against people from elites] this kind of dominance [by the fear gun]... [then] one is [has to be] prepared to fight against it. [16]

Whether it is Plato or Aristotle, thinking about natural states and thinking about duty and role of the prince (e.g., Niccolò Machiavelli) is quite different thing to base one's political philosophy. Philosophy of natural state and prince cannot alone overcome discrimination, caste system, gender, marginality, racial problems and such. Only fearism can cover all aspects holistically. Fear, in its positive aspects, is the source of robustness. Only fear can conduct, direct and control the people and nation. Regardless of these differences, however, comparisons with the developed Western nations are still important to analysis of India today.

In the United States, for example, we cannot see traffic problems as in India. We see many troubling traffic problems in India. People are driving dangerously, and crossing lanes without any fear of rules and regulations. It is near chaos. It causes many costly road accidents. When we see accident rates, robbery, kidnap, murder, rapes, protests, India has higher numbers than the USA. The public generally fears the rule of law and traffic regulations in the USA but not in India. These fears help to control, conduct and direct them. Nearly nobody crosses red lights or drives the wrong way in the USA. They know the punishment of wrong driving. Fear of police and CCTV is controlling them. Everyone feels comfortable, free, and secure under the minimal but necessary fear of government.

This relatively fearful environment regarding authorities guides them to progress and development. Fears are everywhere even it is applicable to the President. In the USA the President is also afraid of the public. Positive fears are the base of happiness, peace, and development of a nation. Nation must consider this theory and try to apply it. Fearism would be helpful. Many kinds of theories were already applied in the world. If India takes to positive fear, it would be the first nation to change and step into advanced futures. The progressive nation is guided by proper principles. Principle of fear when not applied, because nobody coined it as theory, is a problem. India need a basic education on fearism (see also Appendix 1). Recently fearism came into currency, eventually, it can be applied in many countries as well. When we see daily life, political disputes, panic, anxiety, worry of life, we can find fear in depth. Fearism is a solution to discern better how to manage fear.

Fear of insecurity and a dark future with pessimism leads people to be selfish. In the last stage of life, nobody cares about anybody, they only care about the self because everybody is afraid to die and tries to prolong the valuable life. Some years back, Nepal had a big earthquake. Two young friends were talking in their room. Suddenly, the earthquake struck. They ran out from the room. They didn't remember property, family members, society and nation, but just remembered to self-rescue. When they safely came out, then only did they remember everything, including their mom.

Their mom was inside the room. This is the reality. Family, friends, we need them in the healthy course of life. But when scarcity of food occurs, acute danger of life comes, and then nobody said, you survive, I die for you. This kind of sentence is good for movie dialogue or good for drama.

Unethical Slowness: Bureaucratic Practices

India has many kinds of corruption. For definition of corruption we used to think of cash or goods only. Nobody wants to come directly under the eye of CBI (Central Bureau of Investigation). Particularly, bureaucrats because of fear of being caught, use invisible methods to perpetuate their corruption. Bureaucrats or civil servants can produce mental torture for many and add delays even with simple works. People don't want to waste time by having to make many visits. Official files take long periods to move from one place to another place. It delays projects and increases costs. Contractors and public are too tired of hanging in same tree. They know why it is taking long time to forward normal files—it has to do with money. So, they offer beautiful amounts of money to expedite work. It is a kind of corruption. It plays some role to block ease of developments. Capable people can offer bribes to do the work. But masses of people are not able to make these offers. Then their files sink to the bottom of the bureaucrat and civil servant files.

Such barriers exacerbate the already backwardness of those struggling. These kinds of activities push the lower castes towards more ineffectiveness and lack of growth. They have no hope to come forward. It is the responsibility of the nation's governance by leaders and bureaucrats. They are unfortunately too busy in taking and giving bribes. Lower castes must be dealt with fairly, where money is not a factor, for it is the time to directly bring them forward by fast tracking to create some minimal equity in the overall population. Otherwise they will never come forward and one day lower castes will disappear from the national scene of India.

Government employees intentionally delay initiatives thereby troubling many citizens. These people don't know they are hitting the axe on their own foot. They are setting habits of corruption from the high level officers and ministers. Sometimes courts, lawyers, judges also become the part like *Kabaddi* game. How can the nation be developed?

It is unethical leadership that the public are not involved, that transparency is not a policy. They endorse corruption. Such players also fear losing their jobs and quality of life if they would go against the system of the Kabaddi game and corruption. It is not a difficult task to remove and give smooth flow to the system, but we need honest government. To be honest and loyal to the public, says a fearist perspective, the leaders must need to fear the public. In United States, Japan, and UK the governments are afraid of their people and people are afraid of the system. No one is above law and order. To make a more active and powerful system, they need to fear the law. Good law and order must be followed by everyone. Only good laws on the books are not enough to keep a good system; the public and leaders need to respect and fear the law. If the law has no fear creating power on those who are harmful to the nation, that law is of no use. It is the major difference between the developed countries and the developing countries. Developed countries have developed fear; under-developed countries have not developed fear and good fear management. Fear is multi-conductor socket. It can connect many cables at the same time; when it goes to a good handler, it plays well and in the hands of the bad, it plays bad.

Governments need to learn from good business management practices. Good fear has been suggested by organizational business researchers to be essential. "Fear is a healthy motivator" as Schechtman talks of how best to build organizations/communities to survive and thrive in a risky business world:

> [A]ccountability is hard to achieve when your consequences are meekly presented [or non-existent]—or, to put it more bluntly, when you fail to use fear as a motivator. Contrary to common belief, fear is a healthy motivator. Many people wouldn't drive at the speed limit or pay their taxes if it weren't for their fear of the consequences [i.e., punishments]. Many couples remain monogamous despite their natural attraction to others; they do so because they are afraid that affairs would disappoint and hurt their partners. When fear is part of a respectful personal or professional relationship, it is a healthy emotion. It's only when two people have no respect that fear turns unhealthy. When a boss views his [or her]

employees as mindless slaves, for instance, fear is used solely for the purposes of intimidation. [17]

We can take lessons from organizational and leadership research on effectiveness and a healthy use of fear, and we ought to always remember it is not power that corrupts but fear—that is, the unhealthy kinds of power built upon untrusting, non-respecting relationships [18].

Less Attention: Machines

India is giving a popular message of caring about high speed development. It is only good for election campaigns. The slogan cannot gear-up real or fast development for the state or society. Almost at the same time, China and India opted for an open door policy. It looked good. India was running its own *Chakravyuha*, whereas China broke through the Economic *Chakravyuha* of the world. India and China are rich in labor force power. By contrast, India takes it as curse and China takes it as boon.

How to manage the human power/labor, and how to make workers enthusiastic, it all depends upon the state policy and its effectiveness in implementation. For truly activating higher work production base on policy has to be backed-up with an infrastructure in place. Governments makes good policy and bureaucrats work as snails and ignore fear of law, slow the work—so, how can it reach the target goals? It is a major problem in India. Employees are not supporting development projects. Government also follows the traditional methods in the name of creating new jobs. To build bridge, tunnel, fly-over, road, anywhere. Unfortunately, the Indian government is using humans as machines not respectful management-labor relations. In contrast, China emphasizes modern, faster, and stronger machines. One machine is equal to 10,000 human machines. So, they ran faster as leopard in terms of development.

China lowers down its poverty level very fast and became the No. 1 foreign currency reserve in the world. 2025 is the target time to reach to this position but 10 years earlier they met the target. The main pushing force is neither military rule nor equipment. Its main force is the fear. In China, anybody gets a death penalty who is involved in corruption. Law is supreme in China. Even if a political leader, or in high office there is no excuse. We see in the media that every year many corruptors are put to the death penalty. Fear of death penalty prevents them to commit corruption. Less corruption means progress, development, peace and happiness. China is enjoying its victory over poverty. In other terms, we can say it is stepping up to become a superpower.

It is time for Indian government to fear public and develop constructive machines and gear up quality of the human power. It takes psychological fear to activate the human forces at a base of motivational direction. No doubt India can do this long jump, not run. In this long jump it must take all including the masses and relay together. In a relay game, one runner reaches the target but the rest is backing them up—a team matters. India is trying to run without the participation of the lower castes, in absence of which country cannot be a winner, it will be a loser.

Pollution, Garbage, Dirty Sea & Rivers

One of the important factors of development is the hygienic system of a country. In one sense we can say India looks like cities of garbage. Nobody is willing to clean the garbage and not even clean public toilets. We can see huge mountains of plastic garbage in many corners of cities like Delhi and Mumbai. Sea water and rivers are used as a waste bin. This undermines healthy growth and development for all.

Most all developed countries take seas as a natural asset of the state. India is taking it as rubbish bin. The basic concept of country is different. Meanings of sea, river, and natural things are different. Meaning of these things plays an important role to understand one's nation and its assets. There are many hygienic problems, even in their hospitals. It is not a big problem for a nation to solve. But the question remains: Who will initiate it?

Unfortunately, most everyone runs away from social responsibility. Citizens behave as though it is the task of some alien 'outsider.' They believe an alien will come one day and help them to clean it. As a result, average death rate is higher in comparison with other countries. Basically, in this case the so-called high castes have believed that it is the compulsory work of low castes. If educated people revolt it, they threaten them showing fear of EBCP and treat them as slaves, das and low castes. Scheduled castes have no power to protest against them because they are afraid of EBCP.

In the United States there is no culture to keep servants or helpers. Even in old age, they have to do work themselves. Less public transport is concerned with self- service in the US. Everybody has to do work if they are capable. In Japan, citizens not only clean up their own rubbish, they help others too.

One of the other dangers is human organ smuggling. It is developing in India in human organs trade business. It is an easy business to earn profit. Politicians have connections here. In this easy business, mostly lower castes are losing their life by selling organs. They have not enough income to eat and do some expensive treatment; they are selling hearts, kidneys and other parts of body. RPB has no such problem as they are the buyers of the organs to prolong life.

The rich upper castes have been exploiting the poor for thousands of years. It is not the result of the present system. Roots of it go to the beginning of civilization and changes that led to an unsustainable culture. When concepts of property were developed, the game of manoeuvre and cheating began. Everyone was afraid of insufficient food stock. To store food, strong people started to dominate the weak (see Kumar in Part 1). Since then, the caste system was developed in the Indian sub-continent. The weak and the defeated were treated as human-animals. Condition of human-animals has never been changed. It is true and possible the dominating RPB's game of inequity could be turned upside down—it will take a transformation. When they put *Khouf* (fear) only into the hearts of the unprivileged, the RPB could rule over the lower castes, without recourse to justice.

Different Kinds of Corruption

Corruption has multiple names. To exploit the property of lower castes, they used the fear of EBCP and wasted duty hours, taking more time on breaks, taking unnecessary allowances, taking more leaves to escape from offices. These can be taken as forms of corruptions. Lower castes are not sufficiently employed in the government jobs. Police and army are also another kind of corruption.

Since five thousand years, some people of the society have been prohibited to work or do business. Then how can they compete in the social marketplace? Mass peoples of India are out of work because that is the 'fate' of their name, classification, of lower castes. This caste is not born as untouchable. It was and still is humanly-made. It was made by so-called upper castes in ancient India for their benefit. They are repeating the same blunder displacing the lower castes aside even today. RPB are responsible for such mass corruption.

Governments distribute budget but budgeted items are only enjoyed by RPB. Does this not amount to corruption? Why do they not want to share the resources and privileges of a successful nation? Are they only the authorities to enjoy it? Who gave them this privilege? Is the government distributing budget properly to all people and areas? Of course not. In some of areas the majority population is lower castes, minority is upper castes. But budget is allocated for high castes. It is hundred percent injustice. RPB has a power over treasury of the nation and only they are enjoying it in many sources of project, employment, social welfare and education etc. Misuse of power (and fear) and illegally taking advantage is a corruption. So, higher castes are doing mass corruption. Now is the time to review. From the government level it is not properly evaluated. The nation must distribute budget without any prejudice. Maximum level of balance makes a country progressive in development. Many icons of India have come from oppressed lower castes like Dr. Ambedkar and Darshan Majhi, but they are rare cases of having overcome their oppressions—yet, they can teach lessons for everyone.

In the name of religion, politics, education, culture, RPB takes more facilities, and gets budget privilege from the Government. Lower castes are always put out of the budget. Over time, upper castes became richer and richer whereas low castes became poorer and poorer. One good example is Nepal. In Nepal, *Rana* regime ruled country for 104 years as dictator-based rule. Shah royal family was in house arrest. Only, family members of *Rana* came into military and government posts. Public were not allowed to take education. Some priest families (Brahmans) were allowed to study Sanskrit on government scholarships. They were taking government privileges in the name of Sanskrit. Students were provided lodging, allowance and food. Name of the school was *Tin Dhara Sanskrit Pathshala*. It is in Kathmandu. It was established in 1889.

It produced every year 150 educated students. For higher education, they went to Banaras, India. It is still running. It was started around 130 years ago. What the literate people are in Nepal today, are products of *Tin Dhara Sanskrit Pathashala*. Many ministers of democratic government and secretaries were (are) students of this school. 75% civil service and private service is covered by its students. Only first category of *Branasrawan* (Brahman, *Chhetri, Baishya* and *Sutra* are four hierarchy castes in Branasrawan) allowed and the rest, *Chhetri, Baishya* and *Sutra* were not permitted. Normally production of that school's students can be 2,106,000 in 130 years. As Malthus theorised that population would double in every 25 years, the students of Pathshala swelled to 2,106,000 at the rate of 150 students a year with the assumption of three children in each student's family over a span of 130 years. But the illiterate population of lower castes just increased as ration of crops. RPB increased geometrically and lower castes increased arithmetically;

150x130x1=58500 (1person average family, 150 students, in 130 years)
58500x3x2=351000 (years 25, double population, 3 average family of 150)
351000x2=702000 (50-year double population)
702000x2=1404000 (100-year double population)
1404000x2=2808000 (200-year double population)
2808000/4=702000 (25-year double population)
1404000+702000=2106000 in 125 years total

At present, total number of civil servants are approximately 100,000 and the whole population is 29.3 million in 2017 in Nepal. Over flowed population is spread all over the country and occupied many institutions. Lower castes are controlled by restrictions. Even as their population increased, their employment, education and living standard remained the same.

This calculation might be applicable in the context of India. India has many such institutes in olden days where only *Brahman* can read and write. After long time, their population increased in the field of education, employment and economic situation. Low castes are highly dominated by all.

This system was run by RPB. It doesn't affect merely one generation, it goes from generation to generation. One community is considered high caste, rich, educated, honest, moral and other community is considered as beggar, cleaner, sweeper, dirty and disgusting by birth. It changes socio-culture and psychology. How the path is different? Path was marked by property. If low caste, people have billion rupees, nobody dares to dominate. Upper castes shut main income source through many tactics, while innocent low castes inevitably believe in their trap of 'fate.' RPB hypnotized lower castes in masses and make them believe they were born in this life to do menial jobs (see Kumar, Part 1).

High Degree of Carelessness

Nominal problems are playing the decisive role in causing obstacles to development. Everywhere is a problem *via* scarcity, disease, murder, killing, raping. Authorities are putting cotton in their ears and sitting in chairs. Somebody calls the police for rescue but often action is not taken immediately. May be this is happening because of not paying handsome salaries? Government's departments are doing the same. It is against moral conduct. If concerned officials are not doing their proper duty it smells of corruption. These are symptoms of south Asian countries. It happens when law cannot make officials fear the people enough. If law is capable and has caliber to enforce then such misconduct has less chance and progress will be more. Misconduct, careless in work, insufficient discipline, is also the result of less fear. This is the negative side of fear. To make them more careful, they need more fear. Only fear can drive them properly to basic moral action and responsibility for their roles.

People are careless because they have no fear of law, rules and regulations. They don't have fear of family, future, health etc. Without fearing, if they are enjoying the facilities of employer then why should they need to fear? When they are afraid of termination, accident, future, unemployment, being scolded, defamed, then surely they are fearful and will not be careless. Being careless produces useless fellows; useless they may not be harmful to themselves but they are harmful to the state. It affects lower castes too. Suppose bureaucrats keep pending lots of files. Due to pendency, it delays many industries and construction works. When business, industries and constructions delay, it affects the labor industry. Already lower castes are not employed, and then less demand is created for their labor industry. It directly affects them.

A little carelessness of employee hampers everyone too. Duty and responsibility of bureaucrats are supposed to be of service to citizens. Just opposed to their duty, they behave like master and public are servants. They must understand they are the servants of the public and nation. They are paid by public taxes. This careless attitude must change. They must develop the habit of a relative degree of fearing the public as a start. Public must also behave like master, not as servant. Reverse thinking is needed to develop the nation.

Nobody is afraid that it is a state of anarchy. Anarchy state is like the natural state of Thomas Hobbes. Idealist Hegel said, "First came idea then came the world." Hegel said, "Head is more important than stomach." Materialistic Marx just reversed the dictum of Hegel and criticized. He said, "First comes the world then the Idea." According to him stomach is more important than the head [19]. In context of India, people believe that the bureaucrats are masters and public are servants. New beliefs must be that public are masters and bureaucrats are servants..

Unfortunately, lower castes are always slower in this race. They have little or no choice of life because they are not independent in a republic nation. It is an intolerable fact, unfortunately. *The best way to bring everyone on track is fear.* Forward castes need to have the same kind of fear as what lower castes have been experiencing for a long time. It doesn't mean that they must live as poor. They have to be given *fear-psychology* training. It means to teach fear, which assists them to change life. Some reason of backwardness is the ignorance of fear knowledge (not general knowledge or philosophical knowledge). Philosophical knowledge has lots of treasures. But in the past it was prohibited to lower castes. The problem we are seeing is the ignorance of lower castes. Fearism and lower castes are similar category in the sense of marginal. Lower castes were knowingly put aside whereas Fearism was not. Fearism was not coined by anybody earlier than Subba in 1999.

Balance of Fear

The fear we [should] try to be rid of is an unnecessary fear.
We can be free from normal fears.... we can alleviate it

> by changing its form, facing it, and considering it a minor
> one.... Fear can be alleviated according to its nature. It
> cannot be alleviated [in ignorance] without any idea about
> it. Fear is a kind of problem, a mental disease. It is also a
> kind of treatment.
>
> — Desh Subba [20]

Fear is both disease *and* can be transformed to be the very treatment we need to overcome fear. It may sound paradoxical at first. With wise study and contemplation, the logic of this dictum is that we need to find a balance. We need to be better educated about fear.

In the previous section we discussed the back-drop of the country India. It is for all common people. How extremely difficult it is for the lower castes and workers to live and struggle for survival. They are part of the nation but incalcitrant hierarchy, culture, religion, tradition, and gender privilege (males) act to dominate them. They have been surviving like less valued female human-animals.

They accept that fear of EBCP and upper castes are dominating these innocent girls and women, especially, through many fears. Fear is the factor which forces them to bend their head and allows them to be removed from schooling at puberty and other forms of confinement (see Fisher, Part 2).

Rather than fear, other forces cannot intimidate them. Particularly when we go through the lives of lower castes they have no good income, education, assets and anything to be grandeur of life. Anxiety, sorrow, insult, domination, isolation, aspersions, torture kills their human emotions, hopes, eagerness. Big population of the country is surviving an animal life. Sometimes lower castes are treated as lower than animals. How can a nation be proud of glory and development? It is the shameful face of nation. How can a nation proudly stand at the world forum in the 21st century with undeclared slaves? What is different between ancient Dark Age and modern slaves? It is a big question. 21st century ought to be optimum for development in human history. India is choosing to keep blind beliefs and a slave mentality. How can one remember its political freedom? Why are caste domination, prejudice, fear imposed on the downtrodden already? Is it justice? Can a nation be that dumb? Life of the lower caste is lower than the average life in India? At least they have the right to live at average human level.

There are many ways to solve the problems. The higher castes are targeting Mandal Commission because they are afraid of losing opportunity as their privilege. They used the other, as their habitual best methodology. The nation was a dumb audience since the beginning of history. How can a nation always play a dumb role?

When some innocent citizens are killed by fear blades; it is more dangerous than other killings. Weapons can kill limited numbers but killing by fear is bigger than any massacre. Massacre kills in some areas but fear can kill nationwide. It is difficult to stop fear killing. Fear killing can be stopped by a fearless injection of misuse of fear. This injection is being developed by Fearism and other projects [21]. When the oppressed are able to be fearless of RPB, give up artificial fears, the nation may transform. Government has to fear the public and public have to fear the rules and regulations. Parliament has to fear the government and judiciary, government has to fear the parliament and judiciary, judiciary has to fear the government and parliament. It has to run in a self-system regulation, a circle of good fear. Checks and balances of fear are the good virtues of a good nation. If there is no balance, then the country will remain in a downfall. Some philosophers and social scientists apply other theories of power, or the state, etc., but for the fearist it is fear which is the most important among all explanatory factors. It is fear that when managed properly, and accompanied by good fear education (*a la* Fisher), then a society may advance. India is no exception.

Misuses of Authority

Fear is a beautiful consciousness.

– Desh Subba [22]

It is harmful to ignore fear, by anyone, but especially by government leaders and their employees. It is a bad luck of those countries where leaders think they are superior and the general public are just like inferior workers. Fear must be kept either in the name of the Lord or any members of the family. In fact, fear doesn't denote the external factor; it is a part of consciousness. What happens if some part of consciousness is missing from our main consciousness? Automatically mindfulness is incomplete. Due to lack of it, we become unable to fulfill our task. It is an intuition of body. Some people think they are making fools of others. It is wrong. They are making fools of themselves. For instance, we can take higher castes. They are making fools of lower castes and taking advantage from them. It is absolutely mistaken. If they are right, then why are they making polluted air, water and harmful environments? Why are they not treating air, water and environments as valuable like developed countries? They are being a part of foolishness because they are creating unhealthy environments which will not support a healthy vibrant nation.

If they did well in leadership, ethically, then they would have a grand life. Indians whomever, rich or poor, are seen by the West on average as rather foolish, arrogant, poor, and uneducated. Dr. Sanjeev, citing the book of Rushdie, said in a book "*Sidhanta* ka Kura" that the Westerners have the power of definition over the East. They define Easterners as foolish and ignorant. This label is not patched to untouchable and low caste only. It is also for the so-called high castes, the powerful and the richest Indians too. Why would Indians put up with this?

Use of political and economic power is made for the welfare of the nation not only a small percent of elites. Without all people there would not be any nation. Nationhood can be only built by harmony of peoples, including lower castes. In the nation everyone has responsibility, duty and rights. Suppose a farmer is not doing his duty, then the nation will surely suffer from hunger. Some authorities are not doing a respectful duty and are misusing power. Power police, for example, is not for harassing, torture and panic. Their duty is to protect and respect civilians (see Kumar, Part 1). Why are they misusing *Khakhi* uniform; because they are not afraid of public? They have set themselves to loot people from top to bottom. If the country is facing difficulties every citizen will suffer. Most employees, generally, are cheaters. Some are good too.

All upper castes don't have the same standpoint regarding lower castes. Mostly 90% standpoint is the same regarding lower castes: for example, if they eat together with lower castes, they feel disgusted. Their psychology says, " they are dirty and deliverers of disease." Before eating if they keep such thinking, definitely it makes them unhealthy and its blame comes to lower castes. It strikes people psychologically. We can call it a psychological and *fearological strike*. It is a *"cultural psychofear."* Theoretically RPB agrees to accept lower castes, practically not so, but they only nod head to such a thought. It is an adopted cultural more since way long ago. It takes time to improve but initiation must start today. When we plant seeds, there are more chances to grow a tree and one day that tree gives us sweet fruits. Without planting seed, it is impossible. Indians can be the *avant garde* in this regard. The great Indian sage Patanjali guides transformation vision to this day:

When you are inspired by some great purpose,
Some extraordinary project,
All you thoughts break their bonds,
Your mind transcends limitations,
Your consciousness expands in every direction,
And you find yourself in a new,
Great, wonderful world.
Dormant forces, faculties and talents,
Become alive, and you discover yourself
To be a greater person by far
Than you ever dreamed yourself to be. [23]

There are many cracks in barriers to development. A very small factor, like consciousness which is invisible, can play the role of making or unmaking blockades. Typically, as citizens, we never take them into account. For example, s like slowness, laziness, road block, cracked roads, licensing, ignoring government rules etc. can accumulate with devastating impacts. Less fear of law causes laziness and slowness. Fear of termination wakes up lazy workers. How big fear has power, it can see pitiable face of lazy workers after termination notice. That *fear power* cannot be replaced by other means. Even money power cannot be subservient to them. Fear is the only ultimate solution to make them labor inspired producers. Seven Wonders of the World was built by fear. Back then money had no importance as it does today.

Masters ordered slaves to do labor otherwise the slave would have to face death. Slaves had no option. They built with breath, blood and sweat. Those were not built by cost. What work was possible by fear that cannot be possible by money? When citizens ignore the fear of law, government, rule, police, court, discipline, code of conduct, it harms development. Less fear of law makes corruptors more powerful. It is the major virus of progress. India is the major victim of such virus. Political leaders collect funds through ransom claimers, kidnappers, and gangsters impact their elections. So, those people take advantage with these corrupted leaders. Between the leaders and corrupters, the public become sandwiched and a country gets destroyed.

Prejudice & Women

Dr. Fisher (Part 2) also spoke to the issue of girls and women and fear in India. We analyze the situation with some independence but also universal ideas. In Indian main stream feminists are not ready to eat together with lower caste women even today. Hypothetical and theoretical or academic feminism is inconsistent in practice. These lower caste women have the experience of domination by upper castes, middle class women and men. Male domination is another part, for sure but it is not alone oppressive to lower caste girls and women. During colonial times, girls and women had the domination of many kinds including the white race. They have been experiencing the pyramid of intersecting domination. What lessons are taken by the lower castes were hard? Did they dominate over their women? Here, prejudice is more important for discussion because they hold more than 50% of the Indian population. The percentage of lower caste women is accountable. Until granting them more opportunities and lesser domination of fear, nations cannot develop progressively.

Thomas Hobbes didn't support the state of nature, but Rousseau supported the state of nature [24]. Rousseau said in the state of nature that nobody had property and no discrimination and no class distinctions. Unfortunately, class and caste came together with property as commodity. Everyone was afraid of sickness, death, and attack on secure life, hence they needed secured property. In India, the case of lower castes they were kept away from property and it was the privilege of RPB. Then the RPB took advantage of the low castes that needed security. The lower castes want to have good life but everyone was struggling for property and secure life and the lower castes lost out. If they someday experience secure life, then they will have peace, happiness and pleasure.

A Few Solutions

Ultimately, India has to acknowledge its Fear Problem and Fear Solution, through a fearist perspective. Philosophy of fearism can offer both analysis and solutions. Without the privilege of elitism, with flexibility as a social practical philosophy, fearism is already at work in popular education within India (especially, N. E. India) for better understanding and fear management. This is led by the important work of many; for example, Rana Kafle in the field with his diverse non-political team of people, some adult educators, cultural workers, and others often utilizing arts and literature as a main vehicle for teaching (i.e., a pedagogy Kafle calls "edutainment"). This is certainly an intuitive direction and works well when there are so many functionally illiterate people in the Indian population.

Arts communicate in ways that other modalities of teaching and learning are not effective, especially with marginalized groups in popular and adult/community learning settings. More research and evaluation of these pedagogical methods is required in the future, in India. Governments and NGO's at all levels in India and otherwise ought give take serious attention to this possibility and help fund operations like "Face To Face" (see Appendix 1). Universal Human Rights and other constitutional laws (as Fisher stated in Part 2) to disband the *fear gun* in India are back-up support for policies and for leaders of all kinds to promote fearism and justice.

In the world, especially two branches are advocating the issue of the backward (marginal, subaltern, feminine, low caste, transgender, bisexual, queer etc.). Renowned feminist Gayatri Spivak Chakrawarti says, "Backward people cannot speak on their own. They need support from someone." According to Gayatri, the underlying reason for the silent of backward people is their backwardness, which again is caused by fear. It's only when they are made fearless of caste and punishment that they would be able to speak. Against that view, Michael Foucault says, "they have to raise their problems themselves. Representation by others is violation of rights" [25]. Lower caste people's voice is seized by RPB. So, they are afraid to speak. When they speak against high castes they must face EBCP. Fear of EBCP chokes off their voice. Till then they don't speak, nobody represents them. Gayatri's way seems more useful.

For example, we have a child. Father is always angry and regularly scolds and punishes the child for small mistakes. Mother is kind. Sometimes both are cruel in the name of education, discipline and moral character. In front of cruel parents, the child never speaks. The child has come with dirty cloths and some wounds. Parents look at him and ask what had happened? Until he stands silent, nobody solves the problem. Even they cannot guess what happened? Shutting one's mouth reveals many meanings: fighting, fell down, or beaten by elders. What parents had to do if the child does not speak? They may scold, threaten, beat, punish, and confine in the room? To frighten sometimes, they use third degree as police do but sometimes it does not work. Make him to speak, it reduces fear. Parents may politely ask," Son please tell us, we do nothing." When he feels comfortable then, he speaks what has happened. When he tells the problem, then parents can search for solutions.

The same methodology can be applied to solve the problem of lower castes. First need is to bring them on track to the talking table. RPB are like cruel parents and lower castes are like frightened children. A frightened child needs to cool down. When lower castes are convinced that they are not going to be punished then they share their life story honestly. By doing so they become part of the nation. Part of nation is a part of community. It gives good fruits for the nation.

****

Appendix 1

Fearism in India: Brief Summary

According to a recent Report (summary of Episodes 1-20) by Budheswar Bordoloi, secretary of "Face to Face":

> "Face to Face" programme is an extraordinary interaction programme which includes edutainment, talks and interactions. It is not an organization but it is a mission to bring awareness among the common people regarding "Fear" in all aspect of life. The programme was totally designed by Dr. Rana Kafle, the co-ordinator, Face to Face, which was upgrade from Basibialo (Nepali : Interaction in Luisure Time) This programme is based on the theory of "Philosophy of Fearism" that lead by Desh Subba from Hong Kong. He was the founder of this new theory who played a vital role to propagate and to promade Fearism in many part of the world.

For the last several years in N. E. India, in particular, Rana Kafle with help from Desh Subba, and Fearism Study Center in Nepal and others, have been organizing, planning and implementing an effective adult education project with several events (Episodes) per year. Rana Kafle is the Co-ordinator of "Face to Face." The purpose of Appendix 1 is not to attempt to give a complete account of the fearism project in India, but it will give some features of its presence (2017-18) through only a few excerpts taken from this unpublished document (below).

> THE GLIMPSES OF AN INTERACTION PROGRAMME `FACE TO FACE," ITS COMPLETION OF ONE YEAR 2017-2018 by Budheswar Bordoloi, Secretary:
>
> A series of 12 "Episodes" have taken place and have been documented. A few examples are Episode 1 – "Programme Report:- The 1st episode Interaction Programme "Face to

Face" was hold at Purana Ghilani, Resident of Sri Maghat Sagra on the 25th july 2017 under the Chairman ship of Sri Bhadra Sagra Assistant teacher. It is an extraordinary programme that includes education in particular and interaction section in general. The programme was hold for the first time in memory of Faimibar Raizung. It is worth mentioning that Faimibar Raizung was a talented Dimasa artist who passed away at the very young age of twenty three years from En-chephalitis on 25th july 2016. The programme was inaugurated by Sri Rubising Sagra and sponsored by TIwa Mathanlai Tokhra, Ghilani Branch ; A Literary Group. Mrs, Sonali Langthasa, mother of Lt. Faimiba Raijung was attended as the` Guest of the month " The programme also present some of the dignitures as --- observer : Sri Bapon Kro, eminent poet, analysis; Sri bishnu Nirola ; president Gorkha yuwa sahitya academy, Tezpur. invited guest : kumud johori ; former president ; Dimasa students union a social worker."

As one official observer of Episode 1 noted:

"sharing of cultural values unites the co- existence of love, peace and brotherhood. In his remarks he also vividly elucidated how the moral values of cultures helps to propagate the common people to keep the strong bonds of mutual love and respects. Lastly, he also vividly demonstrates the need of cultural exchange among the community in the region."

Without biasing the Episodes (i.e., edutainment events) by religion, cultural group, ethnicity, class or caste, there is therefore an open exchange and welcoming atmosphere, with various kinds of groups, from literary organizations, to self-help groups, etc. sponsoring them locally. Guests are invited both from expertise backgrounds but also regular citizens. "Cultural assimilation" is a term used often in the reports describing "Face To Face" objectives. So the focus is not always directly on fear(ism) in many of the Episodes, but it is always implicit in the gatherings, exchanges, and education because excess negative fear can lead to lack of successful growth and development and unfortunate factionalism (conflict) of differences to the point of undermining community well-being in regions in India.

Episode 3:

"<u>Programme Report</u> : ... Interaction programme was held on the 16th September 2016 at gamganagar L.P School. Tumpreng West Karbi Anglong Assam, under the chairmanship of Miss Surabi Phanglosa president Gadaindi SHG. The programme was sponsored gadain di SHG. It was inaugurated by Sri Raju Daulagazau eminent Dimasa playback singer. He was also present as a Guest of the Month in that programme. Some of the dignitaries that have been present in the auspicious programme were —observer Sri Biren Enghi eminent reporter PRAG & KAT channel Analyser Sri Kumud Johori social worker invited Guest Sri Asinta Zidung social worker welcome speech was addressed by Miss Khiwsodi Hojai secretary Gadaindi SHG and the object of the meeting was delivered by Sri Budheswar Bordoloi ; programme secretary` Face to Face" the most interesting part of programme interaction session was led by Sri Rana Kafle; Co-Ordinator `Face to Face".

The programme was held by it was cultural awareness programme which attented large number of villegers and students. The students raise several reasonable questions regarding Raju Daulagazau journey to Dimasa music world." "Statement :Human Being never learn from the mother's womb .what we learn is acquired from the mother's earth. This statement makes us clear from Raju Daulgazau's remarks in the 3rd Episode of Face to Face. Initial stage as a singer he had a disturbance of negative fear in the path of success. But gradually negative fear have converted into positive fear and got established in the society. He had shown an example of converting negative fear into positive fear."

****

NOTES

1. "The fearist perspective is a new dimension [lens] to look at life and the world. The question strikes the mind: How does the fearist perspective look at life and the world?," asks Subba (2014) and he replies: "Fear has completely surrounded all living creatures, especially man.... It is a rule of nature" (p. 11). Fisher & Subba (2016) define "fearist" and "fearist perspective" further (p. 157) within the context of a philosophy of fearism. Subba, D. (2014). *Philosophy of fearism: Life is conducted, directed and controlled by the fear.* Australia: Xlibris. Fisher, R. M., & Subba, D. (2016). *Philosophy of fearism: A first East-West dialogue.* Australia: Xlibris.

2. Subba (2014) called this "fear weapon" (p. 235).

3. Kirsten Holst Petersen and Anna Rutherford named this. Quote is from McLeod, J. (2000). *Beginning postcolonialism.* Manchester, UK: Manchester University Press, p. 175.

4. See Subba (2014), pp. 245-306; Subba, D., & Fisher, R. M. (in press). Dephilosophy as universal discourse. Proceedings of the Indian Philosophy Congress, Jan. 5-7, 2018. Surat, Gujrat.

5. Retrieved from https://en.wikipedia.org/wiki/Desh_Subba

6. See Fisher & Subba (2016), pp. xxv, xxviii. Subba wrote "*philosophy of fearism* has been inspired by my observations, artistic lens of perceptions and expressions, my study of texts (E. and W.) and my passion for thinking critically about important topics of human concern.... I am thankful to the many authors throughout history who have written about it [fear].... my original mentors and scholars of

greatest influence in developing the philosophy of fearism have been
Prof. Dr Tanka Prasad Neupane, Chairman [Fearism Study Center,
Nepal] and Prof. Mahendra Multiple Campus Dharan, Nepal, Prof.
Dr. Govindaraj Bhattarai, Tribhuwan University, Kathmandu, Nepal
[and] Rana Kafle, writer, Assam, India and many more" (Fisher
& Subba, 2016, pp. 50-51). For more details on the activities of
philosophy of fearism in the East, see Fisher & Subba (2016), pp.
84-85.

7.   Details in Fisher & Subba (2016), p. 84.

8.   Cited from endorsements, front matter in Subba (2014).

9.   "It was my first Fearism Educational Tour in India, 2016. Really it
was marvelous. Many universities, colleges, literary programs and
philosophical thinkers were waiting to listen. They were curiosity
about this new prospective of Fearism. It was combo of philosophy,
psychology, critics and spirituality. There has been a lack of a holistic
philosophy which can cover almost all areas of life and universe—
fearism can do this. There were many unforgettable moments in the
tour. Among them, Miriam Girls College at Hojai, Karbi Aanglang
District of Assam. Aassam was the capital of north east India during
British Rule, it is the college, where distinct honour was given to
Rane Kafle and myself. The principal of the college exhibited the
college premises. Around 500 students were present to listen to my
lecture. There was a ceremony there, where I planted a plant in the
memory of my visit. I was the first person to plant a plant after Nobel
Prize winner, Mother Teresa. I hope that plant is growing up now.
I landed in Delhi 13 of May, and entered Nepal 5 June, 2016 from
Eastern border Kakadbhita. With some leisure time I visited many
beautiful hill stations like Simla, Dehradun, Haridwar, Rishikesh,
Manipur, Shilong, Assam. During the tour many organizations
highly honoured me and my work. Philosophy of Fearism educational
Lectures took place in the following Universities and other locations:
Jawaharlal Nehru University, Delhi, India, May 16, 2016; Kausal
Academy International, Ramnagar, Nainital, Uttarakhanda, India,
May 20, 2016; English Tuition Centre, Ramnagar, Nainital,
Uttarakhanda, India 20 May, 2016; Govind Hindi Sahitya Sewa,
Muradabad, UP, India, May 22, 23, 2016; Manipur University

Imphal, Manipur, India May 25, 2016, at morning; Nepali Sahitya Parishad Manipur, Kanlatombi, Imphal, Manipur, India 25 May, 2016 at 3 pm; Purvottart Hindi Academy, Shillong, Meghalaya, India, 27-29 May, 2016; Gorkha Pathashala, Shillong, Meghalay, India, 28 May, 2016, at 4 pm; Guhati University, Guhati, Assam, India May 30, 2016; Nepali Natya Sammelan, Tejpur, Assam, India, 1st June, 2016; Ajmal Mariyam Girl's College, Hojai, Assam, India June 2, 2016 at morning; GorkhShiva Mandir, Assam Nepali Sahitya Sabha Tumpreng, Karbianlang, Assam, India June 2, 2016 at afternoon (this place is home village of Rana Kafle. It is a remote village, we can see wild elephants on the way. It was our fortune, we saw elephants when we are passing through this village.) Rangsina Sarpo Auditorium Hall, organized by Karbi Write's Club, Diphu, Assam, 3rd June, 2016 (morning); Gorkha Mandir, Dewan Basti, Diphu, assam, India, organized by Assam Nepali Sahitya Sabha, Diphu Branch, June 3, 2016 (afternoon); Durga Mandap, Hawaipur, Assam, India, organized by Aassam Nepali Sahitya Sabha Branch, June 4, 2016; Silguri Mahakuma parisad bhawan, Gurung Basti, Siliguri, West Bengal, India organized by Sukuna,Usma Publication, June 5, 2016."

10. Ibid., pp. 84-85.

11. Bordolo, B. (2018). Rana Kafle: In the realm of literature and fearism. *The Hills Times*. Retrieved from https://www.thehillstimes.in/featured/ana-kafle-in-the-realm-of-literature- and-fearism/

12. Fisher, R. M., Subba, D., & Kumar, B. M. (2018). *Fear, law and criminology: Critical issues in applying the philosophy of fearism*. Australia: Xlibris.

13. Dozier, R. W. Jr. (1998). *Fear itself: The origin and nature of the powerful emotion that shapes our lives and world*. NY: St. Martin's Press, p. 13.

14. Cited from endorsements, front matter in Subba (2014). Subba has also had several newspaper and magazines in India publish articles on philosophy of fearism (e.g., interviews); for example, "Desh Subba has formulated how fear is produced—life, consciousness, knowledge, fear, cognition" (quote from: Gyan Bahadur Chhetri,

Aamar Assam, Assames Daily, 9 October 2013, Assam, India)—
from front matter of Subba (2014).

15. Cited from endorsements, front matter in Subba (2014).

16. Cited from endorsements, front matter in Subba (2014).

17. Schechtman, M. R. (1995). *Working without a net: How to survive and thrive in today's high risk business world.* NY: Simon & Schuster, p. 165.

18. Opposition leader in Burma, Aung San Suu Kyi, Peace Prize Laureate 1991, wrote, "It is not power that corrupts but fear" (cited in Fisher, 2010, p. 14). Fisher, R. M. (2010). *The world's fearlessness teachings: A critical integral approach to fear management/ education for the 21st century.* Lanham, MD: University Press of America, p. 14. Unfortunately, since the 1990s, and in the last few years especially, Kyi has shown less than good ethical practices of fearlessness according to many political critics of her handling of various ethnic, religious and political conflicts in Burma.

19. See end note 14.

20. Subba (2014), p. 307.

21. This includes, but is not limited to, the work in North America especially, of the Fearlessness Movement, by founder Dr. R. Michael Fisher, and The Fearology Institute.

22. Subba (2014), p. 13.

23. Patanjali wrote this around 200 BC. Cited in Chaudhry, R. (2011). *Quest for exceptional leadership: Mirage to reality.* Los Angeles, CA: Sage, p. 174.

24. See also discussion on Hobbesian fear in Fisher, Subba & Kumar (2018), pp. 44-45, 157.

25. Cited in Upreti, S. (2068, Nepal). *Sidhanta kura [Aspect of Theory].* Akshar Creation, p. 282.

****

PART 4

B. MARIA KUMAR,
R. MICHAEL FISHER
DESH SUBBA

QUO VADIS (WHERE TO FROM HERE, INDIA?)

It is hardly possible for the development and harmony of any country without fear.

– Desh Subba

Fear can be considered consciousness, as knowledge and as disease. Liberation from fear needs medicine made for fear.

– Desh Subba [1]

F (Fisher): These quotes remind readers of the foundational assumptions and theory behind fearism (*a la* Subba). This is relevant to assessing any situation (e.g., India's state of affairs) by focusing at times on the nature and role of fear—its good-side and bad-side. In some ways, this book is our offering as co-authors to a type of "medicine made for fear" and made for overcoming prejudice in India. I think we also all are calling for a shift in consciousness and a futurist and internationalist vision which India needs to expand to move beyond its enclosing limitations of vision for itself and its relationship to the world and to evolution itself.

As we conclude this book, our primary aim to raise ideas, questions, imaginations, and critiques of India as a nation has been reached. Our secondary aim is also satisfied because of our emphasis on *fear(ism)*, with specific attention to its nature and role in assessing India's past, present and future. Fear and prejudice certainly stand out together as each contributing to each other's potent dynamic and negative impacts. Although, all along we have embraced Subba's notion that warranted fear may be very positive and is basically foundational to shaping human motivation, growth and development. In that sense, there is no country without fear. In India this is no exception; yet, we faced in our analysis of India many of its challenges, some serious problems where it is apparent not 'good fear' but 'bad fear' is ruling the formation of this great nation at all levels of scale. How do you each feel at this point upon reaching our book's aims, and yet also realizing the real India still carries on its common ways? Are you optimistic and why, or have your views of India changed with this book's completion? How so?

K (Kumar): Yes Michael! First let me respond to the optimistic part of your query. One of the greatest optimists of the contemporary world Prof. Steven Pinker, a cognitive psychologist, of Harvard University has a commendable positive outlook to realise that human lives overall at present are much healthier, wealthier and freer than in past history. Famed for his latest book, *Enlightenment Now*, he has also good words for the current Indian scenario in saying that things are getting better in the sub-continent. He quoted a survey according to which Indians are more optimistic than the westerners, overall. He discussed in this book that India has progressed since its independence in socioeconomic terms, as evidenced by reductions in war casualties, famine deaths, extreme poverty and illiteracy. At the same time Pinker too had some surprises for himself when he learnt that the per capita income in India today is the same as that of Sweden in 1920, though its population is huge. He also confessed in an interview to *Sunday Times of India* (Dec, 2018) that Indians at-large are among the world's least tolerant people compared to those of other nations. Studies also point out that most of the Indians tend to be rather ambivalent with the noble ideals like equality, as regards to the people of different races, ethnicities and religions. They remain to not have an affirmative view to endorse full equality to women.

I do concur with Pinker in so far as the betterment trends are concerned, not only for the world but also for India. No wonder that the average life span of Indians rose from 32 years in 1947 to 68 years nowadays, thanks to the increase in nutritional standards and medical facilities. However, on recollecting Pinker's view, I wonder even now as to what made India limp on the road to modernism and is still being unable to wriggle out of the quagmire of the past social inequality and dehumanising practices. Being hooked on the erstwhile demonic customs and regressive traditions does not conform to modernisation of mind. Adopting advanced technologies in space, nuclear and digital fields *per se* as much of India has, does not imply full progress or development of the nation. On the contrary, it results in more harm if social inequality continues rising its head in an era of lethal technologies. Because, unlearning harmful things paves the way for a safe society. Knowing what is to be eschewed becomes pivotal. Nassim Nicholas Taleb said, "Negative knowledge is more robust to error than positive knowledge."

And your last point pertains to my views of India as to whether they have changed with this book's completion. My views stay unchanged. Rather, I am apprehensive about something worse may happen if things go unchecked. The trends are not great in that we are witnessing throughout the nation the following: escalation in socio-political disruptions with the proliferation of acts of terrorism, extremism, militancy and insurgency, caste-based conflicts, religious tensions, linguistic and regionalist disturbances and of course economic problems, which raise anxieties, fears and threats amongst people. Governments in the past or present applied only *status quo* tactics without relief. Unfortunately, the governments are pitting the law enforcement and bureaucratic machinery against the agitating mobs without remedying the actual causes of problems. It's short-term management and policy. The enforcement officers who suppressed the voices and thoughts of protesters are being rewarded. Hence, disaffection inevitably grows in the public mind. The situation is akin to the actions of the Nawab of Khatm in Ruth Prawer Jhabvala's Booker Prize winning novel *Heat and Dust*. The Nawab, in league with dacoits, used to let them loot his own subjects with impunity, for a share in their booty. I am sad that the same cunning tactic is being used in the current Indian scene overall to suppress the wailing masses. I refer to it as *khatmification*, after the vile Nawab of Khatm leadership disasters.

I feel satisfied that our book completion has achieved its basic aims. As the title and subtitle nudge, there are two aims: (a) to clarify and impress upon the people's minds that the root cause of persistent socioeconomic maladies in India lies in the haunting and daunting fears and prejudices risen from the ever perpetuating social inequalities through age old, scripturally-sanctioned caste system structures and dynamics and, (b); to explore ways and means by which we may be able to arrive at new ideas and solutions as to how could all the people of India leap together, without letting anyone behind, *a la* Lia Diskin's Ubuntu race and enjoy the fruits of modern glory. We do hope that our assertions may serve as guidelines for structural reforms to aid law makers and policy framers.

There's no doubt in saying that India still carries on its common ways. *World Happiness Index*, 2019, released on March 20, 2019 shows India's drastic fall to 140th rank among 156 nations from the previous rankings of 118 in 2016, 122 in 2017 and 133 in 2018. Happiness was assessed on certain variables like per capita income, healthy life expectancy, freedom to make life choices, social support, corruption free governance etc. The parameters stipulated for happiness are difficult, if not impossible, to attain because of caste rigidity existing even now in rural India and with covert prejudices in the urban set-up. All government records on welfare schemes, census, recruitment details, public service data etc. contain caste particulars. Practically speaking for example, an ambitious lower caste person can neither dare to run a hotel business nor venture to perform as priest at a temple for the simple reason that upper castes hardly approve of or patronise such endeavours. It can be inferred that for the vast majority there's no freedom to make advancing life-choices. Caste prejudices hinder team building and the spirit of unity, negatively impacting social support and a generous and trusting attitude. Another criterion of happiness is per capita income which is so alarming an issue that there are millions of starving people in India as per government's socioeconomic statistics.

In 2019, the election year for India, there remains no opaqueness to check up how elections are contested in the Indian setting. Political parties allot candidature on caste lines and castes are treated as vote banks for the same caste candidates respectively. Caste unions, associations and clubs become active to campaign for their caste-man. In order to garner solidarity of their caste members, candidates openly flaunt their caste tags or caste names as suffixes to their first names.

Another upsetting trend is that the 'caste monster' has not confined its tentacles to Indian soil alone. It has spread itself across foreign lands wherever the Indians migrated. The people of Indian origin in the UK and US have experienced caste-based discrimination and prejudices over a considerable period. There were deliberations and contemplations in British parliament also for enacting anti-discrimination laws similar to the Indian Act for prevention of atrocities. Dr. B. R. Ambedkar felt that even inter-caste dining and inter-caste marriages are not sufficient enough to eradicate casteism. He said, 'the real method of breaking up the caste system was..... to destroy the religious notions on which castes were founded.' It is absolutely an accurate and profound mind storming assertion. Truly, the institution of caste has been an innate part of scriptural writings and commensurate practices. As long as religion exists, caste exists and as long as caste exists, caste-based fears and caste-oriented prejudices exist. John Naisbitt and Patricia Aburdene's *Mega Trends2000* predicted religious revival in the new millennium. According to Simon Atkinson's 10 Mega Trends, most people in the world today identify with a religion and India tops the list (98%).

F: Maria thanks for these stark diagnostic statistics and realities; not the most pleasant to hear but obviously have to be faced and not diminished because one fears their truths. Speaking out 'truth to power' and calling attention to injustice isn't going to bring a lot of happiness either. Yet, "happiness" obviously is not the only indicator of justice and success in this world. I wish there was a "Truth Index" being assessed in each country that documents how many and how often people actually tell the truth or a "Trust Index," that is constructed from when people vote, if they do, in a country they can put on their ballot a scaled index number that tells how much they trust the particular candidates and the parties they are voting for—be it in the populus and/or amongst the institutions and leaders—where is there going to be the *fearlessness(izing)* [2] to truly want to know what everyone really thinks (?)—then, and only then, we will have a possibility of *freedom* and not until. Entirely new means of policy-making could be structured around such Indexes.

Anyways, in regard to your point about religion(s) and their role in the future, I am cautious of mega-trend data, although it may be somewhat accurate. In the Western world, in particular, there is lots of evidence that religion is less and less popular in the traditional sense—and, fact is, people, especially the younger teens and 20s-30s aged are choosing "spiritual not religious" on various censuses. They are not, in great numbers, any longer impressed by traditional religion overall. I suppose that is a shift that can come as well to so-called less developed nations as they evolve through modernization and into postmodern cultural and consciousness shifts.

I really think in the end the best way to go with facing the traditional and often pathological aspects of religion(s), their chronic fear and prejudice and symptoms, e.g., caste systems, is to bring in more *spiritual education* in many diverse forms to a nation. In Part 2, I recommended several spiritual sages and philosophers in India, e.g., Gandhi, who knew how to bring this forward and many still are attempting such (r)evolutions in spiritual consciousness. They have to be reinvigorated as source curriculum. Unfortunately, this inward-change work does not always bring about changes on the material plane so quickly. We need to do both, work on material and spiritual transformation together through better education, and especially as I have argued in my work using a curriculum with a *pedagogy of fearlessness* [3] and a critique of what is critical thinking so that it truly is "critical" in a powerful way of challenging all oppressions, not merely reform of surfaces of a culture and nation.

The best global resource I know of in terms of understanding the developmental and evolutionary issues and tasks involved with all religions, that has much to offer ways to change and transform—that is, to mature the religions and religious leaders of the world, is by the integral philosopher Ken Wilber, he recently wrote,

This is a book [and an argument based on developmental theory] about what a possible religion of tomorrow might look like. It is meant to apply across the field of the Great Traditions; I believe that all of them will, in fact, most likely end up incorporating many of these elements into their own fundamental teachings at some point, simply because of the [evolutionary] forces driving toward such are so varied and far-reaching and, on balance, indeed make such a great deal of sense.... [it is a world vastly changed since the Great Traditions were born, mostly 3000 years ago] any spirituality that can't pass muster with science will not make it past the modern and postmodern tests for truth, and any science that doesn't include some component of testable spirituality will never find an answer to the ultimate questions of human existence.... [4]

I'm not going to go into Wilber's holistic-integral and developmental offering for religions of the world today, but to say he is not one to trash religion in the typical way most secular modernists and postmodernists may; rather he embraces the vast importance of the core essence of the perennial wisdom in religions but then challenges them to be in the 21st century and to up-date their practices/teachings to help their people authentically "Wake Up" and "Grow Up" and much more; rather than keeping their practitioners 'slaves' to the tradition and its premodern political-institutional archaic and oppressive ways. Wilber's point is that with so many billions of people practicing religion of one kind or another globally, this represents one of the greatest potential forces of advancement for humanity as a whole, because religions have always been known to mobilize people like nothing else can—especially, in crises. The issue is one of good guidance in such a mobilization and it has to be a guidance in an up-dated and informed religiosity available today for all religions to mature—which, is in my view, to move beyond a fear-based motivation to a truly love-based motivation— which is, in my studies, the essence of the perennial teachings of all the Great Traditions of religions and the best of secular philosophies as well. Wilber's integral theory supports this claim as well. This movement from Fear to Love [5] is the basis of any *universal ethic* which can authentically unify the great tensions, conflicts and diversities around the world—"fears of the future" play the major causal role in group conflicts, most everywhere according to some researchers [6]; and yet, keeping those diversities intact as they are, without trying to mash them all up into some forced *faux* "unification" plan or Global World Order scheme. Wilber's integral approach avoids that damaging tendency. Of course, it is a long way from being understood and applied at nation levels. However, that situation of world affairs ought to be a motivator for us educators interested in true emancipation, not a hindrance. India's consciousness, it seems to me, and I hear Desh and Maria saying the same thing in this book, has to embrace a *progressive internationalism* vision and *worldcentric* mission [7] and pull itself up and out of the obsessive ethnocentric isolationism it seems to have predominantly fallen into in the religious, cultural and political spheres. Of course, not only India is responsible for this—all nations are, a point I made in my Part 2 suggestions.

K: Thanks Michael. I wish to continue a wrap-up of my diagnostic concerns for India. With such continued adherence to the past, a considerable chunk of the Indian population observe and cling onto old practices in the 21st century. In 2016, a survey was jointly conducted by the Centre for the Study of Developing Societies, Konrad Adenauer Stiftung and Lokniti about how the Indian youth's attitudes, anxieties and aspirations are evolving in contemporary society. It was revealed that the Indian youth have certainly become modern as far as their dress styles and consumption habits are concerned but their thoughts and views still seemed to be traditional and orthodox.

These instances corroborate the fact that the ancient and traditional ways of outlook and social equations remain almost unaltered. With such a diabolical legacy of forced human inequalities and associated fears and prejudices having a regressive impact on society at large, India does not appear to have an iota of structural transformation to do away with the debilitating perennial social maladies.

F: To be realistic about modernisation, and it's obvious advancements is worthwhile, so I agree in part with your and Pinker's enthusiasm, though

I have my critiques, as do others of Pinker's work. Back to India, however, I think "poverty" is so fundamental an issue, and the Meita and Shephera 2006 major historical study of "chronic poverty" in India shows an open door to new thinking on this issue. They conclude reduction of poverty is vital for "the attainment of the Millenium Development Goals as also national and international goals of development and good governance" [8]. It is important that leaders at all levels look to these modern referents of success and justice for humanitarian purposes. I also think that there's a real problem if India attempts to compare itself with further along "developed countries" so-called because statistics is not everything of truth. In the United States there is a horrible record by international standards of good governance when it comes to child poverty and its connection with race. Again, I'm not here to throw statistics around but it is well know the abysmal low-level and humanity of one of the most modern powerful nations in the world. What the authors of the poverty report said at the end is a hopeful opening for a philosophy of fearism, perhaps. They said "In principle, the field [of development policy in India] is open for new ideas [solutions]" [9]. Now, that's where discussion needs to happen and where more alternatives than merely what modern Western countries have done (e.g., USA) ought to be looked at—and fearism could be part of that new discourse. The other good thing I see in a later 2008 report on India's economic development policy is that authors conclude that "development has to be environment inclusive" or it will more or less fail, and overcoming poverty or caste or racism is only part of the solution. I agree with this so much because of the massive pollution that goes with growth that is rationalized as "development" but is harmful to the ecological net of the nation or world. The very notion of "development" needs re-visioning beyond moving from pre-modern (classic old world) to "modern"—I believe that's barely the best of human potential and sustainability. We require a philosophy of development on a spectrum of consciousness that truly is based on fearlessness and sees "modern" as about ½ way there in the full realization of the maturation of civilization—and of great citizenship, leadership and human-global harmony.

K: Yes, thanks for mentioning those reports and findings. Regarding what has been raised about 'bad fear,' I would like to agree that the psyche of an average citizen in India is unproductively haunted by the fears and prejudices that are associated indelibly with the 'caste monster.' The same kind of fears and prejudices, embedded in the old systems of slavery, serfdom and feudalism in the medieval west had mostly vanished from human civilisation because such anti-human institutions were abolished in law and done away with in implementation with the advent of the modern era. But in India the age old traditional caste propagation does not seem to decline; rather, it shows up as further escalation as is evident from proliferating caste oriented social organisations amongst almost all castes, namely upper, backward and lower.

According to a recent news report that appeared in the *Deccan Herald* (Chennai, Feb 14, 2019), a woman lawyer has officially cast away her caste with the receipt of an authenticated certificate from the concerned authorities. But what about the rest of India? Does a single example test it or not? Does an exception prove it or not? It all depends upon how the woman lawyer would be able to bring up her children. Because, the manner in which tender young minds are groomed determines their future personalities. Whereas fear is instinctual, caste based prejudice is taught and promoted by socialisation processes in the initial stages right from the birth. Apart from parents and siblings, children also learn from school teachers, peer groups, media and nowadays from the easily accessible digital gadgets.

A child normally begins forming its personality around the age of five years. If the feelings of superiority and authoritarianism are indoctrinated *via* fear-based teachings, knowingly or unknowingly by the concerned at such age, the child of an upper caste family tends to grow into a prejudiced authoritarian orientation. If the child of a lower caste family is imparted with feelings of inferiority and insecurity, the caste-based fear gets ingrained as a persistent trait of the grown-up personality. This is what has been happening for eons in India. Bad fear and negative prejudices have been thriving to the extent that India's superstructure is always weak and brittle.

Karl Marx theorised that basic structure of social and economic relations determine the state and fate of the superstructure, which consists of government, religion, legal bodies, the institutions of marriage, education etc. But I would like to add that even the Marxian basic structure in turn is influenced by such undercurrents as instinctual fear, socialised prejudice, learned fearlessness etc., which I would like to refer to as elementary or foundational structure for a society. Unless the elementary structure is supported by the humanistic ideals of equality, fraternity, liberty, freedom, dignity, justice, fearlessness etc, the bad fear and negative prejudice will continue causing havoc to the fabric of the Indian nation in the form of disunity, disharmony, dishonesty and degradation.

S (Subba): It is clear Kumar has many insights to offer and his knowledge of India is superior to my own. I approached this entire book project with humility and strength of philosophical perspective. The philosophy of Fearism is my guide. In general, my approach is not unlike all philosophers who foreground inquiry and interpretation with criticality as their gift. Philosophers never give full set of solutions or advice. This tradition is found among many in classical philosophy. In my understanding of philosophy there is a generic philosophical formula which can be applied according to necessity of the context, situation. place, and time in history. Philosophy pursues possibilities for new and wide ideas, keeping itself free as possible, with no limitations. For India, we applied philosophy in part to the context and particularities within India. Even with this same approach and even the same data collected, we would be advised to not apply such findings or ideas necessarily in the USA, USSR, China and Japan or an African context. There are such important differences for such nations. Economics, education and health are another aspect for acknowledging these differences. Underdeveloped, developing and developed India, we can apply fearism differently.

As to your question Michael, You know, we are human beings. There are some deep universal truths philosophy can rely on. When some people hurt, face injustice and have pain, we too as human have empathy. Indian spirits are not beyond human spirits. How painful life is living by lower caste and untouchable people, we too can feel this in some way. This makes our philosophical inquiry humanistic, social and practical.

Life of Fearism is for humanity. This co-authored book reflects only small parts of the real India. We may use statics, for example, but these are numbers not real people, who have their own uniqueness and interiority that is much less easy to measure and make claims about. Our book's contribution is for humanity of the World, we are merely making a gate way into and through India, as best we can to understand the World.

Assessing amount of progress is not always an assessment of actual progress in quality. External changes, more easy to assess, are also more easy often to change than inner change. Constitution, law, rule and regulation are external. Justice needs to be both external and internal in its scope and understanding. The great philosopher Schopenhauer has given attention to inner phenomena and said, "Our body is a manifesto of will." Our book plays, for the most part, the role of an external documentation and manifesto for change and reform. Transformation goes beyond that and is harder to penetrate, to discover an inner manifesto of every individual Indian. Yes, what is the "medicine" each can find for their struggles, for their fear?

When every Indian realizes pain and suffering and interacts with a fearological or fearist point of view, maybe then, that will be real India in its way to fear management on a new level. As authors we are mirrors, in this mirror we can see where is a dot in the face. Every viewer has to wash/clean themselves. our book is a mirror, in this mirror one can better see the Indian face. Personally I am optimistic, we have filed here the case in the court, now the judge is India herself, how will she give verdict? I personally have one principle for my work, that is, first make good quality knowledge and promote it as much as possible through good communication. Completion of this book is not enough to change a nation. The message must reach every individual through nationwide media and good community and adult education for starters. Rana Kafle's work that was mentioned in Part 3 is one type of grassroots approach to education that perhaps can be adopted further throughout India. Sometimes the outcomes of our efforts can be seen early but sometimes their effects take centuries. Indian leadership is a key ingredient in this but they are not the only ingredient, all people have a role to play in their development and freedom from fear.

F: I feel at a subtle level there is a more human, but even more-than-human, 'soul' of India that I have tapped into with this work with you both. It is hard to put in words—it is arational or extrarational, one might say. It is internationalist and that alters my small-positioning in Canada. It has led me to feeling more caring about India. Yet, maybe it is that I am so removed from the everyday streets of India, and have never been there, that distance allows perspective, gives me a means of standing back from all the scenes and realities of the banal, of the problems and suffering too; and, I am able to envision and invoke a 'spirit' of potential Indian power, and ancient philosophical wisdom already there but needs more spark, that flows within India still and in and through me and potentially all peoples everywhere. India's success and failure is mine, and its success and failure is everyone's. This subtle awareness, albeit, it may seem trivial, is a unity or nondual perspective that lurks and feeds me, so that I do not dissociate from the country and its problems. I am not ultimately separate, even though on the gross surface of life it is easy in my comfortable white-male Canadian privilege to forget and remain only in my ego-personality.

The growing familiarity, empathy, in this extrarational modality of connection with India, is likely due to my life, which has led me in 67 years of struggles as a working poor personal-identity, to see patterns that are much the same in all places. Persistent underlying excessive *fear* is the most common thing that has attracted my attention and led me to become a fearologist. Fear unites us on a common platform of life-struggle, of joys and sorrows. Some philosophers of fear would claim rather, that it be "love" that unites us [10]. I wish of India's leaders and peoples to take a more serious look at the "element of fear" and the relationship of *fear* with *development* at the smallest and largest levels. This element is the human element, is that basis of social capital that often is relegated to the margins in development thinking and projects, a point well made by Clouser's analysis and call for a "rethinking development and fear":

> Among the numerous debates and discussions of development, the element of fear is rarely given explicit consideration....I review current development literature to demonstrate the incomplete treatment of fear, as it is often [only, and meagerly] implicitly incorporated via discussions of security, power, identity, social cohesiveness or resistance....fear shapes, and is shaped by, development at multiple, overlapping scales....[we must be] directly engaging with fear in development analysis.... [11]

Why is it, that in searching a dozen books on economic and development policies in India, rare is it to find the word "fear" even in these books and reports, but when it is used it is a shallow use about some "fears" (fear of x, y, z) that are part of India's challenges but there is never more than one or two sentences about that. The worst of it is, as Clouser has shown in her survey of development literature, and surveys with development workers in Guatemala, that fear is not seen discussed with any nuance as a key factor, yet 90% of the development workers in her study "readily identified fear as a critical element facing development initiatives"—where often it may somewhat motivate, but in its extreme chronic fear patterns in peoples there is a plethora of inhibitions to development in all kinds of ways. It often leads to lack of long-term vision [12]. Among the villagers or almost anywhere, "Fear and mistrust are like antibodies that do not allow [development] projects to enter [a community]," reports Clouser on the challenges of adult and community education [13]. Fear is a very big factor of resistance and it has to be dealt with specifically in restoration work in India or any other nation that has suffered for so long under oppressive conditions. Clouser also reminds everyone that even 'benign' development efforts brought to a nation or community can "be a form of violence" themselves [14]. So, great ethical scrutiny is required to do development work in the *least* intimidating and harmful ways.

I am haunted over and over by Kumar's (Part 1) and his point that India in some ways has become nearly consumed under the umbrella expression of and reality of "The Fearful Vs. The Fearsome" –both sides, the rich and poor are fear-based at core in their approaches to life and citizenship. Like

Clouser, I believe we need to make "fear" and fearism a study itself within development literatures, policies and actions, as was suggested a few years ago by Subba and myself in an article on participatory development in Nepal [15]. It's frustrating that emotional, affective elements, like fear are so under-attended to in their importance, by education and development experts and planners!

S: Yes, the internal is usually forgotten in much of what is done as development work. I wish to state my relationship more historically with India, especially as a born and raised Nepalese citizen. What I have written in Part 3 is some of my witness of the experience of India and yet my knowing goes deeper in my life. My city Dharan is close to the Indian border. In Nepal, India has high influence on culture, political, racial, language and much more. I recall, I believe, in 1989 that I travelled to western Nepal via India. In Nepal there was not good roads, rail and sea travel almost 50 years before. Nepalese used to go from India because Nepal had not bridges on rivers. Education treatment and religious pilgrims from Nepal use to go to India. "Munglan Jane" it was a famous word, it means go to foreign country. India was the main foreign country before. It was a kind of *El Dorado* for Nepalese people. Nepalese went to find jobs, and be recruited in the Indian army. In most all states of India there are Nepalese. North India and north east India are highest numbers of Nepalese. Some parts of North India were Nepalese territory before British India. Sugauli Treaty of 2 December 1815 and 4 March 1816 which some of the territory controlled by Nepal would be given to British India? Who were living in Nepalese Territory was to become Indian. Even today the border is open for both, with no visa required. So, I am very much familiar with India. It helps me to write about it and share my passion and views.

In our writing we have written practical for the most part. Less theoretical. We realize one must have both in development work. Grassroot readers can easily catch our prospects. If even a few members of the public, a few professionals, or leaders adopt our meaning means for a new analysis of India, then we have to consider the writing of this book a success. Of course, there is always more work to be done.

I agree with Michael. Fear(ism) was not considered as attractive to learn about or as a motivator for most parts of the world to date. India is leading, as one among them. When fearism is not taken as serious and a grand matter, then it never gets focused on it. Education institutes, media, political geography, medical studies, economic indexes etc., have been typically unaware of its importance. Nobody coined it as philosophy till our presentation. Before discovered of psychology, political philosophy faced the same problem. After invention of theories, formulas then we are moving into a new modern era. This is the reason authors, professors, and most journals avoid it. Our book provides a special panoramic perspective with a deep analysis—*fearism*. We visualize new horizons, as artists and writers and intellectuals do—through the weaponry of the word. Thomas Hobbes used Newtonian gravity theory in political philosophy; we are using 'Fear Gravity' in the development of a nation, like India. We need to play openly and imagine new ideas to find sustainable, not short-term, solutions to things like victory over poverty, corruption, caste systems, and inhibitive slow development.

K: That is true Desh! India happens to be one of the leading propagators of thought on fear and fearlessness in olden times. Indian myths, legends, puranas etc. are testimony to the fact that the gods and kings in classical literature never backtracked on extending protection to the people in fear. Puranas are the Sanskrit texts of ancient Indian culture, history, religious ceremonies, arts and sciences etc. that date back to several centuries BC. Skandapurana is one of such puranas which gives an account of 'abhayada', meaning *'making a promise of safety'* or simply explained as *'the giver of fearlessness,* 'A' means 'No,' 'Bhaya' means 'fear,' and 'Da' means *'one who gives'* and hence *'the giver of fearlessness'*. It is a common sight in Indian temples, having statues of deities with hands stretched forth in token of offering protection against fear. Such hand gesture is called as 'abhaya hasta' meaning *'hand of fearlessness'* and the hand pose is referred to as the 'abhaya mudra.'

Ancient literature is replete with legends and episodes of offering safety and/or fearlessness to the people in distress. An episode in Mahabharata narrates an incident about Gaya, a king who inadvertently offends Lord

Krishna. Furious over what has happened, Lord Krishna vows to kill him. Fear-struck Gaya approaches Pandava prince Arjuna for protection and Arjuna, without ascertaining the facts, assures 'abhaya' to him. Later, Lord Shiva intervenes and stops the war between Lord Krishna and Arjuna. Such stories are aplenty in ancient literature of India. But, paradoxically at the same time, it was otherwise when it came to the fate of toiling masses at the lower rungs of social hierarchy. Systematic and chronic fear was thrust upon them for exploitation in the name of *karma*, which lays down that the past life's actions would decide future fate and caste profession. And it was the custom sanctioned by religious texts and any violation of scriptural directive amounts to great sin and so on, as I elucidate in Part 1.

K: This paradoxical nature of wisdom available for practices of fearlessness and then doing the opposite as you point out regarding the motivational coercion of fear-based ways from social hierarchy, shows the disconnect to me. I think we could find this disconnect in many places because the economic, social, religious and political spheres are too often in contemporary societies but even in the ancient past, divided from the sphere of *philo sophia*—that is, the virtue of *love of wisdom*—and thus, philosophy seems to frequently thrown out the window for practical and lesser aims of a society, its leaders and institutions. Principle of *abhaya dāna*, as you are speaking about has to be part of a vision and mission within a countries' constitution, in its ethical laws, even in their secular form. That would be a legal and humane responsibility to back-up mass intervening critical education which is required for all. And so philosophies that deeply understand fear and fearlessness have to be taught from cradle to grave. It takes a bold nation to make a big commitment to this, of course.

However, as far as the study of fear and fearlessness in modern context is concerned, I have no words adequate in regard to commending you both, Desh and Michael for holding the reins independent of each other since more than three decades in pioneering the cause of fearism and fearlessness philosophies respectively, in a methodical manner. It is a fantastic terminology Desh that you have mentioned about your coinage 'Fear Gravity' while referring to development. It is a fact that unless the 'bad fear' is driven off, people will not be able to either choose their life choices freely or grab opportunities uninhibitedly. As earth's gravity pulls us towards itself, fear gravity too holds us to itself. The more the mass of the object is, the stronger the pull of earth's gravity is. In a similar fashion, the bigger the threat is perceived by the subject, the stronger the hold of fear on the subject. As you pointed out, poverty, corruption, caste systems etc., are severe threats to the well-being of people that make the fear gravity to pull them more strongly towards itself.

F: Now, to shift focus a bit. There are four tensions, perhaps conflicts, that I have detected in this book, like an 'elephant in the room' that are not easy to speak about, even amongst us as co-authors. They could be messy and confusing to readers. If care is taken in our own work and by readers of what we write about, it seems there's justifiable heuristic purpose for discussing these matters. Perhaps, they will be too theoretical for some. Yet, let me try to articulate them and have you respond to them. It is not that I am looking for a solution to them, but rather believe they are tensions that will be in the minds and value-systems of many others as well as us. So, here are the four that I have brought forward for this dialogue, to at least begin to address in brief, as I realize they are complicated and would need more space to do justice to:

1. "modernization" of the so-called lesser developed countries is *not* a panacea and in fact seems to bring with it the baggage of colonialism, W. imperialism, and greater problems, to the point of threatening quality of life in lesser developed countries—and to counter the modernism discourse as the 'only direction to go' for improvement, I would say that is why postmodern thought and analysis of "development" has evolved as a criticism of the one-way short-comings and disasters of modernism (e.g., 18th century Western Eurocentric post-Enlightenment mind-set and its fears) and,

2. you both seem to equate the great gains of modernism with humanism and you are advocates for more humanism as the solution to India's developmental problems—I think a case can be made that humanism is also part of the problem of modernism and many postmodern and post-postmodern critics have attacked the narrow-focus of humanism when it goes too far as the guiding ethical

imperative and leaves behind the premodern Indigenous worldview and wisdom, which was the worldview of 99% of human evolutionary history as a species before modernism and humanism philosophies, the latter which are all very Western and part of the colonialist mindset; don't you think India has had enough colonization by the West that it ought to be very cautious in taking on humanism?

3. you both use "fear" and "fearlessness" at times in this book and your other writing in ways that I do not think adequate or complicated enough, or holistic-integral enough; and thus, it appears we are speaking about the same thing and people may assume they understand what is being referred to yet, it is uncertain really if we are communicating about the same thing with what readers are interpreting as well—for example, Subba has 21 definitions of fear [16], I have 15+ definitions/ meanings of fearlessness that I can use at any time [17], the Indian sages and philosophers I quoted in Part 2 use these terms and yet, there's no consensus that they are using them the same as us either; yet, they are all valid from different perspectives—and, thus this seems to become problematic doesn't it when it comes to applications for improving fear management/ education in India or anywhere for that matter?

4. you both seem to agree that *more* "fear," and its cousins like guilt and shame, are required to have social and moral order and thus better development in a society; it seems people are not enough afraid of authorities and don't follow rules and laws enough, and you both say India needs more of this fear as a way of managing its state and commons; how is this to be taught as curriculum in India?—for my part, I am overall not in agreement with this direction of education and this kind of mind-set as it focuses on fear as a solution when I would rather focus on fearlessness as a solution [18], as I have argued all along with the great Indian sages and philosophers in Part 2.

How are these four tensions going to be better dealt with for the field of fear(ism) and applying fearism to development—like in India?

S: Modernism is another side of the coin, one side was the Dark Age. Modernism criticized the Medieval era where life was dark where the realm of religion dominated as was life of the priest. The priest of church was like superman. They had entitlement of magical power by definition. They defined fate of a man and the universe. They tended to rule over science, philosophy, psychology, culture, literature, art, evolution and capital. Many bright fathers of future generations, the most creative and advanced spiritual leaders, philosophers, scientists were burned alive by The Church, for example Giordano Bruno and Galileo. The priestly caste and world had lots of slave as payless workers. The slave castes built many historical monuments. The priests collected plenty of assets and enjoyed heavenly life in earth. They were not ready to share that privilege. To take their elite advantage and happy life, they fabricated many belief, superstitions and rituals. Using fearmongering, they established themselves as supreme commanders. They were all in one-means; they were central of all. And yet, paradoxically, in their privilege and control, they too feared, and mostly fear losing their shinning life.

The majority in premodern times was a life often in suffering, pain, torture, starvation, confines, and banishment to the margins of society, if not death at the will of another more powerful than them. Yet, they were people of the "allegory cave of Plato." Someone came out from the cave and saw the sky of the multicolor rainbow, sun, moon, and nature. Postmodernism started to see life and the world from *parole* (marginal in Fr.) eye. These *parole* viewers were activists. Parole criticized the *longue* (center in Fr.).They criticized the past life of modernism and premodernism. In Marxist terms we can say the Dark Age was thesis, modernism was antithesis and postmodernism is synthesis. Dark Age and modernism were particularly possible just because of the fear gun. The gun was being held by the priestly and/or elites sitting near the religious and political table.

Postmodernism is advocating the freedom of power, culture, economy, rights, equality etc. It is possible to somewhat overcome the fear gun and burden, when they get fearlessness exercise. Modernism forcefully trapped masses of people and handed them to the handful of elite men. Postmodernism is feeling proud, and says we are in the world of the latest model of life postmodernism and a new man. Such came about ultimately because of existing and distributing public education system. Today, to maintain these gains of history, I recommend putting a good *fear education* into the public syllabus. The Education system is the master of social reform. They are teaching this system culturally in universities. It is looking like gold color in a brass cover.

Many countries, unfortunately, are still developmentally in the world living in/with much of the traditional confines of the Dark Age and modernism. We cannot excuse India. In India, still there is domination of castes and religions. It is intolerable for me to witness. Religion, politics, economy, science, education and culture are under the hold of a controlling upper class. What these elites desire and will is equated to the desire and will of a whole nation. This isn't just. How can we argue or even imagine the majority of Indians are living in the postmodernism realities? The upper class doesn't want to lose control of institutions of power, income and grandeur life. They are enjoying rule and regulation, and India's Constitution guarantees that everything is in their favor, whereas lower castes, marginals, and woman are just playing character roles like in a movie. The producer and director of the movies are upper class.

Education means awareness and ability to critique, create and take action based on newly gained knowledge, with past wisdom. The present general Education system is still serving a heritage of Dark Age and modernism. The elite systemized education to protect their reign/realism. If Education cannot educate humanity then it has no use. Why is the present Education system still unable to transform society? Why is the country overall still moving the modernism virus from the 20th century and before when it is now the 21st century? Even the country's highly developed mass of people are existing under the poverty line. They cannot reach human potential in that development. Most villages of India have inadequate food, education, water, and health facilities. They are dying by simple flus and other ailments that could be prevented.

Lower castes, for example, are not allowed to go to the temple, participate in politics, economics and are banned from touching water and speaking.

What is the use of education and development? They are living in earthly hell. It is a negative part of humanity. We have many universities supporting growth of humanity. The Humanities itself have many faculties. What is the contribution of these universities if some communities are living in slavery age? I believe basic humanism is essential still in modernism and postmodernism advances. These Humanities must invite these outsiders in to participate in a human project not biased by castes and privileged heritages. Outsiders have been living outside since the beginning of history to now. They are not given right to live as human in this earth. The earth does not belong to the upper class and their dynasty. The earth, sky, water, hill, sun and moon belong, living and non-living things, are everyone's. Why is the education unable to cover this basis and philosophy? Education does not belong to just some people. It belongs to every citizen. There is a big hole in the Education system. Ideally, a whole curriculum stands one one-side and fear education stands on the other-side. One-side of the coin is previous education and the other side is fear education. Present education, overall, is too prejudice. It needs a transformation and fully to mix with fear studies. Fear education must start from nursery to universities. Without fear education, only suffix 'ism' cannot change the society. Without changing society one cannot change the world. Marx says, "Philosophy is not for philosophy, it is for changing the world." But, in India what world was yesterday, same world is today. We can suppose vertical world changing to reach in Mars; horizontal world is left behind in slavery age. Cubic change is possible if we have fear studies enhancement. Only saying this is of course, not enough. There has to be policy. There has to be will and infrastructure so as to follow up on good intentions and designs. Practically, we need to change the world and India can be a leader in this. It is possible by fear education. Every individual has a right to change their inner capacities themselves. They need support from society to attain. Fear education is a machine which first changes the inner, then that proceeds to change the individual and their relationships. Those individuals can then change the world for the better. When untouchables, lower caste, woman, disabled, transgendered, etc. have equal opportunity, power, rights, then we can say world is changing.

First, *fear education* teaches about the "fear self." Socrates said, "I know only one thing, that is I don't know." Same case ought to be in the court of educators today, they know only one thing is, they don't know the *fear self* nearly well enough. This applies to a whole nation as well.

K: Yes Michael! The four tensions raised by you are in fact contextually relevant, especially for our concluding part, in order to rule out ambiguity, if any, lies in our propositions and assertions or understanding gap, if any, remains in the manner how the readers tend to take it. I would like to address one by one your four queries:

1.   What you stated is true that modernisation of the lesser developed countries is not a panacea because development warrants inputs from all facets of growth potential, inclusive of modernisation. On the other hand, it can also be considered that modernisation may have perhaps done better than what premodern thought did to medieval people. The thought in the Age of Reason Enlightenment might have done better than what feudalistic thought did to the people bonded in serfdom or slavery of the pre-enlightenment era. In similar vein, we may infer that as time and human thinking evolved for improvement in the existing systems, postmodernism may have certainly done well in comparison to modernism. It is like how the geocentric model of Ptolemy in the early centuries of Christian Era gave way to the heliocentric theory of medieval period during the times of Copernicus and Galileo, which in turn opened up to the present day models of the physical universe based on quantum mechanics or Einstein's relativity or Hawking's etc.

Apropos to what you said that modernisation brought with it the baggage of colonialism or imperialism accompanied by greater problems, I would like to opine that it all depends upon the contextual situation, place-wise and time-wise. Colonialism and imperialism might have proved bad for the minority royals in India who lost their dynastic authority to the European colonisers turned rulers but it had hardly affected the state of commoners who formed the huge chunk of population. Rather western colonialism might have bestowed a ray of hope on the untouchable downtrodden people for better lives. In 1858, it was the Bombay Presidency under the British Raj that enabled the untouchable castes to study in schools for the first time. It is also a fact that British imperialism had saved the lives of widows by abolishing the Sati tradition. Otherwise, all the widows would have been being burnt alive along with their dead husbands on the funeral pyre. No kings or queens in about six hundred kingdoms of erstwhile India, who were bound by the dictates of premodern ancient scriptures, would have dared to emancipate women from such ghastly customs.

It is not that all traditions and customs of the past are bad but the time tested values of the institutions of family, spirituality, arts etc. still continue to hold their places in the hearts of people. Yoga is another example. It is only certain vile institutions like caste systems, etc., that forced caste professions, untouchability, segregation etc.

So, pre-modernism, modernism, post-modernism etc. are only the evolutionary processes being experimented by humans from time to time to adopt such practices which are found to be good in a larger interest, while shunning the rest that inhibits human potential. Some blatant dictatorial ideologies like fascism and nazism were vanquished. Depending upon the place and time specifics, communism flourished somewhere and vanished from somewhere. Same is the case with monarchy, which thrives in some places whether it was the Age of Reason or the era of modernism or post-modernism. Because, free will of the people ultimately triumphs.

Hence, it may not seem workable to set any philosophical idea aside simply because it is olden or too modern. The test of its continuity in part or total rests on its overall objective merits and if demerits outweigh the merits in public perception and experience, it is fit for rejection. If the latest wave of post-modernism succeeds in realising such standards of development, it is a welcome trend.

The Sanskrit phrase, *Vasudhaiva Kutumbakam* of ancient Indian scriptures, which can be seen engraved at the entrance hall of the Indian parliament building, exhorts that *the universe is one family*. If we go by this adage, which is unequivocally accepted as a noble ideal, we believe that there are no distinctions among the people of the world. As there is no fundamental difference between a king's army plundering the neighbouring lands and a robbers' gang looting the passers-by, there's also no change in the meanings of colonialist emperor or indigenous ruler if the ruled had to subject themselves to the whims of either of the types of ruler.

Therefore a ruler, whether he is colonialist or dynastic is irrelevant to the ignorant and innocent masses. It all matters to them if the ruler is oppressive or kind, irrespective of the ruler's antecedents and/or ideologies. A kind colonialist is better perceived and received than a domestic local or indigenous tyrant ruler. The modern history of India records the battle of Bhima Koregaon, in which the untouchable lower caste people joined the British forces near Pune in Maharashtra to defeat the indigenous upper caste Peshwa rulers on January 1, 1818. The outcome of the battle was seen as the victory of lower castes against the caste-based discrimination and oppression. On January 1, 1927, Dr. B. R. Ambedkar visited the memorial erected at the scene of battle to pay homage to the dead lower caste soldiers. On New Year's Day every year, hundreds of thousands of lower caste people from across the country visit the site to commemorate the British victory over the oppressive upper caste rulers, who were said to be notorious for their rigid enforcement of caste segregation in 19th century.

What some historians exaggerate is that one culture dominates over or destroys the other culture. Then the issue of culture comes in as to what does a culture really hold for the people. Does it enrich the lives of people or does it exploit them for the sake of the dominant few? Does it enlighten the minds of people or does it crush the weak majority to continue to remain in ignorance, illiteracy and mental blockade. In the epic of Mahabharata, the tribal youth Ekalavya was denied education because he was not a royal. Even now in some villages of India, the lower castes have no rights in a practical sense to walk with their footwear on in front of the houses of upper castes or to ride on a horse as part of their marriage celebrations. Recent news reports provide ample evidence for overt violations of people's fundamental rights to life and liberty. Does it show that humanism has already reached its level of saturation in India and is overflowing? When the UN adopted the historic document of the Universal Declaration of

Human Rights way back in 1948, India took 45 long years to enact the Protection of Human Rights Act in 1993. Such is the lackadaisical attitude on the part of Indian authorities towards the noble conception of basic human rights and freedoms.

The generic pre-modern indigenous worldview and wisdom of the west and of other parts of the world might be benevolent and encouraging but not so likely in the Indian context, at least to a considerable extent. Some good old Vedic ideals like that of *Bahujana Sukhaya, Bahujana Hitaya Cha, (for the happiness and welfare of all)*, etc remain only on paper but not in terms of practice. How could the people of India, particularly the common masses, achieve their welfare needs and happiness aspirations and enjoy their rights as humans? By the time of Independence, India had a literacy rate increased from about 5% in the early 1900s to only 18%, which is now 74% at present with 66% of literacy rate among the lower castes. Humanism presupposes that all humans had inherent rights to acquisition of knowledge, maintenance of dignity, participation in democratic socioeconomic political processes, realisation of potential etc. Lack of education, knowledge and skills prevents the illiterate ignorants from seizing the opportunities. The situation about digital literacy and skills is still worse with less than 10% for the total Indian population. It is much less amongst the lower castes. These are some of the instances that call for the realisation of basic human necessities on priority basis. It's here in this context that the philosophy of humanism has to live up to its responsibilities.

If colonial mindset is regarded as something questionable, it has also had its silver lining in exposing most of the traditional Indian minds to the world's view of rationality, spirit of enquiry, individuality, humanity and social justice. Though humanism has stood out as the outcome of western colonialist mindset, it holds hope and future for the betterment of the suppressed people in India. It was only the western humanistic ideological views that inspired the western educated Indian leaders like Gandhi, Nehru, Patel, Jinnah etc. to steer their struggle for the country's freedom and they had achieved it at last from the British themselves. Given the circumstances, humanistic philosophy still needs to play its role in emancipating the unfortunate citizens from the clutches of ignorance, poverty, mental blockades and self-confined cage of the past traditions and customs.

2.   Arriving at consensus on any definition is not easy. So is the case with *fear* and *fearlessness* too. We find hundreds of Bible versions in English alone. Yet, different groups of people read verses with variations as *per* their preferred version of the Bible. In humanities, we come across innumerable definitions for a single term depending upon the number of thinkers. Apart from Abraham Lincoln's definition of democracy, we see many other variations, albeit the former is more popular.

In the same manner, though fear and fearlessness can be explained in more than one definition, people in general tend to have their own version of understanding as *per* their childhood socialisation or belief system or peer influences and so on. Otherwise, to my understanding, I feel that people at-large interpret *fear* in two clear ways. One, is the fear that goes with the expectation of good: fear of God, fear of parents, fear of responsibilities etc. fall within this category. The other type, is the fear with the expectation of bad. It includes fear of war, fear of disease, fear of enemy etc. We normally term the former type of fear as good or *benign fear* whereas the latter type can be referred to as bad or *toxic fear.* I think that Indians on an average look at fear from these two angles, more or less. Most of what Indians experience and make sense of is toxic fear in their day-to-day encounters. Even in the ancient period, the kings and sages offered protection to the victims of toxic fear.

As Michael referenced to Indian philosophers' versions, *gift of fearlessness* as *abhaya dāna* assumed a special significance in an ethical benevolent manner. It is truly amazing that Michael has, in his own right, come up with a new postulate in his well-worded coinage of dictum: *when fear arises, there will be fearlessness.* The phraseology stands to the test of truth in-tune with biological as well as physical laws, established in firm ground. As fear, *inter alia,* is instinctual, arational, fearlessness also comes in instantaneously as core defence mechanism to deal with fear stimulus.

Similarly, as Newton's Third Law of Motion lays down that every action will have an equal and opposite reaction, fear too has its equal and opposite force in fearlessness.

It is logical to infer that Michael's fearlessness treatment could be resorted to for improving fear management education in India. Social evils such as ignorance, illiteracy, superstitions, blind notions, irrational practices etc. reinforce toxic fear to intervene as stumbling blocks in the progress of people. Blinkered by irrational fears, many people barricade their insight and vision, being unable not only to spot opportunities but also to realise their worth or potential. Unless the mastery over unlocking the doors of blockade to knowledge is achieved, fear continues to remain as the mystery of mental darkness. Therefore, fear management education needs to be customised accordingly as *per* the nature of fear, namely social, economic, political, romantic, marital, pedagogical, relational etc.

3.   I don't subscribe to the view that more 'fear' will lead to moral and social order and better development of the society. I hold that a proper blend of father's strong arm fear and mother's tender heart favour will bring in a balanced personality in a child. An age old adage rightly directs that discipline and freedom must go hand in hand. Discipline without freedom is tyranny and freedom without discipline is chaos. Instilling too much of fear or dwelling in too much of fear will not yield positive results in the long run, though the strategy could achieve the targets in the initial phase alone. This is akin to Blake & Mouton's model of 'produce or perish' style of management, wherein the authoritarian and autocratic administration perceives strict rules, stringent policies and fearsome procedures as effective means of controlling people. But in reality, low spirits, demoralisation and toxic fearfulness ultimately not only negatively affect productivity, performance and well-being of the people, but also spark public disaffection and revolt in due course.

What happens in such leadership and environmental circumstances is that the people who are fear-struck severely tend to become resistant to fear itself. As a result, they stop obeying the rules that are harshly thrust upon them, and rules lose relevance. This is precisely the situation that has set in across the current society in India. That's the reason why chaotic conditions prevail off and on, implying disorder. And this fear is malignant or toxic. Everyone, both rich or poor, perceives insecurity psychologically as antisocial and disruptive tendencies take over the devilish idle minds that are countless in number. Be it property offences, combative rivalry, assaults on modesty, organised crimes or sexual attacks, there surfaces a feeling of improbability of safety that lingers on the public mind. On uncertainty front too, the people's anxiety doesn't seem to calm down as most of them get panicky as to what the future holds in the current volatile socioeconomic political scenario.

Unfortunately, on an average, a typical Indian after stepping out of home feels somewhat apprehensive about minute-to-minute uncertainties. Helmet wearing is mandatory but there are more riding heads than helmets. That's the first fear of road safety and traffic violation. Even if there is helmet, no one knows what the traffic cop looks for in terms of deficiencies in the motor bike's mandatory accessories or in the legally warranted list of documents. India is the world capital of road accidents and casualties. Therefore, there's a lot of attention to traffic etiquette. Not only the rider but the whole family is anxious about the rider's safe arrival at home.

Of late, tax authorities have shown up themselves as the most fearsome creatures, especially to the meek. Any investment made in a start-up and/or a new venture calls for detailed verification about the entrepreneur's funds at the hands of the taxmen. Fear of the taxmen is one of the reasons for the diminishing entrepreneurial activism with commensurate disappearance of jobs. If alarming levels of unemployment are cause for survival fear among the jobless, the employees are also fearful of meticulous adherence to too many rules in working environment.

Adulteration has become increasingly common in food manufacturing that the people become hypochondriacs about what to eat and what not to eat. Rule-making and legislation have almost become a day-to-day affair that all citizens are knowingly or unknowingly breaking some rule or law, making them wary of the long arm of law. Legal provisions on marriage, domestic violence, dowry harassment etc. have also increased to such an extent that fear to the point of near psychosis reigns in some households incessantly. On the other hand, fears and anxieties crop up from the effects of crime, terrorism, political rivalries, caste animosities, communal riots, religious conflicts etc. as additional fear causing worries. Besides these fears, prejudices arising out of caste equations, religious sentiments, tribal tensions, political and ideological biases etc. encompass almost the whole of India in their grip. It being the nation of fear and prejudice in such irrefutable debilitating human complexes that India needs for itself a gigantic reformation in a structurally revolutionary manner as recommended in the four parts of this book. As Michael suggested among other things, fearlessness can act as a solution to fear in as much effective way can be explained by Newton's Third Law of Motion.

F: Thanks to you both for addressing my four queries. There remains lots of good 'grist for the mill' of further dialogues in the future. No matter how we come to understand fear, and I believe we are all recommending that India as a whole has to take responsibility for their inadequate understanding of fear, the next issue is what framework of analysis, be it fearism or fearology, etc. is going to serve the best actionable results, especially for the oppressed and marginalized in societies everywhere ?

If some progressive and courageous leaders in India step-up and into facing the Fear Problem and its impact on them, their institutions, their history, and fellow citizens, then I suggest they begin that critical analysis by asking what are the various fear management/systems and strategies are there operating in their nation, and even beginning a classification and mapping them out. For my small part, I have offered a classification system for this identification in *The World's Fearlessness Teachings* text, but more important from the start I suggest that such leaders take a serious look at why people in their nation, including themselves, are in general recalitrant *resistance* to wanting to know more about fear and its management as priority? And because there is not space for this explanation here, I suggest my teaching video as a start [19].

All of us are going to be inhibited in growing a critical literacy on fear and fearlessness if we don't go deeper than merely surface cognitive-behavioral, functionalist and attitude change motivations to deal with fear better. My experience tells me we have to get to the deepest fear levels we don't understand—the levels that operate often without ordinary consciousness, reasoning or any feelings—that is, in the deepest existential layers of our human nature and the way we have been conditioned by culture and history *via* evolution. Again, I explain that in the video and my book.

With all the problems, challenges and opportunities facing India in the future, of which Desh and Maria have so well spoken about in this book, I want to end with the pivotal problem of all problems to be faced by India in the next few years is the "inevitable collapse" of social systems [20] due to dramatic climate extremes, that is, global warming. Maria close off Part 1 with declaring there is "Impending Cataclysm" in India based on several combined forces. Any exceptional leadership in India, or anywhere, must not ignore this, deny this, or only fear this and distract themselves by it. Nothing, in my view, will cause more human and life destructivity and it has already happened. Fear and fearlessness are core to understanding these problems of climate and to building *existential resiliency* to the economic, psychological and social fabric that are the containers for basic human dignity and sanity when we are all put under enormous stresses in the near-times ahead. Panic is not an option, nor is false bravery!

****

NOTES

1.   Subba, D. (2014). *Philosophy of fearism: Life is conducted, directed and controlled by the fear.* [Trans. Rajendra Subba with Bhabindra Kumar Rai]. Australia: Xlibris, p. 25.

2.   I call for all nations to adopt critical educative practices and frameworks of a complex integral change process of everything, using at least, (a) *Indigenizing* (de-colonialist), (b) *fearlessnessizing* (see Fisher & Four Arrows, forthcoming), and (c) *integralizing* (as post-postmodernist or integralist; see Wilber, 2017, for example). Fisher, R. M., and Four Arrows (Jacobs, D. T.) (forthcoming). Indigenizing conscientization and critical pedagogy: Nature, spirit and fearlessness as foundational concepts. In S. Steinberg, B. Down and D. Nix-Stevenson (Eds.), *Sage Handbook of Critical Pedagogies (Vol.1)*. Thousand Oaks, CA: Sage; Wilber, K. (2017). *The religion of tomorrow: A vision for the future of the Great Traditions— more inclusive, more comprehensive, more complete.* Boston, MA: Shambhala.

3.   Fisher, R. M. (2011). A critique of critical thinking: Towards a critical integral pedagogy of fearlessness. *NUML: Journal of Critical Inquiry, 9*(2), 92-164.

4.   Excerpt from Wilber (2017), pp 1, 78.

5.   See also what Fisher has identified as the Fearlessness Movement as meta-context: Fisher, R. M. (2018). The Fearlessness Movement: Meta-context exposed! Technical Paper No. 72. Calgary, AB:

In Search of Fearlessness Research Institute. See also: http://
fearlessnessmovement.ning.com

6.   Lake & Rothchild (1996), p. 41; according to Lake, D. A., &
      Rothchild, D. (1996). Containing fear: The origins and management
      of ethnic conflict. *International Security, 21*(2), 41-75.

7.   There is, according to Wilber (and others) and my own analysis, a
      "global transformation" going on and India can easily embrace this
      internationalist conscious view of global evolutionary dynamics,
      especially its more progressive leaders. This is part of the up-dating
      in thinking I have called for in this book (Part 2). Wilber calls
      this an "integral view" at the "worldcentric" level or perspective,
      which is a matured level beyond the somatocentric, egocentric,
      ethnocentric (or sociocentric)—to finally, worldcentric. There
      is even a more advanced level as theocentric. Wilber wrote, "...
      numerous individuals (and a number of studies) indicate that a small
      but significant percentage of the human population is going through
      a profound transformation, in many ways, a global transformation—
      "global" not just because it is affecting people around the world,
      but because individual consciousness itself is developing global
      dimensions; no longer egocentric or ethnocentric, it is becoming
      worldcentric and even Kosmocentric in its identity, motivations,
      desires, viewpoints, perspectives, and capacities. Nothing like this
      global interior consciousness has ever existed before in human
      history—at least not on any sort of widespread scale. Its impact
      simply cannot be overestimated" (Wilber, 2017, pp. 36-37).

8.   See Mehta, A. K., & Shephera, A. (Eds.) (2006). *Chronic poverty
      and development policy in India.* New Dehli: Sage, pp. 17-18.

9.   See Kapila, U. (2008). *India's economic development since 1947.*
      [3rd ed.]. New Dehli: Academic Foundation, p. 104.

10.   For e.g., Eneyo, M. B. (2018). *Philosophy of unity: Love as an
      ultimate unifier.* Australia: Xlibris.

11.   Excerpt from Clouser (2014), p. 131. Clouser, R. (2014). Facing fear:
      The importance of engaging with fear in development literature.
      Progress in Development Studies, 14(2), 131-46.

12.   Ibid., p. 143.

13.   Ibid., p. 142.

14. Ibid., p. 134.

15. Fisher, R. M., & Subba, D. (2016). The true gift of education for development: A fearist perspective. *Participation: A Nepalese Journal of Participatory Development,* 17 (August), 23-29.

16. Subba (2014), pp. 13-19.

17. Fisher, R. M. (2010). *The world's fearlessness teachings: A critical integral approach to fear management/education for the 21st century.* Lanham, MD: University Press of America, p. 151.

18. I am referring to fear management/education (and all interventions re: the problem of fear, or Fear Problem) from a holistic-integral (2nd-tier) perspective, in contrast to a 1st-tier perspective (more or less fear-based lens and means), see Fisher (2010), Chapter Two.

19. See Fisher, R. M. (2019). Resistance to understanding fear. https://www.youtube.com/watch?v=mfVNktnN3v4&t=388s

20. I am referring to a great recent conversation (March 25, 2019) by David Thorson (of Emerge podcast) with guest Dr. Jem Bendell on "The Meaning of Joy of Inevitable Social Collapse." See https://anchor.fm/emerge

****

INDEX

J

jobless 23, 53, 54, 209; *see also* unemployment, youth
Johansen, B. 128
Johori, K. 172, 173
Joy, K. J. 127
judiciary 165; *see also* government(s), law(s)
Jung, K. 146

K

Kabaddi game 156; *see also* corruption
Kafle, R. 148, 169, 171, 173, 176, 177, 192
Kaliyug era 23
Kalu, O. A. 135
Kapila, U. 213
karma 32, 197; *see also* fate
Kathari, A. 127
Kauravas 13
Kazi, S. 137
Khatiwada, T. N. 153
khatmification 183
King, M. L. (Jr.) 60, 97, 103
Kleiner, A. 130
Korten, D. 124
Kostas, Y. 131
Krishna (Lord) 197
Krishnamurti, J. 98, 133
Kro, B. 172
Kumar, B. M. xi, xiii, xiv, xviii, xxv-68, 71, 73-5, 79-80, 81-4, 91, 92, 93, 95, 99, 101, 104, 105-6, 107, 109, 111, 113, 116, 117-9, 123, 126, 127, 134, 135, 137, 142, 146, 150, 159, 162, 177, 178, 179, 182-5, 188, 189-91, 194, 196-8, 203-10, 211
Kumar, C. 111-2, 137
Kumar, K. 112-3, 115, 137
Kyi, A. S. S. 136, 178

L

labour 5, 10, 31-3, 57, 83, 143, 157, 162, 167; power/ 157; slaves xiv, 7, 66, 143, 149, 157, 159, 164, 168, 187, 190, 200, 202, 203; *see also* caste(s), jobless, power, serfdom
Lake, D. A. 213
Langthasa, F. 172
laterals 18-21, 29-31, 32-34, 37-8, 43, 47, 54-5, 57-61, 105; *see also* caste(s), India(n)(s), literals, political, RPB
law(s) 2, 4, 9, 23-4, 25, 30-2, 48, 56, 83, 99, 109, 110, 113, 151, 154, 156, 169, 184, 190, 192, 197, 199, 207, 209; Ambedkar's 62-4, 66; anti-discrimination 185; enforcement 44, 50, 150, 183, 205; Natural 73, 79, 87, 103, 104, 119; fear of 157, 162, 167, 168; *see also* ethic(al)(s), government(s), Newton's, police
leaders(hip) xiii, xx, xxiii, 22, 71, 82, 84-5, 87, 89-90, 92, 101, 103, 104, 117, 119, 128, 129, 132, 135, 156, 157, 166, 183, 189, 192, 208, 211; *see also* political, spiritual, vision(ary)
learning: trance-based 124; *see also* education, hypnotizing, pedagogy, transformative
Leary, M. 128
legal: *see* law, political, security
liberation 97, 100, 181; *see also* nonviolence, resistance, spiritual(ity)
liberty xx, 24, 25, 30, 34, 46, 47, 63, 84, 107, 191, 205 ; *see also* freedom, modernization, progressive(s), rights
Liddell, E. 14-16

lie(s) 94, 105; *see also* corruption, illusion(s)

Limbu, T. 146-7

Lincoln, A. (Pres.) 66, 207

literacy 147: critical 101, 211; digital 23, 59-60, 206; functional 23, 59-60; rate 206; *see also* economic, illiteracy

literals 18-21, 23, 29-34, 35, 37, 43, 47, 54, 57-61, 83, 105; *see also* caste(s), illiteracy, laterals, oppression

Locke, J. 153

logic(al) xv-xvi, xxi, 9, 28, 29, 41, 63, 109, 164, 208: feminine 111-2, 115-6; *see also* Achilles, illogic(al), rational(ism); Tortoise

Lokniti 188

Luther, M. 67

M

Machiavelli, N. 153

Mahabharata (epic) 13-14, 58, 142, 196-7, 205

Mahendra (Prof.) 176

Majhi, D. 160

Mandela, N. 103

Mann, B. A. 123

Maoist(s) 65, 150

marginalized 49, 169, 210; *see also* literals, oppressed

Margold, J. A. 131

Marx, K. 23, 60, 62, 190, 202

Marxian 6, 191

Marxist 200: French, 149; Materialist 163; *see also* communism, socialism

Marxist-Leninist ideology 62

Maslow, A. H. 99, 128

McLeod, J. 175

McGaa, E. 123

McManus, M. 91, 131

megalomaniacal 27

Meita, A. K. 189, 213

Mezirow, J. 126

military 8, 44, 115, 146, 157, 159, 160, 195, 205

mind(s) xiv, xvii, xix, xxi, 1, 6, 10, 11, 16, 20, 22, 31, 32, 36, 37, 40, 41, 42, 44, 47, 51, 54, 65, 81, 82, 108, 153, 184, 190, 198, 205 ; colonialist 199, 206; ethnocentric 78; fear-based xiii, 152; fear disease of 128; idle (devlish) 209; irrational 82; -less 157; modernisation of 183; open 33; oppressed 21; public 38, 209; state's 113; transcends 167; without fear xxi, 86, 132; *see also* mindful(ness), rational

mindful(ness) 9, 12-13, 15, 99, 166; un-11, 13, 22, 44; *see also* spirituality

mistrust: *see* trust

modernisation xx, 183, 188, 203; *see also* education(al), political

modernism 98, 112, 113, 138, 143, 147, 183, 198, 199, 200, 201, 202, 203, 204; *see also* humanism, postmodernism, rational(ism), secular(ism)

Montaigne 135

moral(ity)(s) xvii, xx, 18, 40, 54, 55, 76, 90, 91, 96, 108, 161, 162, 170, 172, 199, 208; de- 8, 53; im- 41; *see also* conscience, corruption, discipline, ethic(al)(s), order, religious

motivation(s) 8, 92, 121, 197, 211, 213; affective 91; deficit 99; dual- 128; fear and 158, 182; fear-based xiv, 82, 90, 148, 187; fear-force (meta-) 128; growth

psychofear (cultural) 167; *see also* culture of fear

psycholog(ical)(y) xx, 1, 7, 10, 12, 15, 16, 32, 91, 98, 105, 129, 130, 136, 141, 153, 158, 162, 166, 167, 176, 196, 209, 211: cognitive 162; cultural therapy 123; defence 106; deficiencies 47; developmental 108, 130; ethical 47; fear- 158, 163; fearlessness 130, 136; fearological strike 167; lower-caste 166; matrixial (psychodynamic) 114; priest and 200; science 128; social 16, 126; split 113; *see also* affect, ego(ic) (ism), existential(ism), fear(s), health, humanism, integral, self-actualization, therapy, transpersonal

psychosis (near) 210; *see also* pathology

psychotherapy 123, 135, 137; *see also* cultural, psychology, therapy

Pthiti, H. 131

Ptolemy 203

Puranas: see Sanskrit

Pyszcyznski, T. 128, 136

Q

quantum: leap 86; mechanics 203; of fear 43, 82, 127

Quotient (Fear) 88, 127

R

RPB (ruling class + priest class + business class): defined 141; 143-5, 149, 150, 159, 160-1, 162, 165, 167, 169, 170

Rai, B. K. 212

Rai, L. L. 144

Raijung, F. (Lt.) 172

Rama (Lord) 57-8

Ramakrishna 96

Ramchander, S. xi

Rana (regime) 146, 160

Rao, K. L. S. 134

racism 102, 189; *see also* oppression(s)

rational(ism) xv, 6, 16, 21, 33, 42, 46, 50, 52, 76, 77, 78, 84, 91, 118, 131, 189, 206: -centered 76; discourse 114; extra- 193; planning 112; -pragmatic 132; scientific- 108; stage 78; vs. irrational 82; *see also* arational, irrational, logic(al), modernism, science

reason xxi, 6, 9, 21, 39, 40, 57, 71, 211: Age of 76, 103, 203, 204; *see also* Enlightenment (W.)

reform(ation)(s) xvii, xviii, xx, 82, 102, 105, 107, 111, 118: eco (movements) 79; education 201; India (revolution); radical 66, 67; social 19, 86, 96, 128, 133, 184, 186, 192, 201; true 90; *see also* religious, transform(ation)

regionalism xxi, 65; *see also* separatism

religion(s) 6, 9, 37, 38, 39, 52, 83, 95, 96, 111, 112, 120, 123, 134, 142, 147, 148, 160, 164, 172, 182, 185, 186-7, 191, 200, 201: afraid of 113; based on fear 132; *see also* Buddhism, caste(s), Christian(ity), ethnocentricism, fear(s), god(s), Hinduism, hope, mythical, RPB, superstition

religious xx, 5, 20, 37, 38, 39, 41, 45, 65, 67, 108, 118, 129, 141, 188, 200: casteism and 185; conflicts 37, 178, 183, 210; cultic 95; cultural dialectic systems 142; history 112, 113; fear of 83; intolerance 37; narratives 71; pilgrims 195;

selfish 2, 18, 27, 54, 65, 154; *see also* ego(ic)(ism), motivation(s)

separatism 65; *see also* regionalism

serfdom (and feudalism), 190, 203; *see also* capitalism, elite(s)

sex(ism) 102

sex(uality) 48-9, 54, 83, 91, 113, 116, 124, 137, 169, 209; *see also* HIV/ AIDS

shadow(s) 37, 77; *see also* pathology, unconscious

Shah (royal family) 160

Shambuka 57-8

Shephera, A. 189, 213

Shiva (Lord) 197

Shiva, V. 114

slave(s): *see* caste(s), labour

social species (humans) 3; *see also* security, wounded

socialism 62

socialistic, 141

sociality 104, 108; *see also* trust

socialisation 45, 190, 207

sociopathic leaders 123, 124; *see also* pathology

Socrates 97, 142, 203

Sorensen, M. 123

Spinoza, B. 91, 131

Spiritual (and Natural, Cultural) 119, 120, 132

spiritual(ity) xx, 37, 54, 80, 84, 86, 94, 95, 96, 104, 106, 108, 112, 137, 176, 187, 204: Buddhist nun 129; consciousness 186; education 186; integral 123, 124; leaders 200; not religious 186; philosophies 186; (r)evolutions 186; -self 99; transformation 186; -un 36; *see also* leaders(hip), mindful(ness), religious, ritual(s), sages

starvation xix, 19, 200; *see also* poverty

State (the): fear of 49; *see* government(s), political

Stiftung, K. A. 188

Subba, D. xi, xiii, xiv, xvii, xxiii, 56, 74-5, 88, 90, 92, 93, 98, 100, 101-2, 109, 117, 124, 126, 127, 130, 131, 132, 133, 134, 136, 139-78, 179, 181, 182, 188, 191-3, 195-6, 197, 199, 200-03, 211, 212, 214

Subba, R. 212

superstition(s) xxi, 1, 3, 9, 15, 20, 33, 37, 41, 42, 51, 96, 200, 208; *see also* fear(s), ignorance, illiteracy (India(n)(s)), taboo(s)

Supriya 115-6

Sushmita, S. xi, 11, 17, 137

T

taboo(s) xiv, 31, 32, 75, 96, 108, 126; *see also* superstition(s)

Tagore, R. xxi-xxii, 86

Taleb, N. N. 64, 68, 183

Tangney, J. 128

Tathagatananda (Swami) 133

technology 25, 33, 35, 43, 60, 61, 125, 131, 141: hypnotizing 124, 135; *see also* science(s)

terror 150: century of 102; culture of 131; *see also* fear(s)

terrorism 73, 124, 135, 150, 183, 210; *see also* fearism-t, insecurity, security, war(s)

terrorists xix, 65, 105, 150, 151; *see also* extremists

Thapa, B. B. 153

Tharoor, S. xiii, xxiii, 73-4, 75, 78, 122

theophobia 36

therapy 130: cultural 79, 87, 100, 106, 108, 120; *see also* fearanalysis,

W

X

Y

fearless 96; precariat 12; *see also* education(al), Ekalavya, jobless

Z

Zedong, M. 65
Zeitler, D. M. 135
Zeno of Elea, xv, 28-30
Zidung, A. 173